Cargo of Lies

Cargo of Lies

The True Story of a Nazi Double Agent in Canada

DEAN BEEBY

UNIVERSITY OF TORONTO PRESS
Toronto Buffalo London

© University of Toronto Press Incorporated 1996
Toronto Buffalo London
Printed in Canada

ISBN 0-8020-0731-7 (cloth)

Printed on acid-free paper

Canadian Cataloguing in Publication Data

Beeby, Dean, 1954–
    Cargo of lies

    Includes bibliographical references and index.
    ISBN 0-8020-0731-7

    1. Janowski, Werner Alfred Waldemar von.
    2. Espionage, German – Canada.   3. World War, 1939–
    1945 – Secret service – Germany.   4. World War, 1939–
    1945 – Secret service – Canada.   5. Intelligence
    service – Canada – History – 20th century.   6. Spies –
    Germany.   7. Spies – Canada.   I. Title.
    D810.S8J35 1996   940.54'8743'092   C95-931976-X

University of Toronto Press acknowledges the financial assistance to its publishing
program of the Canada Council and the Ontario Arts Council.

For Lisa and Richard

Behold, how good and pleasant it is
when brothers dwell in unity!
It is like the precious oil upon the head,
running down upon the beard,
upon the beard of Aaron,
running down on the collar of his robes!

Psalm 133:1–2

Contents

Contents

Acknowledgments

Bill Kaplan, a good friend from graduate-school days, first drew my attention to the mysterious case of Watchdog, the Nazi spy landed by U-boat in 1942 near New Carlisle, Quebec. We had contemplated a collaboration, but for various reasons Bill became entangled in other worthy projects and graciously left to me the telling of this story. Our early discussions have left an indelible mark on this book. The backbone of the narrative that follows is the RCMP's 3000-page Watchdog file, obtained after a request to the Canadian Security Intelligence Service under the Access to Information Act. The file offers a fascinating inside look at the recruitment and running of a German double agent during the darkest years of the Second World War, when the Allies seemed powerless against U-boat predations in the Atlantic. Even the acknowledged masters of wartime double agentry, the British counter-intelligence agency MI5, have never permitted such close scrutiny and free use of individual case files. Professor F.H. Hinsley's officially approved access to British intelligence files, which resulted in the multi-volume series *British Intelligence in the Second World War*, was still subject to significant restrictions. Some sections of the RCMP's Watchdog file were partially withheld to protect personal information and to safeguard material obtained from the British and American governments, both of whom were kept intimate with the case. But the resulting gaps in the dossier could be readily patched over by other means. U.S. Federal Bureau of Investigation material on the case was extracted from their archives piecemeal over several years, through the U.S. Freedom of Information Act. The FBI eventually released 217 heavily censored pages from its

Acknowledgments

1911-page Watchdog file, but the documents none the less add an important North American perspective. Canadian Naval Intelligence files held by the National Archives in Ottawa also filled many holes, as did dozens of other documents obtained under the Access to Information Act from the Justice Department and the Canadian Security Intelligence Service. Cyril Bertram Mills, the former British MI5 agent who helped oversee Watchdog in Canada, kindly offered his insights about the case in the year before his death. Two brave merchant mariners, Gordon Hardy and Pierre Simard, dredged up memories of narrowly surviving a torpedo attack by *U-518*, the submarine that days later delivered the spy. Marguerite Beebe, Geraldine Langham, and Simone Loubert told me simply and eloquently what it was like to meet and catch a Nazi spy. All these people cheerfully put up with my near-interrogations, for which they have my admiration and profound thanks.

Many others helped in the research, especially John Annett, Halifax; Bill Beahen, RCMP Archives, Ottawa; Robert Dietz, Halifax; W.A.B. Douglas, Director of History, National Defence Headquarters, Ottawa; Sharon Farrell, *Gaspé Spec*, New Carlisle, Que.; Michael Hadley, Victoria, BC; Suzanne Le Rossignol, Montreal *Gazette*; C. Herbert Little, Ottawa; Doug Luchak, Ottawa; Paul Marsden, National Archives of Canada, Ottawa; Steve Neary, St John's, Nfld.; Andre Ruest, Gaspé, Que.; Dorothy Sheehan, Saint John, NB; Michael Sheehan, Ste-Foy, Que.; Gilles Soucy, Rivière-au-Renard, Que.; David Stafford, Canadian Institute for International Affairs, Toronto; Sylvia Strojek, Edmonton; Wesley K. Wark, Toronto; Nigel West (Rupert Allason), London, England; Glenn Wright, RCMP Archives, Ottawa; Eric Yarrill, Sherbrooke, Que. They have all helped to strengthen this book, but blame me – not them – for any lingering weaknesses. Special thanks must go to Wesley Wark, whose detailed and constructive critique of the manuscript forced me to rethink several issues and led to many improvements. Doug Luchak, who has kindly assisted on this and many other projects over the years, was especially helpful in obtaining photographs and other visual materials. Gerry Hallowell and Robert Ferguson of the University of Toronto Press were supportive and enthusiastic throughout. John St James was an astute, sharp-eyed copy editor. No government grant or direct aid from taxpayers was used to prepare the manuscript, though much research was carried out in Canada's publicly supported libraries.

Acknowledgments

In the pages that follow, espionage aficionados will immediately recognize my reliance on J.C. Masterman's *The Double-Cross System in the War of 1939 to 1945*, a model of brevity and the first full account of Britain's success in strategic wartime deception. Nigel West's pioneering espionage histories, including *MI5: British Security Service Operations, 1909–1945* and *Garbo*, the volume he co-authored with Juan Pujol, were also invaluable. The Hinsley volumes cited above also provided a reliable foundation of fact, as did David Kahn's two masterful tomes, *Hitler's Spies* and *The Code-Breakers*. C.W. Harvison's *The Horsemen* was helpful, despite the frequent inaccuracies and generally misleading account of the Watchdog case in chapter 11. Michael L. Hadley's meticulously researched *U-Boats against Canada* was also a mine of essential information. I have forsaken endnotes in favour of a sources section; all research materials, including transcripts of all interviews, will be deposited in due course at a Canadian archive. Specific queries about sources can be made through the publisher.

My wife Irina and our children, Nikolai and Josef, taught me much of what I know about good storytelling. I hope they enjoy this little wartime yarn.

Dean Beeby
Halifax
June 1995

Gordon Hardy, 18 at the time, was asleep in his bunk aboard the ore-carrier *Rose Castle* when it was hit by a torpedo fired from *U-518* off Bell Island, Newfoundland, on 2 November 1942. Hardy saved himself by diving into the frigid waters of Conception Bay just as a second torpedo finished off the vessel.

An RCAF photograph of the *Rose Castle* in convoy off Sydney, Nova Scotia, on 11 September 1942. The ship, which transported iron ore from Bell Island, Newfoundland, to the Sydney steel mill, narrowly survived two U-boat attacks on 5 September and 20 October before falling victim to Friedrich-Wilhelm Wissmann's *U-518*. Twenty-eight men died.

Pierre Simard, 18, dove off the ore-carrier *PLM-27* after the ship was rocked by a torpedo from *U-518* on 2 November 1942. Simard, torpedoed once before off the New England coast, managed to swim to Lance Cove on Bell Island, but had to be helped ashore because his legs were too damaged for him to walk out of the water.

Friedrich-Wilhelm Wissmann (centre), commander of *U-518*, and his four officers, 1942. *U-518*, on its maiden voyage when it attacked the Bell Island anchorage, was Wissmann's first command since joining the U-Waffe in 1935.

A 'most secret' Naval Intelligence map of the route of *U-518* between 30 October and 8 November 1942, based on Lieutenant Wilfred Samuel's interrogation of Janowski.

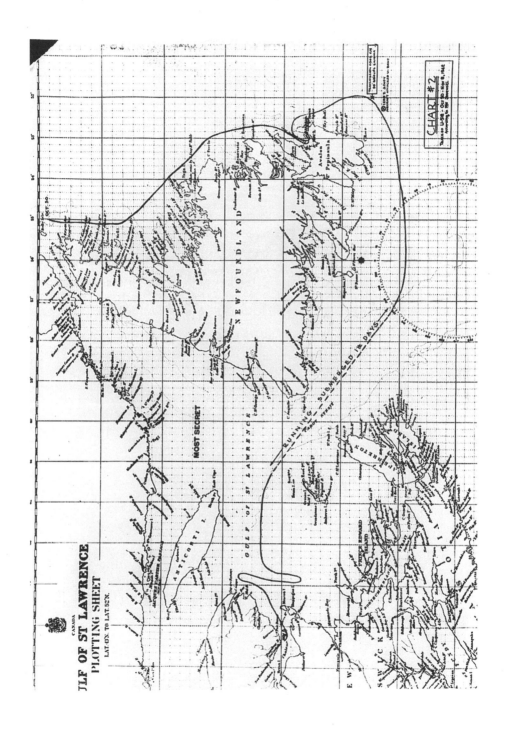

Rocky cliffs four miles west of New Carlisle, Quebec, where Werner Alfred Waldemar von Janowski landed in the dark from *U-518* on 9 November 1942. The Annett family, who were instrumental in Janowski's capture, later purchased the property.

The Carlisle Hotel in New Carlisle, Quebec, where Janowski stopped for a bath and breakfast early on 9 November 1942. Arrow shows the front sitting-room where young Earle Annett retrieved Janowski's discarded Belgian matchbox to gather evidence against the suspected spy.

Cover of the Belgian matchbox that, together with some outdated Canadian $1 bills, helped to arouse the Annetts' suspicions about Janowski. Earle Annett Jr noticed that the yellow matchbox lacked the required excise stamp.

Earle Annett Jr (left) and Constable Alphonse Duchesneau of the Quebec provincial police in front of the Poiriers' gas station in New Carlisle, Quebec, on 12 November 1942. Annett deeply mistrusted Duchesneau as a policeman and was upset about lax security after Janowski's capture.

Barry German, commander of Fort Ramsay in Gaspé, Quebec, in June 1943. German, a former Naval Intelligence officer, desperately wanted to interrogate Janowski but was thwarted by the Quebec provincial police and the RCMP. He lost his left arm in the 1917 Halifax explosion.

The New Carlisle courthouse and jail, where Constable Duchesneau finally placed Janowski for fear a raiding U-boat party might try to spring him from his room at La Maison Blanche hotel. The RCMP's Cliff Harvison conducted his first interrogations of Janowski in the jailer's office.

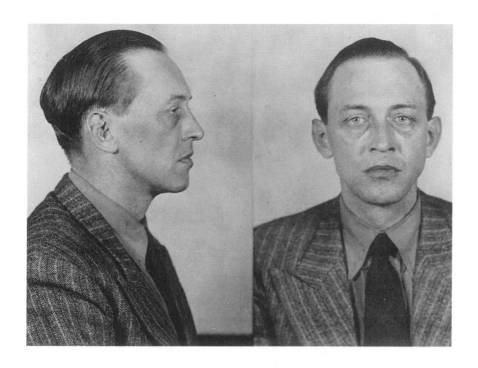

RCMP mug shots of Janowski, 38 years old at the time of his capture. A seasoned veteran of Abwehr sabotage and counter-espionage missions, Janowski presented himself to his RCMP captors as a mere soldier reluctantly pressed into low-grade espionage work.

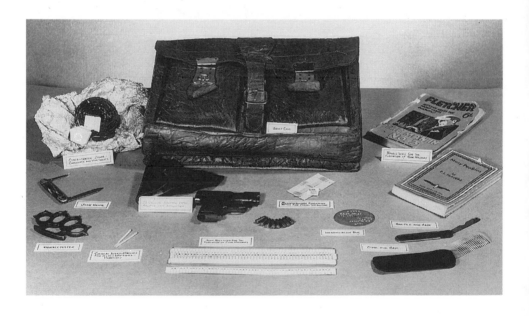

Some of Janowski's effects, including the two paperback books that formed the basis for his radio code system and a slide rule that added a measure of security to the coding. All the items were contained in the briefcase that Janowski carried in addition to the suitcase-sized Afu, or 40-watt short-wave receiver-transmitter.

Janowski's naval uniform, which he wore on landing so that in case of immediate capture he could credibly claim he was a military officer, rather than a spy, and thereby avoid execution. The clothing was carefully buried at his landing.

RCMP Commissioner Stuart Taylor Wood, staunch anti-Communist and anglophile, who persuaded Justice Minister Louis St Laurent to approve Canada's first double-agent operation on 24 November 1942. Wood also invited Britain's counter-intelligence agency MI5 to send an officer to help run the case.

Cliff Harvison, the man who ran the Watchdog case, and who became the 11th commissioner of the RCMP in 1960. Harvison had a well-deserved reputation as a tough, effective cop, but was out of his depth when it came to counter-intelligence matters.

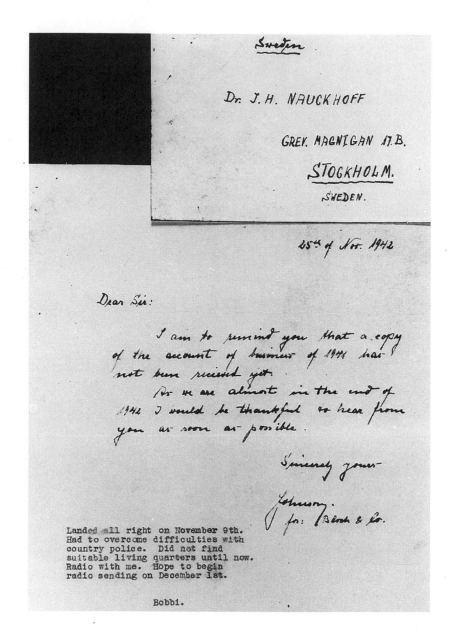

Photostat of the letter and envelope Janowski sent to an Abwehr mail drop in Sweden on 25 November 1942 to inaugurate the RCMP double-cross. Typed copy lower left is a translation of the invisible-ink message that lies beneath the visible message.

Cyril Mills (left) with his brother Bernard in England in the 1930s. Mills joined MI5 during the war, eventually to become a top double-cross officer, and was posted in Canada from December 1942 to September 1945 as MI5's North American liaison officer.

RCMP mug shot of Alfred Langbein, aka Alfred Haskins, taken on 27 November 1944. Langbein landed from *U-213* near St Martins, New Brunswick, on 14 May 1942 and lived quietly in Montreal and Ottawa. He turned himself in to Naval Intelligence on 1 November 1944, and convinced the RCMP and MI5 that he had not carried out any espionage.

Cargo of Lies

Prologue

Just how many enemy spies washed up on Canadian shores during the Second World War is anybody's guess. Like subatomic particles, their existence can often be inferred only from the faint flash-traces they leave across the historical record. Alfred Langbein, rowed ashore from a U-boat near St Martins, New Brunswick, in the spring of 1942, is one of only two documented arrivals. Apparently never intending to carry out his mission, Langbein travelled with little trouble to Montreal and Ottawa, where he lived for more than two years on money supplied to him by the Abwehr, the German military-intelligence service. Running short of cash and resigned to Germany's eventual demise, he turned himself in one fall afternoon in 1944 to a naval lieutenant at No. 8 Temporary Building in Ottawa. Under RCMP interrogation, Langbein freely confessed his mission, saying he had been trained in Bremen alongside another German spy who was to be landed by submarine somewhere in Canada shortly after him. That mysterious agent has disappeared from history. RCMP wartime files also refer obliquely to an Italian agent landed by submarine in the Gulf of St Lawrence. That spy, too, is a phantom whose footsteps have left no imprint on the official record. A captured German U-boat engineer claimed in 1944 that the captain of one submarine, Friedrich-Wilhelm Wissmann of *U-518*, had landed five agents in Canada and the United States – not just the lone agent known to the RCMP. Any such spies were apparently swallowed up by the intrigues of war, never again to surface. The 1943 War Diary of the German Naval Staff cites several agent reports from Canada that cannot be traced. Who were these Nazi moles who had quietly burrowed into

3

Canadian cities and towns? How many Langbeins chose not to reveal themselves? How many agents dutifully carried out their missions without detection? Did any of them remain safely and anonymously in Canada after the destruction and dismemberment of Germany?

Among the spoils of war is control of the historical record, especially in the murky world of espionage. Captured enemy documents, not always complete in the case of the German intelligence services, finally provided the Allied victors with an eagle's-eye view of the war. Wartime theories and assumptions about the enemy could be checked in peacetime by patiently sifting through filing cabinets and interrogation reports. Perhaps it is not surprising that the main Allied counter-espionage agencies, the U.S. Federal Bureau of Investigation, Britain's MI5, and the Royal Canadian Mounted Police, concluded in hindsight that they had effectively rebuffed the German espionage and sabotage threat. A prostrate Germany was in no position to challenge that interpretation, and so an Allied consensus seemed to jell: the German intelligence services were incompetent, disorganized, easily duped, and crippled by petty politics. Such a view has persisted to this day, supported in great part by the reluctance of Western agencies to release the full wartime record of their counter-espionage efforts, despite the passage of more than half a century. Contemporary newspapers and other media, caught in the swirl of jingoism, added their own slanted accounts that frequently ridiculed the German agent.

The Watchdog file, the story of the RCMP's capture of a Nazi agent in 1942, pokes a hole in the traditional picture of sharp-witted Allied spymasters outfoxing the stumbling Teuton. Werner Alfred Waldemar von Janowski, code-name Bobbi to his German operators, created havoc within Canada's nascent intelligence service with consequences that have reverberated down the decades. The release of the RCMP file on the case, with missing pieces supplied through interviews and other formerly classified documents, provides a unique opportunity to balance the historical scales. The Watchdog operation has been called a 'key event in the Canadian experience of counter-espionage' and the Mounties' 'entry test into the spying big leagues,' predating by almost three years the better-known Igor Gouzenko defection from the Soviet embassy in Ottawa in September 1945. It was an inauspicious début on the world stage of espionage, revealing as it did that the RCMP was largely incapable of the subtleties of counter-espionage and strategic deception. The episode was like an early-warning signal, particularly for MI5 officials, that Canada's intelligence service was clumsy and amateurish. The Watchdog case helped cement the RCMP's junior and dependent role in the world of espionage, a reputation it was unable to shed throughout the Cold War. Janowski's bold deceits were thickly layered, one woven into another, creating a tangle of deception that eventually ensnared his captors. Precious police resources were drained by the Watchdog case, pinning down RCMP manpower and perhaps allowing other agents a clearer run at Canadian shores. The sleek U-boat that disgorged its shivering passenger at the base of a boulder-strewn Gaspé cliff in November 1942 had dropped off more than a mere spy. It was also delivering a cargo of lies.

ONE

Broken Boats, Broken Bodies

Gordon Hardy, steward aboard the iron ore–carrier *Rose Castle*, prepared to dive from his ship into the frigid, choppy waters off Bell Island, Newfoundland. Sweeping searchlights from the shore regularly rolled into the pitch black that November night in 1942 as Hardy raced onto the deck, dressed only in boxer shorts and a thin life-jacket. 'Where are you going, Hardy?' barked one of the engineers standing on deck. 'I'm going over the side,' he announced, climbing with determination onto the railing. 'Don't jump in that cold water. It's too cold. It'll kill you,' came the shouted reply.

But Hardy knew better. Born and raised in the Cape Breton Island fishing port of Ingonish, he had been diving from ships into the North Atlantic for most of his eighteen years. Ingonish, near the north-east tip of Nova Scotia, was then a bustling centre for fishing companies, all of whom had their own fish stages and wharves stretching far out from shore. Dozens of boats from Newfoundland bobbed in the harbour each spring as a groaning catch of cod was unloaded or supplies brought aboard for the next trip out to the Grand Banks. The port was a wonderland for Ingonish's young boys, with its forest of masts, its fleets of wooden dories and schooners, its sailors and fishermen prowling among the barrels, crates, and nets along the wharves. Hardy's gang would hang out here spring and summer, befriending captains and crew members who would let the boys dive from the decks or rigging. Hardy was the local daredevil, diving from the highest spots, plunging into the coldest water, and holding his breath for as long as possible. Often, a fisherman would accidently drop a fish-splitting knife or some other equally valuable object over the side. Hardy would grandly offer to help, diving and swimming all the way down to the sandy bottom of the harbour to fetch it.

At age seventeen, in 1941, Hardy went to sea. His father had been working as a fireman aboard the *Lord Strathcona*, which regularly transported red hematite, an iron ore, from the world-famous mines at Bell Island on the east side of Conception Bay to the blast furnaces of the steel plant at Sydney, Nova Scotia. The voyage across the Cabot Strait and into the North Atlantic was perilous and nerve-wracking, exposed as it was to German U-boat attacks. Crew members willing to brave the dual risks of fierce Atlantic storms and enemy torpedoes were difficult to find. Hardy had no work in Ingonish and was too young to sign up for the war. But the merchant marine, starved for men, readily accepted his application in Sydney to become a trimmer aboard the *Lord Strathcona*.

By September 1942, Hardy had been a year aboard ship and long overdue for a visit home. After a short trip back to see his mother in Ingonish, he returned to Sydney only to find that the *Lord Strathcona* had sailed for Bell Island ahead of schedule, leaving him stranded. Just as well. On 5 September, a German submarine, *U-513*, plugged two torpedoes into the hull of the *Lord Strathcona*, sending it 140 feet to the bottom of Lance Cove off Bell Island. All of those on board made it safely into lifeboats, including Hardy's father. The crew of the *Saganaga*, another ship destroyed in the same attack, were not so lucky, with more than twenty losing their lives. Another torpedo narrowly missed the 7800-ton *Rose Castle*, docked at the ore-loading pier, but it did blow up a large chunk of the wharf. Badly spooked, many of the *Rose Castle* crew – including the captain – called it quits. On 17 September, Hardy, his father, and several others who had served on the now-broken *Lord Strathcona* transferred to the *Rose Castle*, its sister vessel built at the same British shipyard and also owned by the Dominion Iron and Steel Company of Sydney.

Some weeks later, on 20 October, the *Rose Castle* was part of a convoy headed back to Bell Island for another load when a terrific storm blew up. Her holds empty, the ship was high and light in the water, and extremely difficult to control. The blasting gale forced the vessel a hundred miles or more away from the convoy to a point sixteen miles southeast of Ferryland Head. The heavy seas tossed the ship like a cork, its spinning propellors rising into the night air, the blades loudly slapping the surface of the water. Suddenly hearts sank as someone on deck spotted a white streak several hundred yards off, pointed directly at the bouncing hull, the unmistakable wake of a churning torpedo. Miraculously, there was no explosion. Either the torpedo was a dud, not uncommon with German U-boats, or the boiling sea had tossed the hull up and out of harm's way just as the explosive was about to ram the ship. Everyone was immediately ordered onto the boat deck to be ready to abandon ship when the next torpedoes arrived. As fate would have it, the torpedo was the very last carried by Ulrich Graf's *U-69*, which six days earlier had sunk the ferry *Caribou* in the Cabot Strait, killing 136 people. After a bitterly cold and tense night on the deck of the *Rose Castle* awaiting the next attack, Hardy's father came down with a severe case of pneumonia. 'I got cold, like the rest of them, so I said the devil with this, I'm going down,' Hardy recalled. 'I wasn't the nervous type, so I went down and went to bed.' The night passed without incident, and the charmed *Rose Castle* again survived a close encounter with a marauding U-boat.

Hardy's ailing father was admitted to hospital on the ship's return to Sydney, and was unable to join his son for the next run to Bell Island. The trip proved uneventful, and on the evening of 1 November 1942 the *Rose Castle* lay at anchor about a mile from the island's Scotia Pier, fully loaded and ready to run the submarine gauntlet the next day back to Whitney Pier, on the outskirts of Sydney. Hardy – now a steward – finished serving supper to the engineers and cleaned up the dishes and mess table. His day's work complete, Hardy visited the cabin of fireman Freddy Burt, a Newfoundlander from Rose Blanche who was always cracking off-colour jokes. Their youthful banter inevitably drifted to the subject of girls. Sometime before 11 p.m., Hardy headed back to his own cabin with a 'Good night, I'll see you tomorrow on deck somewhere.' 'Yes,' said Burt, 'we'll see you tomorrow.' Back in his steam-heated cabin, on deck at midships, Hardy stripped to his underwear and lay down. No need for a book to put him under – the work of a typical day readily overwhelmed his wakefulness. Under his pillow, a heavy canvas life-jacket was always at hand, ready for the day the *Rose Castle*'s luck might run out.

Out in Conception Bay, Friedrich-Wilhelm Wissmann peered through a light rain at the vague silhouette of the *Rose Castle*. The commander of

U-518, Wissmann was on the prowl for the first kill of his boat's maiden voyage. All the ships in the anchorage were carefully blacked out as he stood gazing intently from the front of the conning tower. But the army searchlights on shore, meant to expose or drive away submarines, drew Wissmann forward, mesmerized. For as the beams mechanically swept across the bay, their stray luminescence also flickered across his prey, trickling through the rigging, dimly caressing their hulls, leaving their edges burned briefly onto the retina. Like a cat in the grass, Wissmann and the hushed crew silently tensed, ready to pounce.

Their boat was a 750-ton long-range submarine, known as a Type IXC, newly built at the Deutsche Werft in Hamburg. The vessel had departed its Baltic Sea base at Kiel just thirty-seven days before, to the farewell strains of a navy band. Provisioned for an eight-week North Atlantic cruise, the vessel carried twenty-two torpedoes, though as many as half might be duds based on early fleet experience. The fifty-odd crew members were mostly young men out on their first mission in this much-desired branch of the German navy, which in 1942 had almost single-handedly choked Allied supply lines to Europe.

Operation Drumbeat, or Paukenschlag, launched in January 1942, had inaugurated a concerted U-boat assault on American coastal shipping. The operation was a direct result of the sudden entry of the United States into the war following the 7 December 1941 Japanese attack on Pearl Harbor and Germany's declaration of war four days later. Hitler removed previous restrictions on attacks on American shipping and set loose his pack of sea wolves. The first six months of 1942 were known as a new 'happy time' in the U-Waffe, matching the string of Atlantic successes in the summer and fall of 1940. Through inexperience, the American navy was inept at locating and destroying submarines, and coastal defence was sloppy as cities, towns, and freighters remained well lit at night, helping the U-boats to target their prey. By the end of January, sixty-two Allied ships were sunk, about 327,000 tons. To the German architects of the carnage, it was a 'merry massacre' or the 'American hunting season.' U-boats, of course, had probed Canadian waters even before Operation Drumbeat, since Canada had been an enemy from 1939. The first, *U-111*, had investigated potential convoy egress points off Newfoundland in June 1941. But Operation Drumbeat was the bloodiest time for Canadian shipping. A U-boat first penetrated the Gulf of St Lawrence in May 1942, and by the fall twenty vessels had been torpedoed before Cabinet closed the St Lawrence to ocean-going shipping. By July, however, the easy pickings of Operation Drumbeat were over. With British help and growing experience, the United States and Canada were becoming more effective at countering the threat. In the fall of 1942, the scales were better balanced and Wissmann's crew faced some daunting counter-measures.

As his U-boat left Kiel on 26 September, Wissmann was accompanied by a 300-ton captured Dutch submarine and a minesweeper. He took on additional diesel fuel and fresh water two days later at Christiansand, Norway, then passed submerged through the heavily patrolled North Sea. Later surfaced, the submarine entered a violent storm, leaving many in the crew prostrate with seasickness. Woodwork was smashed and plates buckled as the gale battered the hull for several days. With clearer weather, *U-518* continued unimpeded south of Iceland, though it apparently ran into a volley of 'Schreckbomben' – literally 'scaring bombs' – intended to keep all U-boats at a distance rather than as a direct attack. The submarine appears to have rendezvoused with another U-boat mid-ocean, though for what purpose is unclear. As *U-518* continued towards the southern tip of Greenland, a large, fast ship was spotted but not attacked – provoking a complaint from the gung-ho torpedo officer, Oberleutnant zur See Seehausen, that Wissmann had failed to act quickly enough. Many of the crew regarded Seehausen, ambitious for his own U-boat command, as the real chief of the mission next to the ineffectual and reserved Wissmann.

At about midnight on 18 October, the submarine arrived at a point about sixty miles north-east of Belle Isle, at the eastern entrance of the strait of the same name separating Newfoundland from Labrador. For the next ten fog-shrouded days, the boat remained submerged during daylight, the crew idling or sleeping so as not to further deplete the stuffy air. Personal radios were ordered turned off to ensure the sets did not re-radiate signals and so expose the submarine to ready detection. Music picked up from broadcasts by one of the boat's main radios, however, was piped through the vessel. Surfacing the submarine at night to search for convoys, Wissmann grew increasingly uneasy at finding no targets for days on end except the odd fishing vessel. The unmarried son of a First World War U-boat officer, Wissmann was out to prove himself on this, his first command since joining the service in 1935. But it was becoming increasingly clear that the strait, the mouth of which they entered at least once, was not the presumed conduit for Allied supply ships bound for Europe. The crew began to grumble about the monotony and the bitter cold.

Wissmann eventually headed south along the east coast of Newfoundland and intercepted a coded signal from BdU, Admiral Karl Doenitz's French command post, intended to alert *U-521* and *U-520* to the ore-loading operation at Bell Island. 'Favourable possibilities to attack' was the message. 'Endeavour to force your way into the harbour.' Wissmann decided to get in on the action himself. Once the surfaced boat was in Conception Bay, Wissmann could see automobile headlights, on both Bell Island and the mainland, as well as a searchlight. As the vessel nudged closer to the *Rose Castle*'s anchorage at Lance Cove, Wissmann noted that army searchlights strafed the surface of the water regularly, every twenty minutes. The clouds suddenly parted to expose the bright moon ('Always comes when it is not wanted,' Wissmann typed in his war diary) and minutes later a searchlight came perilously close, forcing the boat to withdraw.

The next searchlight sweep, though, played into his hands: it exposed two looming shadows between him and the shore, the ore-carrier *PLM-27* and the *Rose Castle*, both of them sitting ducks. Coming ever closer, Wissmann spotted a third ship in the distance, the *Flyingdale*, anchored alongside the Scotia Pier. Unexpectedly, another probing searchlight edged close to the submarine. 'The next seconds are decisive,' Wissmann noted in the diary. 'If it goes farther, he will have caught me. But exactly in front of us, he turns back and off.' Then the moment of decision, as the beam swept away, leaving the boat again enveloped by the night. 'It has to happen now – the 10 minutes until the floodlight illuminates again have to be taken advantage of.' Wissmann's enterprising torpedo man, Seehausen, fired from Tube 1 at the farthest ship, the moored *Flyingdale*. The hiss of escaping air could be heard throughout the sub. Seconds later, Seehausen let loose from Tubes 2 and 3 at the *Rose Castle*.

The two men on watch that night aboard the *Rose Castle*, second mate Jack Savery and Gordon Hardy's cousin George Hardy, glimpsed the tell-tale airstream of at least one torpedo bound like a demon for the ship. They immediately lunged to trip the ship's internal alarm system, but it was too late. Forty-eight seconds after launch, and a few seconds after it was spotted, a torpedo ripped apart the hull of the *Rose Castle*.

The force of the blast knocked young Gordon Hardy out of his deep slumber and almost out of his bunk. Groggy, he grabbed the pull-chain of the light at the head of his bunk, but the bulb would not illuminate. He then knew for certain that his own ship had been hit. In the pitch dark, he grabbed the life-jacket, opened the door to the alley-way, bounded along its twelve-foot length in seconds, and was out on the deck amid the shouting and confusion. Damn! The life-jacket turned out to be his pillow. Back down the alley-way and blindly into his cabin again, Hardy found the life-jacket and put it on like a vest before dashing out again onto the steam-covered deck, now listing badly. Instinctively, he knew that another torpedo was already on its way: that's how it had been with the *Lord Strathcona* in September at this very spot.

The ship's second and third engineers were on deck with a flashlight, warning their near-naked steward that the freezing waters would finish him, not save him. But as daredevil Hardy stood on the railing, there was no hesitation. A thousand and more boyhood plunges from schooners into the Ingonish harbour, and hours spent swimming underwater, had prepared young Hardy for the dive of his life. 'We're due for another torpedo,' he shouted at the second and third engineers, as others in the crew scrambled to get off a few shots at the sub with their four-inch gun. Hardy's legs launched him into the void at the very moment another torpedo hit on the opposite side of the *Rose Castle*. Hardy and his ship, separately but side by side, both sank swiftly into the stinging, numbing waters of Conception Bay. 'I can see, even in the dark, this big thing. Me looking back as I jumped and struck the water, this big thing above you sort of rolling over,' Hardy remembers from that bleak night. 'It seemed like she was coming on top of you.'

In the few seconds he dropped thirty to forty feet through the air, Hardy suffered ear damage from the concussion of the explosion. And as he hit the water, the powerful suction of the sinking *Rose Castle* – already heavy with a full load of ore – dragged him down deep, one hundred feet or more. The water pressure damaged his ears further as he swam furiously against the downward torrent to break the surface. Water began to seep into his chest, slowing him as he clawed upward. Finally, after more than a minute, he was gulping the night air and bobbing amid the flotsam. Blood oozed from his ears and nose and his hearing was badly damaged. But in the distance he could still make out the screams of his drowning crew-mates crying out to God Almighty and the Blessed Virgin Mary. He swam as best he could, with the wind and away from the disaster, growing ever more stiff and numb. He came across an empty lifeboat that was upside-down, and tried desperately to crawl onto it. But his fingers and hands were so cold and weak that he could not haul himself up, so he shoved off again, alone and in the dark. The life-jacket provided some buoyancy, but in the confusion Hardy had neglected to turn on its small, battery-powered red light that sat on the left front pocket. When he finally did remember the light, intended as a beacon for rescuers, his fingers were too stiff and numb to slide the switch.

Seehausen had fired a third torpedo, from Tube 5 at the U-boat's stern, towards the *Rose Castle*, and Wissmann noted in his log that it struck home forty-five seconds later. One of the first two fired at the ship, then, either missed its mark or was a dud. The Tube 5 torpedo – the one Hardy had narrowly avoided – completed the kill. Wissmann then turned on the third and last big vessel in the anchorage, the *PLM-27*, a Free French ore-carrier owned by the Paris-Lyon-Marseille line. Seehausen let fly the fifth and final torpedo of the attack, from Tube 4, at *PLM-27*, which was anchored between Bell Island and the now-broken *Rose Castle*. Thirty-five seconds later, the warhead tore into the stern of the heavily laden ship.

Pierre Simard, able seaman aboard the *PLM-27*, was already on deck when his ship was rocked by the blast. The attack on the *Rose Castle* had rudely alerted the crew to the presence of the U-boat, and the men had time enough to get to the First World War–vintage three-inch gun in a brave attempt to protect themselves. The submarine itself was a barely visible silhouette several hundred yards off. Simard, born in Montreal but raised in Quebec City, had already survived one other surface gun battle with a U-boat. Just seventeen years old and looking for adventure, Simard had signed on to the *Skotland*, an aged Norwegian cargo ship, in September 1941. In May the following year, the *Skotland* steamed from Philadelphia with a load of timber – and three days out encountered a surfaced U-boat that boldly began to pump shells into the ship from the deck gun. The *Skotland* crew returned fire from their lone gun. They were accurate enough that the U-boat captain hastily abandoned the shelling and launched two torpedos. The massive explosions splintered the load of timber, driving a shower of wooden spikes into human flesh. Simard, on the gun platform at the time, was sent skyward and badly twisted his legs and back on landing. He and the other surviving crew members managed to clamber into a lifeboat with a salvaged case of whiskey. Three days later they were picked up and taken to Boston to recover.

Wissmann, however, had no time to waste on a gun battle, efficiently dispatching the *PLM-27* with a single torpedo. Simard's recovering legs were again badly twisted in the blast, as the deck suddenly lurched upward under his feet. He managed to make the railing, and jumped into the water with his life-jacket. The shore was about a half-mile off, and Simard – six feet tall and a lean 140 pounds – struggled towards it. His poorly made life-jacket got more and more waterlogged until he finally had to throw it away. Wissmann, meanwhile, was already making his escape around the south end of the island to then loop towards the west side of Conception Bay. As the submarine sped off, Wissmann observed the *PLM-27* in its final death throes. About an hour later, safe now in the deeper waters of the bay, he noted smugly in his war diary that the 'searchlights that were supposed to protect the ships sealed their fate.' The sweeping beams had helped illuminate the prey, and their regularity – contrary to army standing orders – allowed Wissmann to time his attack with confidence. Shells from the ineffective shore batteries had landed harmlessly in potato gardens near St Phillips, miles from their target.

Hardy, meanwhile, was getting badly played out in the water. Just over five feet, seven inches, his 140-pound frame had little insulating fat to protect him from water that was only a few degrees above freezing. During the excruciating hour or two he spent drifting with the wind, virtually naked, Hardy's thoughts turned to his mother, who had already lost a son to the war in June the previous year. He vowed to survive for her sake, that her burden of sorrow be made no heavier. Miraculously, Hardy came upon a life-raft carrying a few other *Rose Castle* survivors and was quickly hauled aboard by Savery, the second mate. The crude vessel consisted of oil drums and planks lashed together in an open square, the centre exposed to the sea. The raft was normally carried in the rigging, and the crew had somehow managed to launch it in the confusion of the attack.

Soon, all on board could see a faint light on the water in the distance that slowly made its way towards the life-raft. Eventually they could make out the form of the third engineer – Jimmy McDonald, the man who had urged Hardy not to jump – and grabbed an arm to haul him aboard as well. McDonald was still clutching the flashlight he had been carrying while on watch, its light steadfastly burning even under sea water. Hardy's knees had buckled in the life-raft, unable to support his weight as he tried to clamber around the primitive craft. Still dressed only in his underwear and badly whipped by the chill November winds, he did the only thing he could to warm up: he hopped back into the water, in the centre of the life-raft, where at least there was no wind to frost his flesh. A small navy boat finally took everyone off the life-raft before dawn, but the ordeal wasn't quite over for Hardy. Wrapped only in a blanket, he froze in the back of an army truck that took him up to the village, then stubbed his toes as he stumbled to the second-floor home of a local family. Soon he was tucked into bed, with a shot or two of rum to calm his nerves and help him sleep. Twenty-eight crew-mates had died in the attack, including funny Freddy Burt, who likely died instantly with the first torpedo blast.

Simard spent thirty minutes or more in the water, swimming laboriously towards the Lance Cove beach. Among the other struggling *PLM-27* survivors was 'Papa' Henri Lemesle, an aging alcoholic, once a captain but now an assistant cook. Loved by the whole crew, he had befriended Simard, trading apples for Simard's daily mealtime ration of French wine. In the distance that night, Simard heard 'Papa' Henri call out his name, asking for help. 'Mon petit Pierre,' came the anguished cry. 'Viens m'aider!' But the old fellow slipped forever below the waves before Simard could reach him. Once at the beach, Simard found that his legs were too mangled and numb to carry his weight on land, and he lay there helpless among the breakers. He was eventually found by a local fisherman, given a bone-chilling ride in the back of an army truck, and taken in by a mining family who placed him on the floor next to a pot-bellied stove to warm up. They offered him and his crew-mates some

Screech, Newfoundland's famous rum. 'They had to pour it down our throats because we just couldn't relax,' Simard recalled. 'After a little while, I was okay, felt good, and I slept for nearly twenty-four hours; we all did. It takes a lot out of people to be torpedoed.' The attack took the lives of a dozen fellow crew members.

Whether from confusion or wartime secrecy, word went out to Hardy's ailing father at the Sydney hospital that no one had survived the attack on the *Rose Castle*. For six black days, the elder Hardy and his wife coped with the anguish of a second son lost to the war – the very news young Hardy had hoped to spare his mother. He had no money to telephone home and simply assumed the steel company would notify relatives about who had survived. Savery, the *Rose Castle*'s second mate and the only officer still alive, eventually persuaded a Canadian government official to give $20 to each of his recovering crew members in St John's. Hardy immediately called home, like a voice from the grave. The three-minute call, reduced to just one minute because of interference by switchboard censors, was a shock to the family. His sister Gladys screeched, 'It's Gordon!' but the censor would not allow much more to be said. By the time he put down the receiver, Hardy had spent $10.40 of his small store of cash.

On the ferry trip back to Sydney, the torpedo attack continued to play on Hardy's nerves. He'd be asleep in his bunk when a big steel door would slam – and in an instant, he'd be on deck ready again to jump into the North Atlantic. Eventually Hardy contracted pneumonia, then double pneumonia, and spent six months recovering in hospital. Giving up on the merchant marine, Hardy soon joined the army. Pierre Simard, by contrast, was not yet through with the sea – though he'd now make sure his ships had better fire-power than an antique three-inch gun. He joined the Canadian Navy in 1943, serving aboard the destroyer *Saskatchewan*, and was never again torpedoed.

Wissmann's escape from the Bell Island anchorage was without incident, but he did run into trouble two days later as he rounded Cape Race, surfaced, and headed for the Cabot Strait entrance to the Gulf of St Lawrence. A Digby aircraft on submarine patrol spotted the conning tower about 3.5 miles away, despite the boat's new camouflage – bluish-white for the upper parts, grey for the hull – designed specifically to thwart aerial detection. Wissmann made a crash dive at the approach of the Digby, which dropped four 450-pound depth charges into the swell left by the submarine. 'Oil patch 100 ft in diameter appeared after attack,' the pilot reported. 'Fog closed in 10 minutes later.' Below the surface, one of the exploding depth charges jolted the submarine and its neophyte crew, most of whom were suffering through their first under-water assault. The boat's compass and other glass-covered fittings were shattered, but the damage was minor and easily repaired. Wissmann con-tinued his cruise on into the Gulf.

On 5 November, the boat picked up a German-language broadcast from Berlin directed at North and South America, boasting of twenty-six Allied ships destroyed in the past week. 'Of the ships sunk near New-foundland, there were three heavily loaded with ore,' said the report – though in fact the *Flyingdale* was undamaged, as the torpedo slammed into the Scotia Pier instead. The sinkings were a testimony to the techni-cal skills of Seehausen, formerly a torpedo instructor at Flensburg and regarded by the crew as the most enterprising of *U-518*'s five officers. (It was Seehausen's second celebration of the voyage – he had learned weeks earlier by radio that his wife had given birth to their first child, a boy, an event the officers toasted with champagne.) Even Wissmann, stiff and high-strung, had ably led his crew into their first successful engagement and escaped unscathed. He seemed to be living up to his nickname – 'Wissmannchen,' or 'smart guy,' a pun. This second deadly U-boat attack on the Bell Island ore operation within two months severely disrupted Canadian shipping schedules and forced authorities to string anti-torpedo nets to protect the wharves. The locals now felt so exposed to attack that soon a story was making the rounds: the U-boat commander had gone ashore in disguise the night before the *Rose Castle-PLM* attacks and had taken a local girl out to a dance. The officer, so the story went, later had the audacity to send her a postcard.

Wissmann, meanwhile, ordered the submarine to remain submerged for the next day and a half as he entered the Gulf for the next stage of his mission. There was some discussion aboard about moving into the St Lawrence River to a point between Métis-sur-Mer and Matane on the Gaspé Peninsula, but the daring sortie was ruled out for reasons that remain unclear. On the morning of 8 November, *U-518* headed instead into the mouth of the Baie des Chaleurs, the deep inlet that separates northern New Brunswick from the Gaspé Peninsula. The bay was named by Jacques Cartier in 1534 for its relatively mild climate, compared with the chill waters of the Gulf. Its eastern basin offered clear passage for a submarine, with no shoals and depths exceeding two hundred feet. For Wissmann, anxious about being spotted, the bay's special attraction was its rather thin coastal population. The periscope was raised to gauge the ship traffic, but no vessels were sighted and the submarine withdrew. That night, taking advantage of the dark sky of the new moon, *U-518* returned at periscope depth. No ships or automobile lights were seen, so the submarine rose to the surface, relying on its diesel engines. As the boat travelled down the bay, automobile lights could be seen on the shore roads on both sides. Approaching a spot on the coast about four miles west of the Gaspé community of New Carlisle, Wissmann switched to the silent electric motors. The submarine was nudged to about seven hundred yards from shore while a twelve-foot wooden boat, stored vertically in a special receptacle, was removed and readied for launch. The forward diving tank was flooded and the submarine was gently beached on the modest slope at about twelve minutes past midnight, local time. Two men climbed into the dinghy with baggage and equipment, and one of them – a seaman named Roeseler – began to row his passenger towards the forty-foot jagged cliff-face along the shore.

Suddenly, the headlights of a car swung out over the water as the vehicle hugged a curve in the road heading east towards New Carlisle. Wissmann's mouth went dry from the shock. 'Involuntarily, I ordered "Quick, put your heads down,"' he noted in the war diary. The crew ducked – never mind that there was a 750-ton U-boat beached like a whale under their feet, fully exposed to view. The headlights swept across the vessel but then swung back without hesitation onto the land, briefly illuminating some residences. The boat had not been spotted. Wissmann felt compelled to record that 'the houses make a very poor impression.' About forty-five minutes after setting out, Roeseler returned alone in the wooden boat. It was quickly stowed, the forward diving tank purged, and *U-518* returned to the middle of the deep bay to retrace its route back to the Gulf of St Lawrence. 'The mission was completed silently and unobserved,' Wissmann typed in his war diary. The successful landing had come just one day after Operation Torch, the British and American invasion of French North Africa that began finally to roll back the German empire.

18

TWO

The Stranger in Room 11

Sleepy New Carlisle, on the south coast of Quebec's Gaspé Peninsula, is today little more than a gas stop on the shore highway that dips and curves wildly towards the tourist haunts around Percé Rock. A town brochure meekly promotes its CN Rail station, a war veterans' monument, an Anglican church, a local museum, and a restored house as visitor attractions. But the few tourists who do stay briefly seem more interested in a two-storey, white frame house on a corner lot nearly obscured by trees. For New Carlisle is perhaps best remembered as the boyhood home of one of Canada's most famous political personalities. 'It thought of itself as the bellybutton of the world and was very, very WASP, the microcosm of a blissfully dominant minority,' René Lévesque recalled in engaging memoirs about his youth there. 'Although immersed in this English micro-climate, we were no less French for all that. Well, Francophone. Even a bit too much for my liking.'

The little community was first settled in 1784 by seven boatloads of British Loyalists, who had fled America to Trois-Rivières before accepting a British offer of land along the Baie des Chaleurs. The three hundred or so refugees, most from the New York area, sailed to nearby Paspébiac and soon established themselves a few miles west at Petit-Paspébiac. 'The shores of the Baie des Chaleurs share with many other lands' ends in the world a vocation for picking up the shipwrecked,' as Lévesque had put it. The group set about creating a proper British enclave, soon rechristening it New Carlisle after the fortified English town near the Scottish border, the birthplace of their lieutenant-governor. These displaced and exhausted people emulated the battlements of

Carlisle by erecting cultural walls, the better to live in peace away from the bloody currents of war and revolution. The town soon had its wharf, courthouse, jail, Masonic Lodge, and assortment of Protestant steeples overlooking the grand bay. A lush forest of lovingly planted hardwoods soon spread along the lawns and roadways, eventually overwhelming most of the New England–style buildings. From its earliest days, the community was a legal and administrative headquarters. In the twentieth century it became a rail centre of some importance, with a repair shed and marshalling yard serving the narrow-guage trains that huffed along the Gaspé cliffs.

By the Great Depression, New Carlisle was home to about one thousand people, not all of them English. There was a substantial francophone population, many descended from Acadians who had been deported from the Maritimes almost two centuries earlier by the British and who returned to rebuild in more remote areas. Their numbers had grown enough that in 1933 station CHNC confidently signed on the air, the first French-language broadcaster on the Gaspé Peninsula. Lévesque's father was a French-Canadian lawyer forced by illness to flee to the purer air and languid pace of rural Quebec. He settled in New Carlisle, at first doing legal work for a local Irish businessman until he got 'sick of shady dealings whose bad smells emanated from every drawer,' according to Lévesque. He opened his own practice and soon prospered, working in French with francophone clients. Indeed, the town seemed to epitomize the 'two solitudes' of modern Quebec, as each language group clung to its own cultural and religious traditions, crossing over only when business required – sometimes not even then. Children, though, were another story.

By all accounts, young René Lévesque was a swirling dust devil of mischief. Even before he was old enough for school, his mother fastened him to the back-porch railing with a cord to keep him from tearing up and down the neighbourhood. And once he was old enough to be free of the leash, Lévesque roamed with his friends like a hyperactive savage, stirring trouble all the way from the beach beside the dock to the dense bush in back of town. 'He was a hellion,' recalls Dorothy Sheehan, who grew up with Lévesque in New Carlisle. 'We used to congregate at the beach and he was the kind that would come with a handful of sand and pour it right on your head.' Lévesque's friends tended to be French, especially Gérard and Paul Poirier, whose parents owned the gas station down from the Carlisle Hotel, just past the beer shop. Lévesque was fluently bilingual – indeed, his French had become muddied with borrowings like 'le post office' – but already there was a vague sense of separateness from the anglophones. ' "Les autres," the ones on the other side, which included the majority of the bosses and exploiters, weren't they also the English conquerors?' Lévesque recalled half a century later. 'That had never bothered me when we chivied each other good-naturedly by exchanging stones or snowballs and countered their "French pea soup" with "English crawfish." One name was as silly as the other. It was all in fun and we had never taken it seriously.'

At the Poirier gas station / hangout in the 1930s, the gang of kids often included Earle Annett Jr and his tomboy sister, Geraldine. Their anglophone parents had arrived in town in the spring of 1931 after buying a property alongside the Gaspé highway where a hotel once stood but had burned to the ground. Earle Sr had a new hotel – the Carlisle – built on the site, and everyone moved in 29 July to operate it as a family business. Earle Jr, fluently bilingual, was just three months younger than René and they struck up a friendship. Earle and Geraldine, five years his junior, would often walk to school with René, playing a quick game of kick the can before they went their separate ways to the English and French schools. They'd sometimes meet again after classes and saunter back home, conjuring up whatever trouble they could. The Annetts had originally come from the town of Gaspé, another Loyalist bastion towards the tip of the Gaspé Peninsula, where Earle Sr helped manage another hotel. Earle Jr, then about eight years old, had been riding his bicycle in town one day when a young rowdy driving a car tried to frighten the boy by pretending to swerve into him. Earle was forced up a little rise, where he fell off the bike and injured his knee – a lifelong injury, it turned out. His sore knee slowed him down a little when whipping around town with Geraldine and the boys.

Earle's bad knee took on much more significance after the war broke out in 1939. For as his friend Lévesque later put it, 'unless you were in uniform you couldn't get a girl to go out with you.' When he was thirteen, Lévesque used to earn a few dollars translating press releases for station CHNC and was sometimes allowed to stand in for the regular announcer. He later parlayed that experience into work as a uniformed war correspondent on European battlefields – close enough to real soldiering to impress the girls. His buddy Earle, coming of age in a Gaspé backwater, was desperate for war service, but the wobbly knee made him an instant reject at the enlistment office. So he took the train to Montreal for a hospital operation, and spent six weeks recovering, undergoing intensive rehabilitation. The procedure was a disaster. Back in New Carlisle, his kneecap would repeatedly pop out of place and he could not bend his leg more than ninety degrees. Though he did not quite limp, Earle could never walk very far without feeling pain. He was trapped in New Carlisle and modern medicine was not going to set him free.

The eight Annett kids all pitched in to help run the three-storey Carlisle Hotel, which stood on the south side of the Gaspé shore road, its rear facing the sea. There was a natural division of labour. The eldest, Marguerite, kept the books, ran the office, and was the only one her father trusted to drive the family's $3000 Chevy, which served as a taxi. The roads were wicked, especially in the spring. A brief lapse of attention could easily leave a car upside down in the ditch, its wheels spinning wildly. Marguerite, though, was widely admired as a master motorist. When they still lived in Gaspé and she was barely sixteen, Marguerite would take the car and meet American tourists at the train in Matapédia, driving them safely along two hundred harrowing miles back to Gaspé. When she turned eighteen and finally got her licence, she was the only driver for Annett's taxi service. Her sister Geraldine's job was to serve guests water and butter in the dining room. Gerry, as she was called, never cooked, never made a bed, never touched the cash register, specializing in water-and-butter serving.

Earle Jr was the Carlisle's bellhop. He would sit on the wooden porch beside the hotel entrance listening for the approach of cars. When he spotted potential customers, he would dash out, hop on the running board, and try to get them to stop. The hotel offered 'luxurious log cabins, sea foods, buffalo steaks, salt water bathing, boating, fishing,' he would bark, and all at good prices. Getting their attention was important – the rival Maison Blanche hotel, run by Paul-Emile Roy, was a few hundred yards east, just up the road. Of course that was the French-speaking hotel, while the Carlisle was English, a clear advantage when trying to lure American tourists. Business got so good that Earle Sr even hired maids, boarding them in a nearby house he had bought. The family lived in rooms on the third floor of the hotel, working long days in the summer trying to scoop up as much tourist traffic as possible before the season's end. In the fall and winter, the guests and cash flow would almost disappear, except for the occasional travelling salesman.

After war broke out in 1939, young Earle – confined to the home front because of his knee – assigned himself another job: spy-catcher. Often at night, especially at the height of the U-boat attacks in the North Atlantic, people in New Carlisle would hear strange, unexplained noises out in the Baie des Chaleurs. The dull rumble of pistons, the growl of machinery, strange metallic sounds. Everybody was convinced that U-boats regularly surfaced in the bay, firing up their diesel engines to recharge batteries under the cloak of night. And one evening – who knows? – perhaps they'd try to launch an invasion on the Gaspé shore. A mite of fear would infect the imagination, growing with each unexplained noise out on the waves. During the war, it was sometimes hard to get a decent night's sleep in New Carlisle. But Earle Jr was prepared to do something about the Nazi menace. With his sister Marguerite he made a vow to catch a U-boat spy as their contribution to Canada's war effort. And so every stranger that came to the hotel was placed under secret scrutiny.

Shortly before 1 a.m. on Monday, 9 November 1942, Werner Alfred Waldemar von Janowski stepped off a wooden dinghy onto a rocky beach four miles west of New Carlisle. He swiftly carried his baggage onto the inhospitable shore, at the foot of a forty-foot cliff, then bid Matrosengefreiter Roeseler farewell as the seaman rowed silently back towards *U-518*. Janowski, thirty-eight, was in full naval uniform: blue officer's jacket, double-breasted with two rows of brass buttons, two anchor insignia emblazoned on each side of the collar, green submariner fatigues of canvas, high leather boots, and an officer's cap made in Paris. The uniform fit him closely, having been made to measure in Berlin. Pinned on the left side of the jacket was the Iron Cross, 1st Class. In a pocket were two Army movement orders, dated 24 September 1942, describing him as a 'Leutnant zur See, Sonderfuehrer,' or naval sublieutenant S.B. A petty officer had given him a haircut and shave on board shortly before leaving, but he kept a thin, sandy moustache. He stood five feet, nine and a half inches and weighed 160 pounds, with dark brown hair parted on the left side, medium blue eyes, and a sallow complexion. His pastey face was vaguely rat-like. Dark circles hung under his eyes and his hair was slicked down greasily. The joint of his right thumb was permanently stiff from an injury and his right knee bore a bullet-wound scar. There was also a slight scar above his left eyebrow.

Alone with his baggage, Janowski attempted to make his way up the treacherous near-vertical cliff face in the dark, but without success. Forced to spend the cold night pinned to the rocky shore, Janowski could do little more than smoke his made-in-Hamburg North State cigarettes. By about 7 a.m., chilled to the bone and aching for a bath, he had sufficient light to drag his luggage to the top of the jagged shore, where there was a grassy overhang. There he rapidly changed into civilian clothes – grey turtleneck sweater, grey tweed suit, blue felt hat with a narrow brim, rubber-soled brown shoes, and a dark trench coat. Using a shovel he had brought, Janowski dug a hole into which he placed a rubber bag containing his naval uniform, burying it. The shovel he tossed as far as he could into the sea. At about 8:30 a.m. he began walking eastward along the shore highway towards New Carlisle, carrying a leather satchel and leather-covered briefcase, trying as best he could to look like a businessman setting out on his Monday morning calls.

Janowski had walked about a mile in the chill morning air when he ran into James Coull, a train conductor for the CNR. Coull, who lived in the country about five miles west of New Carlisle, was driving his Ford into town to start his shift. He had stopped to pick up a fellow worker – Charlie Gallon, a section hand also heading to work – when he noticed the stranger and asked where he was headed. To town, was the clipped reply. Coull, sixty-five, offered a ride, and soon the three men were speeding along the rough road towards New Carlisle. Janowski assumed both men, each dressed in overalls, were local farmers. Coull asked Janowski in English about himself, but the stranger feigned difficulty with the language, indicating he was French Canadian. Coull was not fluent in French. Janowski did mumble something about being a salesman for the Northern Electric Company and said he was looking for a hotel. A few minutes later Coull dropped him off in town just a short walk from the Carlisle. Still chilled from his night on the beach, Janowski had passed his first test.

Just inside the front entrance of the hotel, twenty-two-year-old Simone

Loubert was busy cleaning the lobby. A French Canadian from the nearby community of Maria, Loubert was working as a maid and living in the Annett house across the field. Short and a little stocky, with jet-black hair and dark eyes, she had a pretty face and an inviting smile. She did everything rather quickly, whether walking, talking, or cleaning. Janowski stepped inside that morning, about 9 a.m., and asked Loubert for a bath and breakfast. No overnight stay, he said in thickly accented English, just a day room. Loubert went upstairs, awakening Earle Jr to ask how much she should charge and what room to give him. 'He is a plain-looking man but well dressed,' she said. Loubert was told to put the stranger in Room 11, one of the nicest in the hotel. Opposite the office, it was the only guest room on the ground floor, where the hotel dining-room, living-room, kitchen, and sun-room were also located. Room 11 made sense for a man with heavy luggage who would be leaving in a few hours anyway, and it had a tub. Janowski headed to the room, where he had his first hot bath after being cooped up inside a submarine for forty-four days. He emerged within the hour and slipped quietly to a table in the dining-room, where another maid, Léone Poereen, served him breakfast. Janowski had said very little to anyone, but already people were talking in hushed tones about this unusual visitor.

'He was quite a tall man, and slender,' Geraldine, one of the Annett girls, recalls. 'He had a strange-looking face. His face was kind of round-looking and he had very cold eyes. And when he would smile, he had a cold smile. You'd just see teeth.' Marguerite, the eldest Annett sibling, also found him odd. 'We knew that he was a foreigner, the way he spoke,' she says. 'He spoke English, but he had a kind of gutteral speech, in the back of his throat.' Loubert noticed the thick accent as well, and sensed he was nervous. That aroused her suspicions, especially with all the rumours of submarines in the area, and soon she was chatting about him with the other maids.

Janowski might have been a quite ordinary travelling salesman – typically the only guests after the close of the tourist season – except that little things about him did not add up. The first thing young Earle noticed was the clothing. At twenty years of age, Earle was acutely aware of fashion. 'His shoes were quite different from anything I had ever seen,' he later wrote. 'They were a brown-colored summer type with a thick, light-colored sole, which appeared to be rubber, and had an odd-looking welt around the toes. His dark gabardine topcoat was not quite like the Canadian style. It had patch pockets instead of the slip-in type.' The turtleneck sweater was also at odds with the tweed jacket, definitely not the outfit of a commercial traveller.

There was more. The stranger had given Loubert a one-dollar bill to pay for the bath and breakfast, and another for some cigarettes. Both were large-size Dominion of Canada bills dating from the First World War. They were legal tender, still in circulation in some Canadian back-waters, but were becoming rarer. The newly formed Bank of Canada had issued its own smaller-sized bills in 1935 and for seven years had been diligently withdrawing the old bills. Loubert took the strange money to young Earle, and remarked that the man – a heavy smoker – didn't seem to know how much a package of cigarettes cost. Sensing trouble, the lad immediately tipped his father. Earle Sr closely examined the bills at the reception desk, just across from Janowski who was now seated in the lobby, smoking. 'Is the money counterfeit?' the stranger asked. No, just not in circulation any more, came the reply. His curiosity piqued, the older man began to gently probe for more information. Was that a Swedish accent? No, Janowski said, he was from France. And his name? 'Bernhardt,' he said, repeating 'Bernhardt.' Did you come in on the bus from Chandler? Yes, yes, the bus from Chandler. As anyone in New Carlisle could tell you, there was no longer any bus from Chandler, about seventy-five miles east.

But it was Janowski's bad aroma that really bothered the old man. Here was someone who had just bathed and shaved, and yet he stank. His clothes, his luggage, even his money exuded a stale foulness that everyone noticed but only Earle Sr could identify. Some of the Annett clan in Gaspé were fishermen, and an uncle once took Earle Sr as a boy deep into the hold of a fishing boat that had been at sea for weeks. The briny dampness had imparted a terrible smell to everything. 'That's the only time he had ever smelled that smell,' Marguerite recalls. 'It was like a kind of shut-up smell, but it wasn't a smell like anything shut up on land. It was a funny smell.' Geraldine remembers her father remarking to her: 'That's strange, he's been under water. He's been in the water somewhere.' The Annett men were now convinced they had before them a genuine spy who had spent the last few weeks on a German submarine.

The Carlisle, like most hotels in the Gaspé, had its year-round residents. The third floor, where family members were spread out in several rooms, was also home to several young men who worked in the local branch of the Bank of Nova Scotia, the town's only bank. The Annetts gave them a much-needed break on room and board, bank clerks being paid poorly. And on the second floor, in back, was P.P. Johnston. The Annett kids never knew his first name – they rather enjoyed calling him 'pee-pee' to his face. Johnston was a retired banker who had lived at the competing Maison Blanche hotel before moving over to the Carlisle. His mornings were always the same. He'd sit at his little table at a window of the dining-room, glaring at any of the children who dared make fun of him, especially Geraldine, who liked to torment him as she put out the water and butter. After breakfast, Johnston enjoyed nothing better than to sit in the living-room listening to the radio. Here he had a ringside seat for most of the comings and goings of the hotel. If he got lucky, Johnston could engage a visitor in conversation. And that's exactly what Earle Sr needed now, someone to delicately draw the stranger into more damning conversation. After first alerting Johnston to his suspicions, he introduced him to Mr Bernhardt, formerly of Paris.

'I was quite aware that I had someone of unusual interest and governed myself accordingly, without giving him the slightest inkling of my suspicion,' Johnston later wrote about this conversation, which he estimated took place over two hours. Janowski claimed to be a Parisian who had come to Canada in 1921, and had since taken out naturalization papers. That made the odd tailoring of his clothing seem even more strange for someone who had supposedly lived in Canada for twenty years. At some point the Annett dog intruded and Earle Jr joined them. 'It's a clever one,' Janowski said, referring to the animal. The boy chattered on about the dog, but the stranger was distracted as he peered out the window, shifting in the leather-upholstered chair. Janowski finally asked about the arrival time of the next train to Matapédia, where it intersected with the rail line to Montreal. About 11:10 a.m. was the answer. 'The road to the station is that way?' he asked. 'I am going to the train and I'll give you a lift,' Earle offered. Janowski declined, saying, 'I think the walk will do me good.'

Earle suddenly spotted a yellow matchbox that had been dropped beside the chair, and barely stopped himself from blurting out the fact to Janowski. Here was a possible clue, hard evidence to show along with the old dollar bills to any sceptics. But there was no way to retrieve the matchbox without arousing suspicion. To make matters worse, Earle's little brother Stanley, not yet two years old, had also spotted the matchbox and was crawling at a rapid clip to grab it. Just then, Janowski took his bags and darted from the room and out the front door. Earle dived for the matchbox, loosening it from Stanley's grip. The box said 'Camp Safety Matches' over a picture of two pipe-smoking men seated on logs before a campfire. 'Made in Belgium. Average contents 50.' The Belgian origin was by itself suspicious, but then Earle saw that it lacked an excise stamp, required of all such imports.

Earle was already convinced he had his first spy, but the matches now provided enough physical evidence to get the police involved. The train would leave within the hour, so he had to move fast. He hopped into the family Chevy and drove down to the station, where he planned to get on the train to find the naval policeman who was always on board. In the meantime, Janowski had arrived at the station and was buying train fare at a wicket manned by Dewey Smollett. 'He put his grip and briefcase down beside him at the ticket window,' Smollett later recalled to a newspaper reporter. 'Then he asked for a ticket to Matapédia. He pulled out a big roll of bills. I noticed that. Then he peeled off a twenty – it was a new-issue bill – and handed it to me. I gave him his ticket and his change. The ticket was $3.40. I gave him sixty cents in silver, five ones and a ten. I couldn't find another one, so I gave him four quarters. "That's twenty," I said. "Twenty," he repeated after me, kind of gutteral. I was in the army of occupation in the last war. Immediately I spotted the way he said "twenty." I knew it was a German accent. He even acted suspicious. He kept his head down all the time. Wouldn't look into my eyes.'

Janowski headed over to the station restaurant, where he ordered coffee. Earle, still awaiting the arrival of the train, slipped into the seat beside him and offered a cigarette. 'Kind of cold out,' he said nonchalantly as he put another cigarette into his own mouth and waited for the stranger to offer a light. Sure enough, Janowski drew another box of Camp Safety Matches from a pocket, another link in an incriminating chain of evidence. 'Is the old gentleman at the hotel your grandfather?' Janowski asked as he held the flame to Earle's cigarette tip. 'No, he is a retired banker who lives there.' Janowski stepped outside for five minutes, then returned to the restaurant, asking, 'What kind of place is Matapédia? A small place, I suppose?' 'Yes, quite small. There is really nothing there,' said Earle. At last, the train chugged into the station for a twenty-minute halt before continuing west. Janowski got aboard, and a minute or two later Earle followed. There he sought out Johnny Lozinsky, an on-duty naval policeman stationed at Gaspé who kept the sailors in line as they rode the trains.

'I was approached by E. Annett, and informed of the presence of a suspicious character who had just boarded the train at that point,' Lozinsky later told investigators. 'I went back in the train followed by Annett who showed me the passenger in question [but] owing that this man was a civilian I had no authority to act.' Here was a real spy within their grasp, and Lozinsky was hair-splitting on jurisdiction. It was frustrating for young Earle – and an ominous start to the police work on Canada's most important wartime espionage case. With precious minutes slipping away, the pair felt they quickly had to find a real policeman to make the arrest. Gus Goulet, the deputy sheriff, was a possibility, but this was much more than a local matter. With no RCMP detachment in town, Lozinsky and Earle did the only thing they could. They jumped into the Annett Chevy and sped off to get the Quebec provincial police.

Constable Alphonse Duchesneau, the senior provincial officer in town, was going to be a problem. He and his partner lived in rooms at the Maison Blanche hotel, the French-Canadian rival of the Annetts' Carlisle. Duchesneau (the anglophones pronounced it *doo-shay'-nee*) was firmly on the francophone side of the town's two solitudes, or at least that's how the Annetts saw it. There was a perception among the anglophones, whether fair or not, that the Quebec police were slow to act on anglophone complaints. 'He was a French Canadian and we had a lot of trouble even in those days with the French Canadians,' Geraldine recalls. 'It was hard to get them on the move.' Duchesneau, in particular, was 'not very pleasant at all. Very sure of himself, not very helpful at any time.'

Compounding this mutual distrust was young Earle's spy mania. More than anyone else in town, he saw Nazi U-boat agents behind every bush. The town was already nervous about the strange night sounds that drifted inland from the Baie des Chaleurs. That September, lighthouse-keeper Joseph Ferguson had reported a U-boat sighting in the Gulf of St

Lawrence from his post atop the Cap-des-Rosiers lighthouse at the tip of the Gaspé Peninsula. Ferguson's report helped inflame fears of invasion in the region, and local authorities were constantly asked to check out dead-end tips. Just the previous month, the Annetts had alerted the police to a young hitchhiker in a white turtleneck who had stopped by the Carlisle for breakfast. The fellow claimed to have just come up from Los Angeles, saying he had been hitchhiking for four years, even though his pale colour suggested otherwise. He boasted how easy it was to get across the Canadian border, and was apparently planning to take photos at Gaspé, location of the Fort Ramsay naval station. A sceptical policeman came over, but merely offered the hitchhiker a lift to Bonaventure. The Annetts came to believe the mystery man was a Nazi spy who had been sent to test security along the Gaspé Peninsula in preparation for other agent landings – other landings like that of Mr Bernhardt, formerly of Paris.

'They seemed doubtful about my spy theory,' Earle wrote about the hasty meeting he and Lozinsky had with Duchesneau and his partner. His sisters Marguerite and Geraldine remember it the same way. Duchesneau 'just thought that it was a joke probably, because he didn't want to go down and check the fellow out or anything,' says Marguerite. Perhaps it was Lozinsky's presence that tipped the balance. Duchesneau, a stout man, ducked into the police car with his partner, Lozinsky, and Earle and headed to the station, where the train was just about to pull out. Duchesneau and Lozinsky hopped aboard, while the other policeman sped to the next train stop at Bonaventure, nine miles down the track. Lozinsky immediately pointed out the suspicious traveller to the policeman. Duchesneau, in uniform, sat down beside Janowski and demanded to see his papers as the train rolled out of the station.

Janowski, claiming to be a travelling salesman, handed over two cards, the first a Canadian National Registration Certificate. The document identified the bearer as William Branton of Danforth Avenue, Toronto, but the card was bilingual – English on one side, French on the other – issued only to Quebec residents. The other card was a 1940 Quebec driver's licence, no. 79878, but also bearing the Branton name and Toronto address. This jumble of French and English Canada simply did not make sense. Duchesneau then asked to examine the stranger's luggage, at which point Janowski's nerves got the better of him. 'I am caught,' he blurted. 'I am a German officer.' Duchesneau carried on his search, turning up spiked brass knuckles, $5995.11 in various bills and coin, pills and tablets, a loaded .25-calibre automatic pistol and leather holster, eight rounds of ammunition, and a 40-watt transmitter-receiver nestled inside the suitcase. It was a dream arrest, a career-making arrest, barely twelve hours after Janowski had stepped ashore.

The train rolled to a stop at Bonaventure, where Duchesneau escorted the prisoner and his rich trove of espionage paraphernalia into the idling police car. Janowski, trained for this very possibility, immediately issued forth a torrent of lies. He was a submarine officer, he insisted, who in full uniform had made three landings along the Gaspé coast – at Métis, along Gaspé Bay, and at Paspébiac – to determine what shipping was in the harbours and whether the lights at each place were decoys for U-boats. The Paspébiac landing was on Wednesday, 4 November, and the U-boat was to come to retrieve him again on Saturday. For some reason, he truthfully told them the submarine was *U-518*, commanded by Wissmann. Janowski said he had spent Saturday and Sunday nights signalling in vain for Wissmann, before deciding to change into civilian clothes and travel to New Carlisle. He had buried his uniform and insisted on being allowed to retrieve and wear it, and on being treated as a prisoner of war under the Geneva Convention. Janowski's unspoken fear? That he would be hanged as a spy.

His story made no sense, though. Paspébiac was a few miles east of New Carlisle – why change into civilian clothes, travel four miles past New Carlisle to bury the uniform, and double back to town? And why does a submarine officer planning to spend a few days at an isolated location need $6000 cash, a small fortune? Duchesneau inexplicably acceded to Janowski's request about the uniform. They drove to the landing spot, where the prisoner was allowed to put on his naval lieutenant's jacket and officer's cap. The trio then tooled back to the Maison Blanche hotel, where Janowski was put under guard in one of the guest rooms. Duchesneau got on the telephone to ask his superiors what he was supposed to do next.

New Carlisle was soon abuzz, as word of the arrest swept over backyard fences, zapped down telephone lines, sped by automobile to neighbouring communities, and crackled across the ether on commercial radio broadcasts. Within hours, it seemed, the entire Gaspé Peninsula knew some version of the story – the very U-boat incursion everyone had feared. The news also entered official police pipelines, and within hours forces in a dozen U.S. states and in Canadian provinces from Nova Scotia to Ontario were placed on high alert.

Among the first officials tipped that Monday afternoon was Detective-Sergeant Doyon of the Quebec Provincial Police detachment at Gaspé. Doyon and another officer immediately called on Captain Barry German, commanding officer of the Fort Ramsay naval station. German, a recent transfer from signals intelligence in Ottawa, had lost his left arm in the 1917 explosion in Halifax, where he had been serving during the First World War. The men agreed that the two QPP officers and two naval lieutenants, Cumming and MacDonald, would proceed by train to New Carlisle to investigate this astonishing story. After a four-and-a-half-hour trip, and following limited questions and conversation with Janowski, Cumming telephoned back to say he was convinced the prisoner had indeed been landed by submarine. German told them to bring Janowski back to Gaspé as soon as possible for a full naval interrogation. Doyon agreed. German contacted Naval Intelligence in Ottawa to ask for help. Lieutenant Wilfred Samuel, on wartime secondment to the Canadian navy from the Royal Naval Volunteer Reserve, was soon making his way by train from the capital to Gaspé.

At 10:30 p.m. that night, the assistant director of the Quebec Provincial Police, Lieutenant-Colonel Léon Lambert, called from Quebec City to alert the RCMP commanding officer for C Division (Quebec), Superintendent Henri 'Harry' Gagnon in Montreal. Gagnon tipped Inspector Alexander Drysdale, of the RCMP's small intelligence division in Ottawa, who in turn alerted RCMP Commissioner Stuart Wood. With the extremely poor telephone connection between New Carlisle and Montreal, the name 'Branton' had become garbled to 'Braulter.' As a result, this became the RCMP code-name for the case in its earliest days. Gagnon also ordered RCMP Sergeant Paul Chapados of the Chandler, Quebec, detachment to travel the fifty miles west to New Carlisle in order to fly the lone Mountie flag amid the growing crowd of naval and Quebec officers. RCMP reinforcements were likely to come down from Montreal, Gagnon told Chapados, but it would take time.

As officials descended from every direction, Janowski pulled a stunt to help bolster his shaky story about awaiting a submarine rendezvous.

An hour before midnight that Monday, he startled the Quebec Provincial Police guards at his hotel room by suddenly sitting bolt upright in bed and saying, 'My God! My boat!' Janowski then rushed to the window. The detectives claimed they heard a sound offshore like the low rumble of diesel engines, the sound so many townspeople had claimed to hear in the Baie des Chaleurs over the early war years. The officers decided to take Janowski down by the wharf to see what they could see.

Meanwhile, Earle Annett Jr – the lad whose keen eye and suspicious nature laid the groundwork for the arrest – was intensely curious about how the police were handling the case. His mother had inspected Room 11 after all the excitement and discovered a piece of strapping from Janowski's luggage jammed behind a radiator. It was the only physical evidence remaining to the Annetts, since the money and matchbox had been turned over to the provincial police in whom the family had little faith. Earle Jr showed up at the Maison Blanche at about 11:25 p.m. with a neighbour, 37-year-old lawyer John Sheehan. Earle's sister Geraldine tagged along uninvited. The trio arrived just as Janowski and the police were heading out the door for the supposed rendezvous. 'As we entered the door the German was coming down the stairs, but he stopped on see-ing us,' Annett later recorded. 'He was wearing his uniform coat and hat, and a civilian topcoat and pants. He was escorted by three P[rovincial]. P[olice]. but not very closely guarded. As the German left the Hotel he apparently covered his face by adjusting his cap.' Geraldine similarly remembers Earle walking into the hotel just as Janowski was being escorted down the stairs towards the front door. 'My brother walked in and he [Janowski] stopped dead, and he wouldn't move. He wouldn't come down or go up or anything because he knew it was my brother who had reported him. And he wouldn't move – he stood just like a Ger-man soldier.'

Earle continued: 'They all got in a car and drove slowly down to the wharf, which is in front of the hotel. The manager of the hotel and his wife, and the lawyer and myself watched from a large plate glass win-dow overlooking the water. The car lights were put out, then on, then out. After that we noticed a flashlight signalling out over the water from the wharf. At 11.40 PM distinct signals came from the water in the form of a very bright light, at two different intervals. The lawyer and myself decided to go down and see what was going on, we, by another lane, (without lights so as not to arouse suspicion). By this time the car was leaving the wharf, so we followed it.' To an incredulous Annett, the provincial police seemed to be cooperating with the spy and even inviting the crew of a U-boat ashore. This was a conspiracy of such frightening proportions that he felt compelled to report it early the next day to RCMP and naval officials. Many others in town witnessed the same purported attempt at a rendezvous that night. One anonymous letter-writer sent an urgent warning to Major-General Leo LaFleche, newly appointed head of National War Services. 'Our detectives permitted this spy to send a message to the submarine that had been the means of landing him here ... There are some people here on the Gaspé Coast playing directly into the hands of the enemy.'

The QPP officers were clearly spooked by the episode that night, especially when lights seemed to flash back to shore from the middle of the bay. Instead of returning Janowski to the Maison Blanche, they immediately hauled him off to the courthouse that also contained the local jail, run by J.A. 'Gus' Goulet, the deputy sheriff with a bad arm from a First World War wound. If there were a U-boat invasion to try to rescue Janowski, the jail was far more secure than flimsy hotel walls. The detectives then roused Lieutenants Cumming and MacDonald out of a sound sleep at the Maison Blanche and told them the story of the apparent U-boat out in the bay. Cumming immediately tried to telephone German, his commanding officer at Fort Ramsay, to get instructions, but could not get a connection. The two navy men then took up a four-hour watch till dawn at the seacoast, squinting along the horizon for any sign of an inbound U-boat. Neither could hear anything that remotely resembled the rumble of diesel pistons.

Cumming finally got through to German that morning and told him what was happening. German later called back and asked Cumming to re-interrogate Janowski about submarine movements. Nothing more of value was obtained, but Cumming suggested an anti-submarine patrol of the Baie des Chaleurs. In fact, this was already being carried out by two Bangor minesweepers, HMCS *Red Deer* and HMCS *Burlington*, with no results so far. In the meantime, the provincial police had a change of heart about their promise to turn over their prize prisoner to the Canadian navy. They would instead await instructions, a much safer course of action. The decision was frustrating for German, who believed Janowski automatically fell within the jurisdiction of Naval Intelligence because he was an officer currently wearing a naval uniform. Duchesneau, however, had muddied the jurisdictional waters by allowing the stranger to change from civilian into military garb.

Chapados, the lone RCMP officer at the scene, arrived after midnight at the courthouse, where he was briefed by Detective-Sergeant Doyon. He placed a call to Gagnon in Montreal at 3 a.m., and was assured that two Mounties and a translator were speeding down to New Carlisle even then. Early the next morning, at about 6:45, 'Gus' Goulet awakened his newly acquired prisoner for breakfast. 'I told him to get up and dress,' he later told a reporter. 'He spoke pretty decent English and good French. But his accent was funny in both tongues. Even if I didn't know, I think I would have taken him for a German or a Dutchman. I gave him a good breakfast. He said: "This is a very good breakfast. You don't get eggs in Germany this time of year."

'He got to bragging. He said he had served with Rommel in Africa for two years. I thought that was funny because he had told the police he was a submarine commander. His only explanation was that he had been transferred to the submarine service. "Rommel took quite a pasting in Africa," I remarked. He shrugged his shoulders. "C'est la guerre," he said.' The Quebec Provincial Police took Janowski back to the Maison Blanche at about 9:30 a.m. for further questioning. At 10 Chapados finally met the mysterious visitor, but expecting fellow Mounties from Montreal at any moment, he did not question Janowski. Instead, he busied himself examining the spy equipment.

That same morning in Ottawa, RCMP Commissioner Stuart Wood informed Canada's justice minister, Louis St Laurent, about Janowski and asked for clear instructions about which police force was to take custody. St Laurent sided with the RCMP and the decision was duly conveyed to the Quebec Provincial Police, who agreed to hand over the prisoner to the RCMP officers driving down from Montreal. German, the commanding naval officer at Gaspé, was aghast when he learned of St Laurent's decision by telephone that afternoon. Janowski and his priceless information on U-boats might not be available to Naval Intelligence officers, who knew precisely the questions to ask. German, rashly putting his military career at some risk, immediately instructed Lieutenant Cumming to demand that the QPP surrender the prisoner to navy custody. Detective-Sergeant Doyon refused. Cumming and MacDonald could do little else but board the train back to Gaspé without Janowski and report the grim news to a frustrated German, who informed his superiors in Ottawa that the navy was being excluded from a major spy case. Lieutenant Jackson of Naval Intelligence in the capital then got on the telephone to plead the navy's case with the chief of the QPP, but a war censor cut in, refusing to allow the subject even to be discussed. Trying to salvage the situation, German sent a telegram ahead to the Matapédia train station that night for the arrival from Ottawa of Lieutenant Wilfred Samuel, the Naval Intelligence officer who was expecting to interrogate the prisoner at Gaspé. Stop instead at New Carlisle, German wired, and extract what you can from the prisoner.

Janowski's landing on the Gaspé Peninsula came at a time of high alert along the eastern seaboard of North America for Nazi agents arriving by U-boat. The blockbuster news in the summer of 1942 was a sabotage mission the Abwehr code-named Operation Pastorius, after Daniel Pastorius, an early German immigrant to the United States. Eight men, all of them German-born but who had lived for a time in the United States, were given intensive sabotage training at the estate of Quentz Lake, just outside Berlin. For more than six weeks, they learned how to shoot, toss grenades, build bombs, and use secret writing. They practised by staging mock attacks, including a night assault on the Berlin railway yards. With more than $175,000 U.S. distributed among them, they boarded *U-201* and *U-202* at Lorient, France, in late May for passage to America. Their targets: more than a dozen key transportation and industrial points, including the hydro-electric plants at Niagara Falls, New York. This planned rampage, intended to halt aircraft production, was also meant to strike fear into the populace.

One group landed on 12 June at Amagansett, Long Island, where a U.S. Coast Guard patrolman ran into them and sounded the alarm. The other four rowed ashore safely at Ponte Vedra Beach, Florida, on 17 June. All the men landed in naval uniform, to avoid being executed as spies if caught, and changed into civilian clothes on the beach. One of the saboteurs, George Dasch, betrayed the operation to the FBI, and within two weeks all eight men were in custody. President Franklin Roosevelt ordered the arrests made public to discourage other such Nazi sabotage attempts. After trial before a military tribunal, Dasch and another man who also cooperated were given lengthy prison sentences, while the rest were sent to the electric chair. After the war, the Abwehr official responsible for the mission, Colonel Erwin von Lahousen, called it the sabotage section's biggest blunder ever. Operation Pastorius dominated headlines in July and August that year, and highlighted how vulnerable North American coasts could be. It also suggested that Abwehr strategy for U-boat missions in North America was to land agents in groups rather than singly.

Janowski had told his captors he was a lone officer on a strictly military mission, but the similarities to Operation Pastorius were striking: a night-time landing on a secluded coast, an agent in a naval uniform that was buried and exchanged for civilian clothes, a wad of cash. It was no great leap of logic to assume there may have been others landed with Janowski. Police reports of his arrest – crackling across the primitive electronic web from New Carlisle to Montreal, Ottawa, and Toronto and across the eastern half of the United States – had a quite practical purpose: to trap Janowski's fellow saboteurs. The 'Braulter' case in fact was the 'Braulter et al.' case, as RCMP, FBI, customs, and local police officers stretched a dragnet across dozens of cities, towns, villages, hamlets, and isolated border crossings.

In Montreal, Superintendent 'Harry' Gagnon had only the most skeletal information about the New Carlisle incident. Telephone links to the Gaspé Peninsula were notoriously poor, and neither he nor the officers at the scene had any experience in espionage matters. In addition to alerting Ottawa late the Monday of Janowski's arrest, Gagnon called the RCMP commander in Halifax, Superintendent Alex Eames, at 11 p.m. to say that additional U-boat spies may be travelling in the area, possibly headed for the U.S. border. Eames then tipped his counterpart in Fredericton and was assured special New Brunswick patrols would begin immediately. Gagnon also placed a call to the RCMP's 'O' Division headquarters in Toronto, which alerted detachments at Windsor, Leamington, Wallaceburg, Sarnia, Fort Erie, Thorold, Niagara Falls, Cobourg, Sudbury, and Sault Ste Marie. Extra patrols were conducted. And following the usual procedure used when a prisoner of war escaped, calls went out to the FBI, Michigan State Police, customs and immigration officers in Canada and the United States, Ontario Provincial Police,

Trans-Canada Airlines, U.S. Naval Intelligence, Detroit city police, CP and CN Rail police, all branches of the Canadian armed forces, and security officers at the Ford Motor Company. Ontario Premier Gordon Conant, who had taken office in October after Mitchell Hepburn resigned, was also informed. In Ottawa, RCMP Commissioner Stuart Wood alerted the intelligence arms of the Canadian navy, army, and air force, the FBI's J. Edgar Hoover, and William Stephenson of British Security Co-ordination in New York, then the North American liaison office for British intelligence. Within twenty-four hours of his arrest, Janowski's landing was known to thousands of military, police, and security officers along the eastern seaboard, as far west as Chicago and St Louis, in Memphis, Tennessee, and deep into the southern United States. Sketchy details clattered out of dozens of police teletypes.

Twenty-four-hour patrols were begun immediately along both sides of the Baie des Chaleurs. Guards at the Matapédia bridge, which crosses the Restigouche River separating Quebec and New Brunswick, were among the first to be notified. Railway stations and hotels were scoured, and all cars encountered on the road were stopped. Security guards at key industrial operations in New Brunswick were tipped about potential sabotage, including the McLellan Foundry and Machine Works in Campbellton, the Restigouche Company in Atholville, and the International Pulp and Paper Company in Dalhousie. RCMP officers, with reinforcements ordered up from Moncton, travelled as far east as Miscou Island, where residents were told to be on guard against strangers stealing boats. In Halifax and other points in Nova Scotia, local hotels, and bus and train stations, were searched and the Allied Merchant Seamen's Club and Seamen's Manning Pool were tipped. A bridge over the grassy marshes at the New Brunswick–Nova Scotia border was placed under special watch. The commanding officer at Halifax, Superintendent Eames, ordered that 'particular attention must be paid at coastal points to possible flares by night at sea. In this regard you are advised that such flares were observed in the Bay of Chaleur during the night of the 8th instant and may be connected with the present incident.'

The FBI's Boston and Albany offices spearheaded the special security operation in the north-east United States. Special agents were dispatched to Canadian border points, where twenty-four-hour patrols were begun on Tuesday, 10 November, and continued for eight days along highways and roads and at customs and immigration stations, restaurants, and coffee shops. Police activity focused on northern Maine, from Fort Kent, Madawaska, Van Buren, and Fort Fairfield down to Houlton and Vanceboro. All highway traffic into the United States was halted, papers examined, and trunks searched. Pedestrians were required to produce identification, and everyone was asked about strangers in the area. 'Automobiles, trains, and buses were stopped and their occupants checked along with all pedestrians and bicyclists on the highway [between Madawaska and Van Buren],' said one FBI report on the operation. 'In the majority of cases men and boys were requested to produce their draft registration and classification cards ... Special emphasis was placed on the inspection of credentials presented by Canadian Service men.'

Inevitably, information became distorted and magnified in the taut anticipation of Nazi sabotage and invasion. The FBI received an urgent warning on 15 November that an unidentified submarine had landed men dressed as American soldiers near Beverly, Massachusetts. The story was meticulously traced through a New England utility company to a garbled version of the New Carlisle incident. A bulletin arrived at the FBI's Newark, New Jersey, office on 10 November about a landing raft the tide had brought ashore near Atlantic City. The 'raft' turned out to be a floating platform used to help paint the sides of ships. That same day, a U.S. Coast Guard patrol opened fire on what they believed was a man emerging from the water near Wellfleet, on Cape Cod. No agent was found and a bureau official suspected the jittery patrolmen had likely blasted a wooden post driven into the sand. Security officials at Houlton, Maine, assured the FBI in New York that the Gaspé U-boat had in fact landed ten men. This number was unusual, though. Most officials acted on the assumption that Janowski was one of four landed, based on the recent experience of Operation Pastorius.

Several hours after learning about the New Carlisle landing, the RCMP in Ottawa alerted censorship authorities. 'Since it is very likely that others were landed at the same time and are still at large, it is imperative that nothing gets out about his arrest,' Superintendent K. Duncan said in a letter delivered by special messenger to Colonel O.M. Biggar, Canada's director of censorship. 'This will afford a better opportunity of conducting investigations and catching up with any others who may have come ashore.' RCMP Commissioner Wood was also concerned that news of the arrest 'would unnecessarily excite the public.' Biggar's officials soon telephoned dozens of newspapers, especially those in Quebec where a break in the news dam was most likely. Gagnon in Montreal had insisted on confidentiality when getting word out to police forces overnight. But so many people were briefed on Janowski – from desk clerks at Chicago police headquarters to security guards at the New England Power Utility in Millbury, Massachusetts – that it was only a matter of time before word trickled out to the press.

In Detroit and Cincinnati, city police had not fully appreciated the secrecy of the case and alerted local newspaper reporters. These immediately contacted their regional Associated Press offices, and calls were soon placed to Ottawa reporters, who contacted RCMP Superintendent Duncan for details. When Duncan refused comment, they protested that the *Detroit Times* had said it was about to publish the story. The *Windsor Daily Star* also had a story ready to print and threatened to go to press with it if the Detroit paper published its own version. Other Canadian newspapers began to inundate the chief censor of publications with requests for permission to print the story. The first was the *Toronto Telegram*, which called at 10:05 a.m. on Tuesday, 10 November, the day after the capture. Submissions from the *Montreal Star*, *La Presse*, and the *Toronto Star* followed in quick succession. After some difficulty, Duncan had all these stories suppressed with the help of Canadian and U.S. censorship authorities. In the United States, a Colonel Glavin, public-relations officer for the Eastern Defense Command, was preparing to issue a press release the day after the capture. The FBI managed to intervene at the very last moment. Despite all these efforts, the circle of those in-the-know had widened considerably as the story electrified newsrooms in the eastern half of North America. The question that loomed over the RCMP for the next days and weeks was, Who would be first to break faith with the censors?

American and Canadian censors at first appeared to have stamped out all the flickering embers. But five days after the arrest one flared up again in Memphis. In its Saturday, 14 November, edition, the local *Commercial Appeal* newspaper published a story under the headline 'Nazi fugitives hunted.' 'Sheriff Oliver Perry said last night that his deputies are on the alert for three or four German sailors who the Canadian

Mounted Police reported were suspected of landing from a German U-boat in the vicinity of Quebec, Canada, Nov. 9. One German wearing the uniform of a Canadian soldier already has been captured. The others are believed to have considerable money in their possession.' Although garbled, the story contained enough truth to have tipped the Abwehr that their man was in custody. The RCMP could do little more than complain to U.S. censorship watchdogs about the breach and hope the newspaper was obscure enough to be ignored outside Memphis city limits.

Police patrols and the media blackout were augmented by a special censorship 'ring' around the Gaspé Peninsula and New Brunswick, in which postal, telephone, and telegraph censors were explicitly cautioned against letting the story slip through. 'Most of the letters intercepted by Postal Censorship originated quite naturally in the immediate vicinity of New Carlisle and for the most part these reports were quite accurate,' a 15 January 1943 summary of the ring's effectiveness concluded. 'It is interesting to note the variations and exaggerations that creep in with the spreading of the story. The number of Germans involved increases from one to twenty-two; the variety of weapons found in the stranger's possession includes bombs and a sub-machinegun, and the money carried by him is quoted as high as $30,000.'

The author of the report found no instances of radio broadcasts about Janowski, but in fact there had been at least one. Censors at the Moncton postal station intercepted a 12 November letter from 'Reta' in Petit Rocher – directly across the bay from New Carlisle – addressed to a woman in Oliver, British Columbia. 'I did not see it in the papers, but it was reported over the radio that Germans from a submarine had landed in Gaspe. Later one was caught with American money on him. The Mounted Police 'phoned to our shop to tell the clerk to be on the watch for any stranger. So it makes one feel the war nearer.' The radio report was almost certainly broadcast from New Carlisle's station CHNC, which had a ringside seat to the hottest wartime spy story in Canada. The censors, though, were generally satisfied they had built an impenetrable wall between the Gaspé region and the rest of Canada. 'The effectiveness of the Censorship "ring" seems beyond doubt,' said the 15 January report, 'since although the story spread rapidly throughout the Gaspe, no letters from other parts of Canada made any reference to the incident.'

The RCMP was especially concerned that the independent Member of

Parliament for the Gaspé, J. Sasseville Roy, would blow the case. Since his election in 1940, Roy had been outspoken in the Commons about what he considered the inadequate military protection for his region against the U-boat menace. In this, he was faithfully conveying the long-standing fears of his constituents who believed they heard and saw German submarines prowling the St Lawrence River and the Baie des Chaleurs. RCMP Superintendent Duncan asked the director of censorship to take special steps to censor the MP from Gaspé as well. Roy would not be silenced, and made an oblique reference to the Janowski case in late November in a speech at the north-shore community of Les Escoumins: 'At the present time, when the enemy can land spies on our coast, there are but four R.C.M. Police officers on duty: two at Rimouski and two at Gaspé, and they are over-worked.' RCMP Commissioner Wood was so incensed by Roy's blustering that he asked Justice Minister Louis St Laurent to write to the MP 'pointing out to him the necessity for secrecy in the interests of security of the state and the consequences of any indiscretions on his part.' Gagnon, the RCMP commanding officer in Montreal, urged another tack to suppress the information. 'I believe it is still possible to spread the news that this is merely another rumor and thus forestall the news of this arrest getting abroad,' he wrote to Wood. 'There have been so many wild rumors that this one will not surprise anyone.'

Along the Baie des Chaleurs, residents already uneasy about the U-boat threat now began to report every flicker of light out on the water. 'RCMP report submarine sighted from shore by civilian with [field] glasses,' the Gaspé naval station messaged on 11 November to HMCS *Red Deer* and HMCS *Burlington*, dutifully cruising up and down the bay. The next day the minesweepers were notified about 'a flashing white light sighted about $\frac{1}{2}$ mile off New Carlisle.' Mrs Edward Babin, a New Carlisle storekeeper, reported seeing a submarine about six miles offshore several days after Janowski's landing. The navy was still sorting out similar tips more than two weeks later. 'Various indefinite reports from New Carlisle state flashing light seen to westward at various distances three miles and more offshore over a period of two hours,' a 1 December telegraph message to Ottawa stated. 'It is reported similar lights seen last night at the same time but do not consider reliability justifies further investigation.' The navy recorded twenty possible submarine sightings in November, many of them the product of vivid and pent-up imaginations. Janowski, who at first had led his captors to believe the submarine was coming to rescue him, later falsely implied that Wiss-mann's *U-518* was headed down to the Bay of Fundy. As historian Michael Hadley has noted, Janowski's lies were likely intended to help Wissmann make an escape, which he in fact did with ease. After patrolling the Gulf of St Lawrence until 17 November, *U-518* headed back out to the North Atlantic. Crossing the path of an inbound convoy, Wiss-mann torpedoed the SS *Empire Sailor* about two hundred miles east of Sable Island, leaving twenty-one sailors dead.

Young Earle Annett believed he had uncovered a grand conspiracy when he witnessed the QPP officers helping Janowski signal the submarine at midnight on the day of the agent's capture. He, his father, and others in town were also angry and suspicious that Duchesneau had allowed the spy to don a military uniform. 'There was a lot of talk about him being fed the best of meals down at the Maison Blanche,' recalled former resident Dorothy Sheehan. Annett sent off an urgent note to navy officials at Gaspé, the only officers he felt he could still trust. German, the commanding officer of Fort Ramsay, dismissed the allegations of conspiracy. 'The Naval Officers investigated and were satisfied that no activity of a subversive nature was attempted,' German reported to Ottawa. 'Mr. Annett is a young man who is to be commended for his good work in conjunction with this matter, but who is extremely spy conscious and of a rather talkative and volatile nature.' Annett was indeed on to something, but it had nothing to do with treason. Canadian officials were amateurs when it came to the spy business and the Jan-owski case was to be a painful and sometimes embarrassing learning experience.

THREE

A Fluent and Fertile Liar

Clifford Harvison began his thirty-six-year career with the Royal Canadian Mounted Police in October 1919 with a bold-faced lie. A gangly six-footer, with narrow eyes and a long humourless face that was almost doglike, Harvison stepped off the train at Regina a determined seventeen-year-old. He got a haircut, had his suit pressed, bought a new shirt and tie, and checked into his first-ever hotel. The next morning, spruce and jittery, he hired a taxi to take him to the headquarters of the Royal North-West Mounted Police, located at the edge of the city. At the administration building, he asked permission to apply for a job. He presented letters of reference, was given a brief interview, and was handed an application form to fill out. For date of birth, he deliberately wrote 26 March 1901 – exactly one year before his true birth date, which would have automatically excluded his application. Written tests, a physical examination, an essay on Canada, and another lengthy interview followed, and Harvison's ruse worked. He was sworn in as Regimental No. 8758 to begin an intensive training program.

Born in Montreal to a British father and an American mother, Harvison was raised in modest circumstances in Hamilton, Ontario, where he attended a technical school in his late teens. The family had no money for post-secondary education, so Harvison planned to enlist in the armed forces instead – until the First World War inconveniently ended. He made a first under-age attempt at joining the RNWMP in Hamilton in the spring of 1919, but the canny recruiter insisted the youth produce a birth certificate to back his age claim. Harvison decided to apply directly in Regina, where he could believably claim that, alas, his papers were back in Hamilton. As it turned out, no one even asked for proof. After serving briefly in Halifax and Ottawa, Harvison was posted in 1921 to Montreal, where he would spend the next twenty-four years. Inevitably, he soon acquired the moniker 'Slim' for his reedy height.

As Harvison told it, Montreal in the early 1920s was a stinking cesspool of brothels and opium joints. Counterfeiters, pimps, gamblers, and cocaine dealers rubbed shoulders with gangsters who smuggled liquor illegally into the prohibitionist United States, and the whole slimy underworld was protected by local corruption and graft. The RCMP, resulting from the 1920 merger of the Dominion Police and the Royal North-West Mounted Police, had first arrived in Quebec the same year, when the federal government opened a detachment in an aging building on Montreal's Sherbrooke Street. The Mounties – dubbed 'The Horsemen' by the mobsters – rode into a city every bit as wild and unruly as the western towns of their origins. For Harvison, it was a down-and-dirty education that no university could have provided. 'My transition from parade square to active police work was astonishingly rapid,' he wrote in memoirs appropriately entitled *The Horsemen*. 'I left Ottawa in mid-morning. By nightfall, I was hanging about restaurants on St. Lawrence Main trying to locate narcotic drug pedlars.'

Harvison prowled this dark, seamy world for much of the next seventeen years. 'There was the young prostitute lying naked and screaming on an opium-smoking bunk as she suffered through her first experience with the drug,' he recalled vividly forty years later. 'And there was the searching of brothels for narcotics – brothels graduating from the luxurious houses where dalliance was expensive and the girls young and pretty, on down to the cheap tawdry places where intercourse was handled on a production-line basis where the girls carried tally cards punched by the matron each time the prostitute headed for the bedroom with a new customer, where it was not unusual to find from twenty to thirty punch marks on the card.' The RCMP's early restrictive rules about marriage forced Harvison to leave the Mounties for eight years after his wedding, during which he worked as an investigator for the Better Business Bureau of Montreal. Returning to the force in 1932, Harvison was promoted in October 1938 to command of the Criminal Investigation Branch, which included responsibility for the intelligence arm known as the Special Branch. This sudden introduction to intelligence work came soon after the Mounties had shifted their security focus from infiltrating Communist cells to battling Nazi groups in Canada as the war drums in Europe grew ever louder.

Pro-Nazi emissaries became active in Canada soon after Hitler became chancellor in 1933, promoting a revived Germany among some 475,000 Canadians of German extraction. Most of this population was in Ontario and the three Prairie provinces. At the same time, Nazi organizers formed a kind of party brain trust for Canada, the National Socialist Workers Party in Canada or the NSDAP, with restrictive membership rules that kept its numbers low. The RCMP estimated membership at about 100 at the outbreak of war, though records examined in Berlin after hostilities had ended showed there were in fact about 250. Cells were established in six cities, with Montreal the main administration point, and meetings were held in secret. German companies and consular offices supported their work, and reports compiled regularly for Hitler's high officials were normally spirited out by German sea captains. Another pro-Nazi group, the Deutsche Arbeitsfront formed in 1936, was open to any German national of Aryan descent and good reputation. Again, Canadian administration was handled in Montreal, where the local group was the largest in Canada, at 165 members. The eleven Canadian cells of the Arbeitsfront together included about five hundred members, none east of Montreal. Their meetings were more open. 'The usual Nazi claptrap was much in evidence at such affairs,' said one RCMP report, based on infiltration. 'White shirts with Sam Browne belts and swastika arm bands, German flags and Nazi salutes and heiling of Hitler, rendition of the Horst Wessel Lied and so forth.'

A third organization, the Deutscher Bund für Kanada, was far less political. Formed as a culture-appreciation society in the mid-1930s, its 3000 to 4000 members were spread among 70 locals, with the main administration being in Montreal. 'It may be safely said that many of the rank and file cared little for Nazism,' said the same RCMP report. 'Some were even resentful of its introduction into the Bund. They were chiefly interested in getting together with their countrymen, having their beer and singing German songs.' In addition to these larger groups, there was a smattering of pro-Nazi newspapers, bookstores, and businesses across Canada. One of the most insidious pre-war Nazi operations was a contest run by state short-wave radio in Germany. The station invited listeners to send in snapshots depicting their regions, with date and explanation of the scene. 'It is not known how many valuable photographs of Canadian public utilities and defence works the German General Staff obtained in this manner,' lamented the RCMP report, 'but they no doubt ran into the hundreds.'

Montreal was clearly a key organizing point for Nazi activities in Canada, despite Quebec's relatively small German population of just over ten thousand. The city was home to one of the five German diplomatic missions in Canada, a consulate headed by Dr Henry Eckner, and was an important North American entry port for German shipping. Harvison had been promoted to oversee RCMP intelligence in a city that was a potential hotbed of Nazi activity. In fact, even before Harvison's appointment the Mounties had penetrated these groups by intercepting mail and planting their own undercover officers and special agents. Harvison's new role in late 1938 was to ensure that existing operations in Quebec continued to run smoothly. By the spring of 1939, with the chill of war in the air, many members of the organizations had toned down their activities. Some of the more prescient began to flee the country for the safety of their homeland.

With Britain's 3 September declaration of war on Germany, Section 21 of the Defence of Canada regulations came into effect, allowing the detention of 'dangerous persons.' The RCMP had their lists ready, and early the following morning – still almost a week before Canada's own declaration of war – they arrested 303 Germans, including some who had become Canadian citizens. Most of these were eventually packed off to a heavily guarded camp at Kananaskis, Alberta, and to another in Petawawa, Ontario. Over the next few years the number of arrests rose to 807 and included some proven spies and would-be saboteurs. Harvison estimated that his own men rounded up more than two hundred in the first wave of arrests, most of them in Montreal. RCMP resources at 'C' Division – 164 personnel, 73 based in Montreal – were stretched to the limit and Section 21 operations continued to bog down the force for months to come. 'As for internments, it is painful to recall the enormous, even fantastic amount of work involved in the internment of a mere 800 Germans,' Corporal A. Alsvold, the RCMP's Nazi specialist, recalled two years after the war: 'The searches and seizures, painstaking collection of evidence, endless hearings before Advisory Committees and tedious keeping track of released internees.'

The workload was doubtless onerous, but as several observers have noted the RCMP's anti-Nazi operations were nevertheless inadequate and amateurish. The Mounties put their resources into dissecting the institutions of Nazism in Canada rather than ferreting out true saboteurs and dangerous subversives. Owing to the force's 'total lack and capacity for intelligence work, its officers were unable to distinguish between social or political criticism and subversive doctrine,' said a November 1940 report prepared by the prime minister's office. RCMP headquarters in Ottawa did not even have a German translator until the war. There was also virtually no liaison between the RCMP and intelligence sections of the branches of the military or with External Affairs. One historian of the period, Robert Keyserlingk, has concluded that 'the RCMP and government had been unprepared to deal with the problem in 1939 and 1940. To cover this unpreparedness, they took arbitrary actions against individual Germans and German Canadians to demonstrate to an irate public that they were in control of the security situation and to calm and lead public opinion.'

Shortly after 10:30 p.m. on 9 November 1942, when Superintendent Henri Gagnon had received the unsettling news about Janowski from the Quebec Provincial Police, there was little doubt who would be placed in charge of the case. Harvison had been a good street cop, a tough criminal investigator and for four years now had been in charge of rounding up Nazis in Quebec. This case, the first U-boat spy captured in Canada, was too important and sensitive to be given to anyone but the senior intelligence officer in 'C' Division. Gagnon briefed Harvison, now forty years old, telling him to fly down to New Carlisle if possible, otherwise to take a police car. Harvison was to take along Corporal Joseph 'Pete' Bordeleau, thirty-three, also of 'C' Division. Bordeleau, a native of Hull, Quebec, had joined the Mounties in 1933 in Ottawa, serving at Regina before being transferred to Montreal.

Harvison also took along a third man, a German translator who had long experience in intelligence. For many years, this elusive character was referred to only as 'Johnny' in postwar accounts of the operation. 'This interpreter was a fabulous man who had served on German submarines during World War I and later joined the German Communist Party, in which he attained leadership,' Harvison wrote in his 1967 memoirs. 'The rise of Hitler had forced his hurried departure for Moscow, where for some time he served as lecturer in one of the Soviet schools for the training of saboteurs. Subsequently, disillusioned by Communism as he witnessed it in Russia, he became an agent for the British Intelligence Service. His work for the British had been discovered during an assignment in South America. At that time, the Force had been requesting to provide asylum for him in Canada.'

A 1985 book subsequently identified the mysterious Johnny as Gottfried Treviranus, who during the war tried to live anonymously with his wife Gerta in a small bungalow on an average street in the Montreal suburb of Mount Royal. Treviranus had at one time been part of the famous Z espionage network, run by the British Secret Intelligence Service (MI6) in Europe before the outbreak of the Second World War. The network existed as an independent, parallel and more covert organization than the web of MI6 agents who operated out of Britain's phony Passport Control Offices located throughout Europe. Captain Sigismund Payne Best, an SIS man stationed at The Hague in the late 1930s, ran a section of the Z network and regarded Treviranus as his star agent. Along with fellow MI6 man Major Richard Stevens, Best was kidnapped by German intelligence officers at the Dutch-German border crossing of Venlo in November 1939 and under interrogation revealed details of the Z network. Treviranus, however, had apparently come under suspicion in the late 1930s, well before Best's capture, which may have been linked to treachery by another MI6 man, Dick Ellis, who had sold British secrets to the Abwehr. Treviranus was eventually given refuge in Canada under the care of the RCMP, though precisely why the force offered asylum remains unclear. Treviranus's linguistic skills, combined with his knowledge of intelligence operations, were likely welcome assets for the poorly trained and inexperienced RCMP team in Montreal. Canadian Naval Intelligence records indicate that Johnny's cover name while assisting the Mounties was John Gries. Johnny's wartime service to the RCMP later included a role in a failed plot to lure a U-boat close to shore and in a bold penetration of a Nazi group in Quebec. Even today, he remains a shadowy, little-known player in Canada's counter-espionage efforts during the Second World War. In the Janowski case, he was the most knowledgeable intelligence expert available to the Mounties at such short notice.

Chartering an airplane proved impossible, so the three men were left with no choice but to drive the six hundred miles to New Carlisle in an RCMP squad car, leaving at 2 a.m. Even with a modern divided highway today, the trip along the south shore of the St Lawrence can be a harrowing experience. Northerly winds bearing sleet, snow, or rain often create blinding conditions. Towards Rivière-du-Loup, visibility can so deteriorate that motorists are sometimes forced to travel in crawling convoys, often passing vehicles upturned in the ditches. In 1942, the two-lane road to the Gaspé was a formidable drive even in the best of weather. Harvison's memoirs indicate that freezing rain and icy roads slowed the pace even more. With meal stops, the arduous trip took twenty hours or about three times as long as today.

The weary trio finally pulled in to New Carlisle at 10 p.m. that Tuesday night to relieve RCMP Sergeant Chapados and finally to meet the spy. Janowski, who was kept at the Maison Blanche hotel all day Tuesday, was an object of intense curiosity for the townspeople, some of whom were allowed to meet and talk with him. Earle Jr, still shadowing his prize catch and keeping an eye on the QPP, told a newspaper reporter later that the spy 'was saluting everyone he met with a mock British salute. He seemed very cheerful.' Janowski seemed intent on playing up his phony role as a U-boat officer. His jailer Gus Goulet later noted that Janowski 'stood very stiff, and bowed with a quick snap of his heels whenever he was addressed.' The Annett sisters remember his haughty and arrogant bearing when he wore the uniform, much different from the wallflower Janowski had hoped to remain while at the Carlisle the previous morning. Duchesneau allowed his prisoner to have lunch and dinner that day in the public dining room of the Maison Blanche, and took him out into the streets of New Carlisle for exercise.

Chapados quickly briefed Harvison on the little he knew about Janowski. He also gave a report on how the Quebec Provincial Police had handled – or rather mishandled – the case so far. Harvison was appalled on learning that the prisoner had been permitted to dig up and wear his uniform. He told the police to order Janowski back into civilian clothes, then to bring the prisoner back to the jail from the Maison Blanche. 'The warden [Gus Goulet] permitted me the use of his office, and I had the prisoner brought there a few minutes later,' Harvison wrote of his first meeting with Janowski. 'Corporal Bordeleau and a translator named Johnny were present. The prisoner entered the room in the best Nazi military manner, and after clicking his heels and giving me a curt bow, demanded that he be permitted to don his uniform and that he be treated as an officer and a gentleman.' Harvison recalls telling Janowski: 'Nuts. I believe you are a spy. Sit down and keep quiet until I speak to you.'

Johnny then peppered the prisoner with questions about German U-boats, drawing on his own naval experience from the First World War. Janowski dug himself deeper and deeper into a hole trying to maintain the wobbly fiction about his status as a U-Waffe officer. 'The prisoner could not answer even the most elementary questions regarding the procedures aboard a submarine,' Harvison wrote. The interrogation continued throughout the following day, as Harvison took notes on the possessions Janowski had brought ashore. Astonishingly, Duchesneau had lost the very first item of evidence that his prisoner had produced, the Canadian National Registration Certificate bearing the name William Branton of Toronto. Another blank certificate, for any other alias Janowski might require in Canada, had also disappeared. The wallet-sized cards never turned up again.

Apart from his clothing and various pieces of baggage, Janowski had carried a comb, nail file, fountain pen, pencil, three paper-covered books including *Mary Poppins*, diary, the spiked brass knuckleduster, penknife, four chocolate-flavoured sugar tablets, six sugar-and-wine tablets, twenty-three other pills bearing the initial 'V' (later found to contain a sulpha drug for treating venereal disease), two matches oddly jammed into the spine of the diary, the 1940 Quebec driver's licence no. 79878, and the radio transmitter-receiver with spare tubes, insulators, and antenna. Janowski was also carrying a .25-calibre automatic pistol, manufactured by Spain's Ruby Arms Company, eight rounds of ammunition, and a leather holster. Harvison further examined small city maps of Saint John, Toronto, Montreal, Quebec City, and Halifax and regional maps of Quebec and the Maritimes, the Province of Quebec, and southern Ontario; a slide rule; and instructions for using the radio and for encoding messages. Janowski had also buried with his clothing a German soldier's pay-book cover; a metal identity disc, bearing numbers and issued to all members of the German army; and German military forms for rail-way passage, which suggested Janowski was naval sub-lieutenant.

There was also a great deal of money, including fifty American gold pieces, each with a face value of $20 and all minted in 1924. In addition, there was a wad of 654 Canadian bills ranging in denominations from $1 to $100 and issued by the Canadian Bank of Commerce, the Bank of Montreal, the Royal Bank of Canada, La Banque Canadienne Nationale, the Bank of Toronto, the Bank of Canada, and the Dominion of Canada. The serial numbers were random, and did not run in blocks. Some 135 of the bills were of the smaller size, approximately the dimensions of mod-ern Canadian paper currency. The remainder were of the larger outdated size. Most unusual were the $1 bills Janowski carried. Only five of them were the smaller, post-1935 variety issued by the Bank of Canada in its fifteen-year program to become Canada's only legal issuer of paper cur-rency. And all of these smaller $1 bills had been given to him as change by Dewey Smollett, the ticket-seller at the New Carlisle train station, after Janowski had handed over a new-issue $20 bill. The rest of the $1 bills – 499 of them – were the 17 March 1917 Dominion of Canada issue featuring a portrait of Princess Patricia of Connaught, with a scene of the Centre Block of the Parliament Buildings on the reverse. These were the bills that had sent a perplexed Simone Loubert upstairs at the Carlisle Hotel to alert young Earle Annett to the strange morning guest. Janowski also carried $1.11 in silver, presumably given to him as change at the Carlisle and at the train station.

The hefty roll of money, the false identity cards, and the maps of inland cities all served to undermine Janowski's initial story about being a submarine officer. Detailed interrogation of the prisoner resumed the next day, but Janowski remained adamant: he was a navy officer on a strictly military mission that was now complete. Harvison recalled that, during the questioning, an 11 November Remembrance Day ceremony at the cenotaph outside the jail window caught Janowski's attention. He was allowed to watch. 'He was impressed ... by the crowds that had turned out for the occasion and by the obvious loyalty, confidence and quiet determination of all those who had gathered for the remembrance ceremonies,' Harvison wrote in his memoirs. 'This was not in accor-dance with the propaganda that had been fed to the German people regarding the attitude of Canadians, particularly in the Province of Quebec, where we discovered later he had been told the people were on the verge of revolt.' That evening, a veterans' group holding a Remembrance Day dinner at the Maison Blanche sent a man over to thank Harvison for seeing that the Nazi spy had finally been removed from the hotel and placed day-and-night in jail. Men who had fought bitterly against the Kaiser's army were outraged that an enemy prisoner of war had been treated in so cavalier a manner by the Quebec Provincial Police. They were grateful the RCMP had finally set things right.

Meanwhile, Lieutenant Wilfred Samuel of Naval Intelligence arrived from Ottawa after nearly twenty-four hours of travel by train. He had intended to make for Gaspé, but picked up the urgent telegram in Matapédia redirecting him to New Carlisle after the provincial police had refused to turn Janowski over to the navy. Commander German in Gaspé sent Lieutenant Cumming back by car to New Carlisle with a sheaf of secret documents for Samuel that outlined naval actions taken so far. Samuel contacted Harvison that afternoon, and was allowed a six-hour opening interrogation that included taking Janowski back to the point four miles west of town where the uniform had been buried. 'The prisoner proved a fluent and fertile liar, but I was eventually satisfied that he had no connection with the U-Waffe, other than that he had been brought from Europe to Canada on a U-boat,' Samuel later reported. Samuel, fifty-six, had interrogated many U-boat PoWs since July when he was appointed head of NID-3, the Naval Intelligence unit established to extract information from enemy prisoners. His intimate knowledge of the U-Waffe made mincemeat of Janowski's claims. Harvison had another go at Janowski that evening for about 90 minutes. Janowski started to waver, but still would not confess. 'The story told varied with each question,' Harvison noted.

At about 8 a.m. the following morning, a Thursday, Harvison set off on the long trip back to Montreal with his new prisoner. He and Bordeleau occupied the front seat of the police car, while Johnny and Samuel sat in back with Janowski between them. Before leaving, Harvison may have criticized the provincial police directly for their inept handling of the arrest. The official record is silent, but a newspaper later reported: 'They took him away Thursday morning, but not – according to reports circulating in New Carlisle – before they had severely dressed down the Provincial Police for the manner in which they had handled the case.'

Johnny and Samuel continued to grill Janowski relentlessly in the back seat – both speaking in German – to try to break him. By 1 p.m., when they had agreed to stop at a Mont Joli hotel for lunch, Janowski's story was in tatters and he seemed ready to come clean. 'By then, the position had been reached that Janowski's naval pretentions ... were admitted to be a subterfuge and he was on the brink of making a full confession in the hope of escaping from being hanged,' Samuel reported. Said Harvison: 'The prisoner's story changed many times and as we were approaching Mont Joli he stated that he wanted to tell the truth but that he first wished to talk to me.' The five had lunch, then Harvison and Bordeleau took Janowski to a private room in the hotel finally to have the truth from the prisoner. 'I interviewed the prisoner in the presence of Corpl. Bordeleau,' Harvison reported. 'He stated that he was prepared to tell me the truth provided I would guarantee his life. I told him that I would make no such guarantee but that I would report whatever he told me to my superiors and that the decision taken in the case would rest with them. He then started to tell what I believe to be a fairly accurate story.'

Janowski said he had been born in 1904 at Allcnstcin, in East Prussia, to Alfred Janowski and Berta Krieger. His father was a former prison governor who now lived in the Hamburg suburb of Harburg, with the rank of lieutenant-colonel in the Hamburg Kommandatur. Janowski was an only child, his brother and sister having died young. He became a civilian pilot in the 1920s but, finding the economic prospects in Germany too limited, emigrated to Canada. He arrived in Halifax on the SS *Crefeld* on 6 May 1930, eventually making his way to the tiny southern Ontario community of Ailsa Craig, where he worked for a local farmer. There he met a woman named Olive Blanche Quance, a well-to-do milliner some sixteen years his senior. He proposed and they were married on 20 December 1931. The couple lived in Toronto, where Janowski took a repair course at the Radio College of Canada. In August 1933, with his marriage growing stale, he left Canada for France, where he joined the Foreign Legion, serving in North Africa for five years until his discharge in 1938.

Returning to Germany, Janowski was automatically imprisoned at the Dachau concentration camp for his crime of having joined a foreign army. His father's political connections got him out after two weeks and he was allowed to enrol in the Germany army as a private. Janowski trained for fifteen months at a military school in Brandenburg, then was transferred to the Dutch frontier, where he participated in the invasions of Holland, Belgium, and France. Promotions and decorations followed, and while serving in the occupation forces in Paris he was transferred to Africa, where he served with Rommel, earning his Iron Cross, 1st Class. Janowski was ordered to Berlin in December 1941, where he was recruited into the Abwehr because of his language abilities and knowledge of radio. Transferred to Brussels, he was placed in charge of about seventy-five counter-intelligence agents in Belgium and northern France.

Janowski made some anti-Nazi remarks at a late-night drinking party, which were reported by the Gestapo. (Samuel was sceptical later on learning this part of the prisoner's new story: '[I]t seemed to me far likelier that he had done something more criminal than that, as he gives the impression of being an evil liver and a generally unpleasant person.') Janowski was ordered to Berlin and given the choice of imprisonment or undertaking an espionage mission to Canada. He chose the latter, and was given special instructions in codes and radio work, and travelled to Dieppe, where he obtained identification cards from a prisoner of war from Quebec, a captain in the Black Watch (Royal Highland Regiment) of Canada. Janowski also clarified that he had been landed early on 9 November by a U-boat that quickly left the area. 'His instructions before leaving Germany were to proceed to Quebec City and later to Montreal, to set up a gathering-information [sic] organization,' Harvison reported to Gagnon, his commanding officer in Montreal. 'His instructions before leaving Germany were to correspond by radio code with H.Q. on December 1, 1942. Janowski states that it is planned to land in Canada special "groups one and two" men [that is, spies and saboteurs], at a point to be decided upon by him when he had got settled in Canada and when he gave the signal, but not before the Spring of 1943.' The prisoner, then, was a trained counter-espionage expert who had been assigned the job of ridding Belgium and France of Allied agents and resistance leaders. Janowski did not do this work himself, but had been placed in charge of others. He had taken on the Canadian mission only under duress, and was only to pave the way for other, more important, agents, including saboteurs.

55

Harvison and Bordeleau were now convinced they had their confession. Indeed, Harvison later claimed to have used subtle psychological pressure to prime the truth from this obstinate prisoner. The Abwehr had been careless in preparing him for the mission, it was intimated to Janowski: the large-sized bills, the botched registration card, the gold pieces that were difficult to cash, the weak escape story. Surely this was an organization that had no right to expect loyalty from agents it treated so shabbily. Harvison advised Samuel about the new information, especially the facts about the New Carlisle–area landing and Janowski's non-naval military background. Janowski also suggested that *U-518* had in fact headed directly for the Bay of Fundy after the early Monday drop-off. Samuel, warming to the espionage game, stopped by the train station in Mont Joli to dash off a cryptic CN telegram. Addressed to Herbert Little, Room 218 of the Aylmer Apartments on Slater Street, it read: 'Left Baie des Chaleurs early ninth probably for Bay of Fundy – Sammy.' Little was, in fact, Lieutenant-Commander C. Herbert Little, since July 1942 the first Canadian-born director of Naval Intelligence. The 'Aylmer Apartments' was a reference to the Aylmer Building on Cartier Square, where Little had his office. 'Sammy' was the nickname this retired British businessman acquired in Canada soon after his arrival in Ottawa in February 1941 as a navy linguist. Samuel's main concern was to halt the pointless search for the U-boat in the Baie des Chaleurs and redirect it southward to the Bay of Fundy, Wissmann's supposed destination.

Janowski's claim to a Canadian marriage was already known to the police even before his confession. He had mentioned Olive Quance to Gus Goulet, his jailer in New Carlisle, even endeavouring to get a message to her on Danforth Avenue in Toronto. So the Toronto RCMP had this head start on checking out the Canadian details of Janowski's story. Even as Harvison was driving his catch back to Montreal, Mountie gumshoes in Toronto were carrying out discreet interviews. Corporal G.H. Archer contacted a man, his name deleted from the Watchdog file, who had been a teacher at the Radio College of Canada and had known Janowski. 'Although not naturally inclined to that type of work, [Janowski] had apparently determined that he must learn radio work and applied himself with great vigour to his studies,' Archer reported after his interview. 'Subject was apparently very well liked among other students and was also considered to be quite a ladies man. He received considerable mail from widely separated points.'

The man also mentioned that Janowski had been the subject of an article in the *Toronto Star Weekly* in the early 1930s. The following day, Friday, 13 November, Archer visited the library of the *Toronto Daily Star* and quickly located the article, dated 23 January 1932. The piece, later determined to have been initiated by Janowski, was an attempt by the newspaper to localize the unsettling Nazi politics then evolving in Germany. The headline blared, 'Once German fascist staunch Canadian.' Janowski claimed to have been wounded in the German army as a boy of fourteen, and to have led an air circus over Europe for five years in the 1920s. He assured the reporter he 'would defend the Dominion to-day even against his Fatherland.' Indeed, Janowski got enraptured by his newfound Canadian patriotism. 'The country where I earn my bread, that is the country I will fight for. I love Canada. I shall never leave it.' The article went on to claim that he had studied medicine for two years in Berlin, as well as noting that he was skilled at playing cello, and was studying radio engineering in the morning and English and Spanish at university in the afternoons. The article also featured a photograph of Olive Quance, Janowski's bride of six weeks.

The Toronto detectives rounded up some more essential details. They obtained a copy of a 1932 transit visa Janowski had applied for from the United States government. For some reason, he gave his date of birth as 26 April 1905 – more than a year after his true birthday. He had also claimed to be an employee, rather than a student, of the Radio College of Canada at 310 Yonge Street. And he claimed to have $500 invested in his wife's millinery business. The transit visa was needed, apparently, so he could travel from Buffalo to New York and board the SS *Colombus*, of the North German Lloyd line, to visit his ailing mother for six months in Germany. The document contained Janowski's signature, which was now copied for the RCMP file. The RCMP officers also dug out a copy of his 5 December 1931 Toronto marriage certificate to Quance, in which he gave his occupation as 'aviator.' The Radio College records went back only to 1937 because of a change of ownership, so a direct check on Janowski's time there was impossible.

Several key documents were also found pertaining to Quance. Under Canadian law of the time, Quance automatically lost her Canadian-

British citizenship by marrying a German national. She applied under the Naturalization Act to regain her citizenship in April 1941, saying in her application that she was separated from her husband and did not know his current whereabouts. The form indicated she had been born Christmas Day 1886 at Biddulph Township, Exeter, Ontario, and ran a millinery business on Danforth Avenue. Because she was married to an enemy German national, Quance also had to apply in 1941 for a parole certificate, another document the RCMP examined in Toronto. The Mounties determined she had moved to Toronto in 1918 and had run the millinery business for the last seventeen years, although she had recently given it up. Inquiries showed she had toured Europe, including Germany, about 1934. The capture of Janowski immediately raised questions about her own loyalties, but the Toronto detectives were quick to clear her. 'Her character and reputation are excellent,' Archer's report said. 'Responsible persons vouch for her ... All enquiries to date indicate that suspicions regarding her ought not to be entertained.' The intense secrecy surrounding the case meant that Quance could not yet be directly approached about her prodigal husband's unorthodox return to Canadian shores.

Knowing that Janowski entered Canada in May 1930, RCMP investigators now checked immigration records through the commissioner of immigration, A.L. Jolliffe. Within twenty-four hours, Jolliffe reported back that Janowski had indeed entered Canada at Quebec City aboard the SS *Crefeld* from Bremen on 19 May 1930. He declared his occupation as a farmhand, stated that he intended to work in Canada as either a farmhand or landscape gardener, and was duly registered as a landed immigrant. The department did not keep records of departures from Canada, and so had no way to confirm Janowski's claim that he had boarded a ship in Montreal in late August 1933 bound for France. In many respects, though, the main Canadian elements of Janowski's complex biography were supported by the documentary record. The Mounties became increasingly convinced that they had peeled back their prisoner's initial escape stories and were now down to the truth.

Harvison's team, meanwhile, had arrived back in Montreal at about midnight after driving all day Thursday. Stiff and exhausted, they pulled up to the RCMP's 'C' Division headquarters, at 131 St James Street, located in a former post office building. The Mounties had begun their move to the location in 1939, just nine days before Canada declared war, abandoning the cramped Sherbrooke Street residential building that had been the division's home for almost two decades. Harvison commandeered a small room off the gymnasium on the third floor as Janowski's bedroom, and posted a twenty-four-hour guard of two officers. The sergeants' mess in the front part of the second-floor barracks would now be used exclusively as an interrogation room, with the prisoner's meals brought there.

Efforts were made to block off these sections of the building to prevent the general public from wandering in, but prowling newspapermen would prove to be a problem. There was no toilet in Janowski's bedroom or in the sergeants' mess, so he frequently had to be escorted down public hallways to use the lavatory. His presence in the building was soon widely known among RCMP officers with no connection to the case. A veteran police reporter for the Montreal *Gazette*, Lawrence Conroy, later told officials: 'I saw him at least three times, maybe oftener, but it got to the point where I did not pay any particular attention to him.' RCMP Commissioner Wood grew increasingly alarmed about the inadequate security at the Montreal barracks. 'The repercussions throughout the country against this Force would be most lamentable if ... [Janowski] were to escape from our custody,' he warned Gagnon. 'Montreal does not lend itself to the proper guarding of this man over a prolonged period.' Wood ordered the transfer of the spy to a more secure location as soon as the initial interrogations were complete.

The morning after their return from New Carlisle, Harvison dashed off an 'interim' report to Gagnon, based largely on the story Janowski told after his Mont Joli conversion. Already Harvison was alive to the double-agent potential of the case. 'This man claims to be in a position to communicate with the German intelligence H.Q. in Germany by means of the set now in our possession – and that he is to make the arrangements for the bringing to Canada of the sabotage agents which he claims are now being trained in Germany for work here and in the U.S.A.,' Harvison told Gagnon. 'We are in possession of the code books and he is at present explaining in the minutest detail the workings of the code. It will also be noted that he is aware of the identity of many of these men now being trained for this work and of men who have already been sent to South America.

'Janowski appears to be quite prepared to supply us with every detail in his possession and to use the radio equipment in any manner directed by us. The advantages possible are obvious.' Gagnon was instantly supportive of this double-agent suggestion, advising Wood that 'this man has confidence in Insp. Harvison and it is imperative that at least for the time being no one else approach the prisoner so as not to confuse the issue ... I sincerely believe that the subject will give us the assistance required. Life appears very sweet to him at present and if we can use him we can protect the country much better than by destroying him at once.' Both Harvison and Gagnon understood, though, that the proposed ruse depended entirely on snuffing out any news of Janowski's capture that might trickle back to the Abwehr. The problem was not so much that German intelligence officers, alerted by news leaks, would refuse to take the bait – rather, that they would read his radio transmissions as material the Allies wanted fed to the enemy. The Germans could then occupy the high ground in this complex game. 'The arrest of this man in Gaspé is known to many persons in that area, but I do not think the risk of information, regarding his arrest, reaching Germany is very great unless it appears in the public press or radio,' Harvison noted.

Gagnon's hope that Harvison would be left alone to interrogate the prisoner was quickly dashed. Commissioner Wood had regularly updated Sir David Petrie, head of MI5 at Blenheim Palace, the agency's wartime headquarters in Oxfordshire; William Stephenson, the Winnipeg-born businessman known as 'Little Bill,' who ran British Security Co-ordination in New York City; and J. Edgar Hoover of the FBI in Washington – and all were eager for a crack at Janowski. Among the first to arrive was the FBI. Hoover dispatched an agent from Washington on an early Eastern Airlines flight arriving in Montreal at noon on 12 November, the same day Harvison was driving back from New Carlisle. The FBI agent was later joined at the Mount Royal Hotel by the agency's Ottawa station chief. Stephenson had acted since 1940 as a senior Western Hemisphere representative of the British intelligence and counter-intelligence agencies, MI6 and MI5. High among his priorities was the prevention of sabotage intended to cripple the flow of war materials to Britain. The capture of Janowski, claiming to be a harbinger of saboteurs, was thus of immediate and urgent interest. From the BSC offices at the International Building of Rockefeller Center in New York,

Stephenson dispatched Colonel Walter Thomas Wren to Montreal on 12 November.

Wren was a London businessman who had met with enormous financial success before the war in marketing a popular cooker and heater in Britain. Recruited into MI6 at the start of hostilities, and initially based in London, Wren was a short, cheerful man with a fondness for whiskey. He wore glasses with thick lenses, had thin reddish hair, and was heavily freckled – hence his nickname Freckles, used by close friends and colleagues, including H. Montgomery Hyde, the agent-turned-author. In January 1941, Wren was appointed MI5-MI6 representative for Trinidad, Barbados, British Guiana, and the Windward and Leeward Islands. Wren was unable to leave for the Caribbean immediately, as he was still recovering from burns to his hands and face from an incendiary bomb in October that had burrowed into the London cellar where he was sheltering. He eventually arrived at his new station in Port-of-Spain, Trinidad, on 18 February with special instructions from Stephenson to protect the Trinidadian oilfields from sabotage. Another key responsibility was to safeguard the Duke of Windsor, then living in Nassau as governor. Wren had earlier tipped the former king about an alleged German plot in which a team of commandos arriving by U-boat was to kidnap him.

Wren soon gained some valuable experience of double agentry in North America, in the form of the disastrous Dusko Popov case. Popov was a wealthy Yugoslav businessman who in the summer of 1940 was recruited into Abwehr service through a university friend. Popov immediately contacted the MI6 representative in Belgrade, offering to act as a double agent, and was quickly accepted. Soon he was operating in London and Lisbon, feeding lies and half-truths back to the Abwehr under the direction of MI5. His Abwehr masters were so impressed that in 1941 Popov was sent to New York to re-establish an American espionage network after the FBI had rolled up almost every active Abwehr agent in the United States. MI6 officials, who now took over the case from MI5, intended that British Security Co-ordination would help run Popov, known as Tricycle to the British, Ivan to the Abwehr. But they had the case wrenched away by Hoover, who would brook no British double-cross operation on U.S. soil. The FBI chief was naturally suspicious of all double agents. Hoover refused to accept that they could be a vital source of information about the enemy, or that they could be marshalled for strategic deception purposes. Instead, he regarded doubles largely as a means to entrap other agents. Hoover especially disliked Popov's legendary promiscuity and high living in Manhattan, all financed with Abwehr funds. The bureau ran Popov only half-heartedly, keeping BSC and Tricycle himself largely in the dark about developments.

Wren became involved in the Tricycle case when he intercepted the philandering Yugoslav in Trinidad. Popov was returning to New York by ship after three weeks of meetings in November 1941 with Albrecht Gustav Engels, the Abwehr's top Latin American agent, based in Rio de Janeiro. It was the only way BSC could keep abreast of developments, since the FBI steadfastly refused to share information. Wren, looking 'very British, climbed up the ladder from the pilot boat and a few minutes later approached us and asked discreetly if he might have a few words with me,' Popov recalled in his memoirs. Among other things, Popov told Wren over a long lunch that Engels – code-name Alfredo – had agreed to ship a microdot-making machine to Canada for pick-up. A Portuguese captain friendly to the Abwehr would handle the transportation. Popov was to feign illness at the Château Frontenac in Quebec City, where a doctor would provide him a prescription that would in fact be instructions on where to pick up the machine. Alfredo's precise directions raised grave doubts about whether the RCMP had truly smashed Nazi rings inside Quebec in the early part of the war. Wren immediately informed BSC in New York, and soon received a telegram asking that Popov not confide the name of the Portuguese captain to the FBI, since this aspect of the case was considered to be exclusively within BSC jurisdiction. Popov returned to New York and tried to make his way to Quebec City, but got entangled in red tape at the U.S. border and could not make the Château Frontenac rendezvous – a situation he ultimately blamed on FBI interference.

Alfredo had also given Popov a total of $18,500 U.S. to build a radio transmitter in the New York area to communicate with Lisbon and with the Abwehr's 'Bolivar' station in Rio de Janeiro. The link was established in February 1942 with the concurrence and expertise of the FBI, but almost immediately began to turn sour because the bureau refused to feed legitimate intelligence back to the Abwehr to establish Tricycle's bona fides. In March 1942, MI6 advised that decrypted Abwehr internal communications strongly suggested that the Germans believed Popov was operating under Allied control. The case, once so promising, stalled and Hoover impetuously washed his hands of Tricycle. In August 1942, Popov returned to London dispirited and angry. Partly on Wren's recommendation, he was able to resume his work with MI5 by meticulously rebuilding his credibility with the Abwehr.

Wren was always looking for excuses to travel to New York from his Port-of-Spain backwater. After personally reporting on the Caribbean situation to Stephenson, he would be handed odd jobs to take up time until his scheduled return to Trinidad. He happened to be in New York when the Janowski case broke, and so Stephenson dispatched him to Canada to represent British intelligence. In contrast to Operation Tricycle, British Security Co-ordination was on much firmer ground in Montreal. The FBI clearly had no jurisdiction and the RCMP was a close and cooperative ally. The British cabinet's Security Executive had also been actively promoting closer MI5-RCMP links throughout 1942. An MI5 representative had visited Halifax and St John's, Newfoundland, in May 1942, for example, to help promote greater port security. The Security Executive had turned down Stephenson's request for a full-fledged BSC office in Canada, preferring any MI5 liaison to be directly posted from, and responsible to, London. As will be seen, this plan for direct MI5 representation was fortuitously to be carried out within weeks. But the Janowski case called for immediate action, and so Wren was designated to carry the flag for MI5 in the interim.

Wren and the two FBI agents in Montreal were joined the following Monday, 16 November, by Major-General George V. Strong, of the U.S. military intelligence arm known as G-2. (Strong appears to have travelled to Montreal for previously scheduled appointments, adding a last-minute visit with Janowski.) Commander John L. Riheldaffer of U.S. Naval Intelligence in Washington also asked his counterpart in Ottawa, Lieutenant-Commander Herbert Little, to send Janowski down to the U.S. capital for questioning later. Little could only reply that the prisoner was not in the custody of the navy, and any request would have to go through the Mounties. Riheldaffer eventually sent an officer to Montreal in late December – with little effect because Janowski had already been picked clean on naval affairs and his tiny store of information shipped stateside weeks earlier.

Copies of Janowski's police mug shots were soon turned over to Hoover's two G-men. The photographs were then taken by courier to the FBI's New York office so they could be shown to prisoners George Dasch and Ernest Berger, the only Operation Pastorius saboteurs spared execution because they had agreed to cooperate with police. Both men claimed not to recognize Janowski. Much later, in February, Janowski was shown photographs of the shovels the Pastorius gangs had used to bury their uniforms and declared his own to be of similar manufacture. (The RCMP never attempted to recover Janowski's shovel from the Baie des Chaleurs for fear of stirring up talk of spies again on the Gaspé Peninsula.) But apart from the photos, the FBI men were handed only a few scraps from Harvison's laboured questioning of the prisoner over the next week. The 'interrogation of Janowski is proceeding very slowly,' one G-man advised Washington. The two matches found jammed into the spine of Janowski's diary were quickly determined to be tipped with a secret writing material. The RCMP had technicians scrawl a secret message with them, and handed the sheet over to FBI experts. They were able to make direct comparisons with similar matches seized in the Operation Pastorius case. Janowski passed on the names of some ten to twelve agents he said had been landed in Argentina that spring, but had little hard information on Nazi espionage in the United States. 'He did not attend a [Abwehr] radio school with anyone else and attended no schools, according to his story, directly dealing with espionage or sabotage other than one radio school,' said a 27 November FBI summary of the information gleaned to that point. 'He, therefore, claims to have no knowledge of anyone who might subsequently come to the United States as an agent of Germany.'

Janowski did say that the Abwehr now planned to focus on sabotage because of booming war production in Canada and the United States. And he cited an Abwehr post-mortem on Operation Pastorius, saying the disaster had resulted in a radical change of tactics. Saboteurs would now be landed singly instead of in groups, and those destined for the United States were to be routed through Canada. Janowski also said Abwehr officials were weighing whether future saboteurs should be supplied with cumbersome explosives, which seemed to bog down the Long Island bunch, or whether they should be instructed in 'home-cooking,' the fashioning of bombs with ready-to-hand materials. He also passed on the tidbit that relatives of Dasch and Berger had been placed in concentration camps once the pair's treachery became known in Germany intelligence circles, though all publicity was suppressed. The FBI was eventually allowed its own interrogation of Janowski, their agent reporting that 'when conversing with the writer, he is extremely polite, so much so that it is evident that he not only knows of the F.B.I. but respects the name.' But after a week in Montreal, the FBI concluded 'he is going to be of no material aid to us. He can furnish no specific information as to what might happen in the United States – he does have a great deal of general information which we want, but nothing is going to be of any specific aid as far as apprehending anyone else.'

Harvison's memoirs, *The Horsemen*, provide a fanciful account of his early interrogation of Janowski. He claimed that the prisoner made a clean breast of it back in New Carlisle, rather than at Mont Joli, and only after persistent psychological pressure. According to this version, Janowski confessed that he was a spy and bravely demanded that he be executed by firing squad without delay. He was told that under Canadian law, convicted espionage agents are hanged, not shot. Harvison then feigned interest in the ninety-nine quite genuine and modern $20 bills that Janowski had been carrying. With Bordeleau playing along in the pseudo-drama, he told the prisoner they were obviously counterfeit and were likely planted on him by his enemies, as were the large-sized bills. 'Those God-damn Gestapo. The money was secured from them and they have framed me,' Harvison quotes Janowski as shouting while banging on the desk in Gus Goulet's office. 'They wanted me caught and executed.' The prisoner then mulled over the thought of an imminent hanging, finally breaking down and sobbing: 'I will not be hanged, I will not be hanged.' Throughout this game of cat-and-mouse, Harvison kept suggesting that since Janowski had himself been betrayed he might purchase his life by becoming a double agent for Canada. The prisoner wrestled with the upsetting thought of becoming a traitor to the Third Reich, but finally agreed the next morning to do as asked.

Harvison's tale is simply not supported by the reports he and Samuel submitted to their superiors about the case. Janowski abandoned his U-Waffe story only after five hours of intensive questioning by Johnny and Samuel, the U-boat experts, in the back seat of the police car on the way to Mont Joli. At the lunch stop, the prisoner offered to tell the truth only if his life could be guaranteed – much different from Harvison's portrait of a loyal German soldier willing to face a firing squad. Also, the idea of becoming a double agent seems rather to have been suggested by Janowski himself. 'In addition to telling what he then claimed to be the true story of his career and present activities JANOWSKI intimated that he would co-operate with this Force and use his radio in any way directed,' says an RCMP summary of the case. Janowski's story about preparing the way for saboteurs to arrive in the spring would have been a near-irresistible inducement to run him as a double. Far from having to be pressured to turn on his Nazi masters, Janowski appeared rather to be turning himself by floating subtle suggestions past his obviously inexperienced captors.

One of Harvison's first reports on the case was a thirty-five-page analysis of the 'German intelligence set-up,' delivered to Ottawa less than a week after his return to Montreal with the prisoner. The contents made it clear that Harvison's reach had far exceeded his grasp. With virtually no knowledge of German intelligence, he acted more like a recording secretary than an interrogator, meticulously jotting down names, dates, and places as Janowski gave them with little cross-examination. Harvison's expertise was in the drug-infested streets of downtown Montreal, with some experience of local fascists and Nazis. The Abwehr was completely out of his league, as the RCMP was soon rudely to discover. On 19 November, RCMP Commissioner Wood placed a copy of Harvison's report in a British diplomatic bag leaving for London the following day. Attached was a covering letter to MI5's Victor Rothschild: 'It is being forwarded to you without special comment as it deals with the German Intelligence Set-up of which you have intimate knowledge.'

Among the élite group of MI5 officers with precise knowledge of the Abwehr was Cyril Mills, a British businessman who was to play a vital role in the Janowski affair. In 1920, Mills's father, Bertram Mills, founded a circus at London's Olympia Stadium that soon grew by leaps and bounds, becoming the engine for the family's wealth. Cyril, born in 1901, was sent to Harrow, the exclusive boys' private school, and in 1923 completed an engineering degree at Cambridge. He briefly worked for an oil company in Rangoon before returning to London in 1925 to join the family circus business with his brother Bernard. The brothers established a travelling or 'tenting' version of the Bertram Mills circus in 1930, and one of Cyril's primary tasks was to scout talent in Britain and throughout Europe. He took up aviation in 1933 and three years later was given a de Havilland Hornet as a gift from his father. He would pilot himself across the Continent on business, flying 17,000 miles in the first year alone. These trips would often take him to German cities – Hamburg, Berlin, Düsseldorf, and Cologne in the summer of 1936 – where the airspace was normally off limits to British aircraft. British intelligence seized upon this unique opportunity and recruited Mills to take aerial photographs of key Luftwaffe airfields and other sites. In August 1936, for example, Mills got some rare snaps of the Messerschmitt plant at Ravensberg, near the Swiss border.

Bertram Mills died in 1938 and his circus business went into steep decline with the outbreak of war the next year. Cyril and his brother turned over their Dorset Square offices in London to the French underground, which used the space to train and prepare spies and saboteurs to be dropped in France. In the summer of 1940, Mills was himself recruited into MI5 under T.A. 'Tar' Robertson, the brilliant spy-master who was placed in charge of the service's fledgling double-agent section. Mills, fluent in French and German, was soon running an immensely effective operation against the enemy with an agent code-named Garbo. Juan Pujol, a Spanish national, joined the Abwehr but successfully deceived the Germans as a British double agent throughout the war, running a series of notional sub-agents in a phony Abwehr network. Garbo was initially run by Mills, whom Pujol knew only as 'Mr. Grey.' Although Garbo was one of about forty German agents the British managed to turn, few achieved such stunning success. By the fall of 1942, Mills was a seasoned counter-intelligence officer with intimate knowledge of the German espionage agencies. When the report from Harvison landed on his desk in late November, he was incredulous that a so-called intelligence officer could be so easily duped.

'The products of Harvison's interrogation were sent to London where all those of us who were dealing with captured agents read them and found it difficult to believe that Security was in such incapable hands in Canada,' Mills recalled shortly before his death in 1991. 'Harvison was a good policeman but he had no training, knowledge or aptitude for counter intelligence work ... He swallowed what was a wholly ficticious picture of the whole German Secret Service. The whole thing was a concoction of lies because J[anowski] realized Harvison knew nothing about German or any other Intelligence organization.'

The heavily censored version of Harvison's initial report released under the Access to Information Act, for example, contains a brief biography and description of Colonel Erwin von Lahousen. Janowski assured Harvison that this man was the Berlin-based head of Abwehr III, the counter-intelligence arm. 'To him go reports from all Group 3 units in occupied territory,' said Harvison's report. 'Stout build, bald-headed, cleanshaven, blue eyes, clear complexion, military manners, speaks French and possible [sic] English.' Lahousen, who came from a distinguished Austrian military family, was well known to the British as well. The former head of the Austrian Secret Service had been recruited into the Abwehr by Wilhelm Canaris even before the Anschluss of 1938 that incorporated Austria into the expanding German empire. Canaris placed Lahousen in charge of Abwehr II, the sabotage arm that trained agents to destroy foreign industrial sites and strategic transportation points, often harnessing disaffected groups within other countries. This dark army of saboteurs was also to precede invading German armies, facilitating their rapid advance. Even when later confronted with the truth about Lahousen, Janowski would not back down. 'He states that Lahousen's office is located on the second floor of the building [Abwehr's Berlin headquarters at 72 Tirpitzufer], that he has personally interviewed him there and received instructions regarding Group 3 movements,' Harvison dutifully recorded. 'He points out that it is not unusual for the Chiefs of these various Departments to be shifted to other Departments.' MI5 knew better, though. The RCMP report was riddled with these deliberate falsehoods as well as with misleading terminology. Janowski used the word 'Gruppe' or group, for example, to refer to the four divisions of the Abwehr rather than the correct 'Abteilung.' Harvison's disingenous memoirs say only that 'we were advised by British Intelligence that his story had been checked as closely as possible, and that he was apparently telling us the truth.'

Harvison's interrogation report also painted a suspicious picture of Janowski as a reluctant spy. Incarcerated at the Dachau concentration camp in 1938 after his return from the French Foreign Legion, Janowski said he was asked to return to Africa to do intelligence work, but declined. Recruited to the German army, Janowski said he was asked again in April 1941 to become an espionage agent because of his knowledge of English and French. Again he declined. In December 1941 he was again called to Berlin from North Africa where he was serving under Rommel. Urged to become a counter-espionage officer based in Brussels, Janowski 'expressed some little doubt and [Captain Ernst] Muller explained that the job was quite an honourable one and in keeping with the rank of a commissioned officer and of considerable importance.' According to Janowski's account, he was then taken before Canaris, who assured 'he was considered a valuable man and much was expected of him.' Janowski finally relented and agreed to work in counter-espionage, removing Allied agents operating in Belgium and Northern France. Or so he claimed.

Lieutenant Wilfred Samuel, the German-speaking Naval Intelligence officer who had helped break Janowski in the back seat of the RCMP car, produced a far more professional report. After being dropped off in Montreal, Samuel took a train to Ottawa and there, on Saturday, 14 November, he typed an analysis for his boss, Lieutenant-Commander C. Herbert Little. Unlike Harvison, Samuel cross-checked many of Janowski's claims by using Naval Intelligence files and he found several conflicts. Samuel was also alert for logical inconsistencies. Incredibly, Janowski had told Samuel that he was an Abwehr I man, specializing in foreign intelligence, rather than the Abwehr III counter-intelligence officer he claimed to be with Harvison. Samuel was not yet aware of the contents of Harvison's interrogation report, but felt that Janowski's Abwehr I claim was inconsistent with other facts, and said so in his report. 'I close this section by stressing that all information obtained from Janowski must be treated with suspicion, since he is an inveterate liar,' Samuel told Little. The navy thought it had a prize catch when the first reports from New Carlisle suggested a U-boat commander was under arrest. But Janowski knew only what a layman might glean – he apparently was not even aware that Admiral Karl Doenitz was commander of the U-boat fleet.

Even the Americans, far less experienced than the British in their understanding of the Abwehr and related organizations, found Janowski's confessions to be meagre fare. As noted above, the prisoner had no specific information for Hoover that could help trap agents and saboteurs in the United States. Janowski's overviews also added little to the general store of intelligence. 'This report is not of great value except that it confirms from what appears to be a first-hand but poorly informed source that information already on hand,' a U.S. military intelligence analysis concludes about an interrogation report delivered by the FBI. 'The chart is faulty in that it shows the Propaganda Ministry at the top and does not show any real organization or functional set-up.' A German prisoner of war also advised the Americans that Janowski's information was suspect. A Captain Von Fehrn, formerly of German army intelligence, assured that Janowski 'did not amount to very much in the Lehrregiment, and it appears many of the statements he has made might be questioned,' a U.S. Army analysis recorded.

The problems with the interrogations, however, paled beside new breaches in the censorship net that had been stretched across North America. Shortly after Harvison's team left New Carlisle, a reporter and photographer for the *Toronto Daily Star* arrived in town to interview and photograph everyone connected with the case. On their return trip to Toronto the following week, the pair stopped at Montreal to ask Harvison for police photographs in connection with the case, but were refused. The visit alerted the Mounties to possible trouble and Corporal G.H. Archer was again detailed to visit the Toronto newspaper's offices. Archer spoke with the reporter, William Kinmount, and obtained from him a fairly detailed and accurate description of the events at New Carlisle – information even the RCMP had not collected. Kinmount had also retrieved a discarded candy wrapper from the New Carlisle jail cell, which Gus Goulet had good-naturedly allowed him to inspect. It 'had been screwed up into a tight ball, and it is noted that there is a pencil writing on both sides, but in its present condition is illegible,' Archer noted. The reporter 'consented to hand over this paper to the writer on the condition that it be returned to him when it had served its purpose.' The candy wrapper was rushed to RCMP labs in Ottawa, and identified as having been manufactured for McCormick's Ltd. The mysterious writing turned out to be a barely literate poem from a former prisoner with no connection to the Janowski case. Kinmount, who was not apprised of the RCMP's results, included the poem as a minor scoop in his own story of Janowski's capture, which was eventually published in May 1945.

Assistant Commissioner Vernon Kemp, commander of 'O' Division in Toronto, called editors at the *Toronto Daily Star* to remind them of the censorship placed on the Gaspé spy incident. The managing editor assured Kemp that no story was to be published until censorship was lifted and 'that the owner of the paper, Mr. [Joseph] Atkinson, had even offered to destroy all photographs and copy, but felt it would be wiser if this material were placed in the safe in their building in case at some future time it might be of assistance to the Authorities.' To reinforce the media ban, Commissioner Wood wrote the same day to R.K. Carnegie, superintendent of the Canadian Press news service serving most of Canada's daily newspapers. 'For reasons of hemispheric security ... it is most undesirable that any publicity be given regarding a German agent who landed alone from a German submarine near New Carlisle.' The news blackout, originally designed to help capture Janowski's fellow agents, was now essential for the grander purpose of protecting a potential double agent.

But just as one media brushfire was doused, a conflagration roared over the United States border. That same day, 19 November, the magazine *Newsweek* hit the stands with an entry under the 'Canadian Notes' section that read: 'Watch for an announcement revealing the capture of a German submarine commander near New Carlisle, Quebec.' Unlike the obscure Memphis newspaper that had reported the story five days earlier, *Newsweek* was a high-profile publication read all over North America. The FBI's J. Edgar Hoover oversaw the investigation into the embarrassing breach of censorship. 'The editor reported that he had received many such rumors before and did not feel that this story was sufficiently identifiable and as a matter of fact, he had no idea that it was actually true,' Hoover reported to the U.S. attorney general. 'An endeavor was made to stop the exportation ... but information that the magazine contained this article was received too late and the magazine received its usual wide distribution both in this country and Canada.' There was more damage. The Montreal newspaper *Le Devoir* took umbrage at the *Newsweek* item, and published an article in its 24 November edition pointing out the piece and noting that Canadian authorities had forbidden its publication. A clear double standard, snorted the writer. The article referred mistakenly to *Time* magazine, and a correction was published the next day, further compounding the censorship breach. The writer was contacted and promised not to 'follow up the story, the importance of which he did not know fully at the time,' the censorship authorities reported.

Janowski had told his captors he had a radio rendezvous with Hamburg set for 1 December, the first date at which communication was to be established using the 40-watt short-wave transmitter. Everyone in the RCMP connected with the case could hear the clock ticking: a decision on whether to run Janowski as Canada's first-ever double agent would have to be made swiftly. Harvison made his position clear the day after arriving back from New Carlisle. A good cop, he was alive to the possibilities of trapping more saboteurs headed to Canada. 'There appears to be an excellent chance of protecting Canada against the Agents that are allegedly now being trained for work here this coming Spring,' he told Gagnon, his commanding officer in Montreal, on 13 November. 'If the prisoner can retain the confidence of his H.Q. and establish radio communication with them, the point at which they would land and the time of the landing would be named in that event by the prisoner. At the present stage I believe this to be a decided possibility but the possibility decreases with the slightest publicity.'

That same day, 'Freckles' Wren of British Security Co-ordination made a personal pitch to Commissioner Wood in Ottawa. 'I am taking the liberty of saying that from the information so far available I would say that there is more than a reasonable chance of turning this man round and using him to communicate with Germany,' he wrote in a memorandum on RCMP letterhead from Montreal. 'I understand that owing to the manner in which he was arrested a certain amount of publicity has occurred, but it appears that it would be possible to counteract this publicity and use him as a double agent. I hope I will be forgiven for addressing you personally in this manner, but I am so impressed by the possibilities of the case that I wish to draw your special attention to it.' These comments must have had a powerfully persuasive effect on Wood. As the only MI5 man on the scene, Wren commanded a certain authority and respect. His organization had developed the double-cross system into an effective strategic-deception tool. Here was a chance for Canada to get in on the game. Never mind that Wren had limited personal involvement with double-cross, having never himself run an agent. Gagnon, the commanding officer in Montreal, seemed susceptible to Wren's enthusiasm. 'I sincerely believe that the subject will give us the assistance required,' Gagnon told Wood.

Inspector Alexander Drysdale, the Mountie intelligence officer most closely connected with the case, read these recommendations at RCMP headquarters in Ottawa the next day – a Saturday – with growing unease. Harvison and Gagnon had no special training in intelligence work and were taking a gung-ho, boy-scout approach to a major espionage undertaking. Drysdale was dead set against turning Janowski and said so in writing to his superiors. 'I am very strongly opposed to such action ... It is perfectly obvious that thousands of people knew there was reason to believe a landing had been effected from a submarine ... It is no stretch of the imagination that Germany knows now JANOWSKI was arrested – since so many knew a few of the facts and that the Police on the Atlantic coast, etc. were very very active.' Drysdale continued: 'Since it is almost certain Germany knows now JANOWSKI is in custody, any messages from him will be viewed with suspicion, and, it is within the bounds of possibility that Germany may reply to some communication in such a way as to seriously mislead us.' Drysdale and others in Ottawa were also skittish about rushing into a double-agent operation before Janowski had even been thoroughly interrogated and all inconsistencies eliminated.

British double-cross experts, masters of the game, had found from experience that a thorough interrogation was vital before setting out. 'Almost all unwilling or doubtful agents tend to keep back part of their story and much of their information, presumably in order to have cards up their sleeves to play if the game takes an unexpected turn,' wrote John Masterman, a top MI5 official, in a 1945 manual. 'It is therefore often fatal to start a case until a thorough and systematic account has been obtained of the agent's history, background, antecedents, and connections with the Germans.' The challenge was to carry out the interrogation rapidly so as to avoid delays in establishing contact and thereby give away the double-agent aspect. Only experienced officers could act with the efficiency needed, Masterman said. 'Double agents can only be run by a department which has made some study of the German Secret Service, since any other department will inevitably commit errors of a practical kind in the working of the agents due to a lack of knowledge of the personalities, methods, and peculiarities of the other side.' As Drysdale well knew, Harvison had neither a full confession from his prisoner nor any background in German intelligence.

The *Newsweek* article about the New Carlisle capture served only to inflame the fears of Drysdale and others in Ottawa deeply opposed to the doubling proposal. 'In view of the wide-spread circulation of this magazine it is now impossible to believe that the enemy will not acquire the information which has been guarded so carefully to date,' Lieutenant C.W. Skarstedt, a navy signals expert, wrote to the director of Naval Intelligence on 24 November. The sceptical faction in Ottawa felt the RCMP was sleepwalking into the arms of the Abwehr, who could then tie into knots Canada's limited intelligence resources. Janowski would be a triple agent from the very first contact. Indeed, there were some – like Superintendent K. Duncan, assistant director of the Criminal Investigation Branch – who first wanted a plausible explanation of Janowski's extreme carelessness in concealing his identity on arriving at New Carlisle.

As has been shown, the prisoner himself appeared to be pushing the double-cross operation, which by itself should have induced scepticism. Perhaps still fearful he would be hanged otherwise, Janowski repeatedly made it clear he would fully cooperate in the use of the radio. Less than ten days after his arrival in Montreal, he was grandly cursing his former Abwehr masters. 'During a general conversation he expressed thorough dislike for the whole Abwehr,' says the report of a 22 November interrogation. 'He imitated German Secret Service officials with sneers and snarls, and pointed out that jealousy among them will be the ultimate downfall of the whole service. He expressed it as most inefficient, officials working as short hours as possible (10 A.M. to 4 P.M.) with frequent nightly drinking brawls.'

Despite the publicity and lingering doubts about Janowski, RCMP Commissioner Wood was clearly sold on using him as Canada's first-ever double agent. 'I am very much in favour of an attempt being made to get in touch with that country,' Wood wrote to Justice Minister Louis St Laurent on 23 November. 'We have nothing to lose if the attempt fails. On the other hand the advantages of being able to delay the activities of the saboteurs who will, without doubt, be sent to this country next spring cannot be over estimated.' The following day, Wood personally delivered a secret note to St Laurent asking for written authorization to proceed. 'There is not the slightest doubt in my mind that the landing of saboteurs will be attempted as proposed and that further attempts will be made to send other agents to Canada and through Canada to the United

States,' Wood noted in his closing arguments. 'I am of the opinion that knowledge of his capture, if it has reached Germany, has done so in such a vague form that we can overcome it ... If, by any chance, this scheme should not be successful and the Germans become aware of the fact that JANOWSKI is under our control we have nothing to lose ... I strongly recommend your approval of this procedure.' After some discussion, the minister picked up a fountain pen and scratched 'Louis S. St. Laurent' in a tall, bold script under the word 'Approved.'

FOUR

Bobbi Calls Home

One of Janowski's first Abwehr assignments in Canada was to send a letter back to his German masters announcing his safe arrival. Somehow the material had to get past vigilant postal censors, who inspected all mail bound for continental Europe. Janowski told his captors the initial plan was for him to send an innocuous letter to a Canadian prisoner of war held in a German camp, the pages impregnated with a secret, invisible message. Prison-camp officials would know what letters to forward to the Abwehr by spotting prearranged signatures. The plan fell through shortly before Janowski left for Canada, however, when the Germans learned that all letters bound for POWs in Europe were photographed in Switzerland and only the photos forwarded to the camps. Plan B was to post letters to Abwehr mail-drops in neutral countries, again with invisible-ink writing beneath the visible message. Janowski had been supplied with three mail-drop addresses, one in Sweden and two in Switzerland, with specific instructions on the wording to use in his *en clair* writing. Concealed inside his diary's spine were two 'safety' matches whose heads had been replaced with a secret writing chemical the German spy-masters said would last for years. The Operation Pastorius saboteurs had been supplied with similar matches, but Janowski assured his RCMP handlers that his pair contained newly developed chemicals, though he could not identify them.

On 25 November, less than twenty-four hours after St Laurent gave the double-agent operation the green light, Janowski sat down in the sergeant's mess at the St James Street RCMP headquarters and scribbled a short business note in English. 'Dear Sir,' it began. 'I am to remind you that a copy of the account of business of 1941 has not been received yet. As we are almost in the end of 1942 I would be thankful to hear from you as soon as possible. Sincerely yours, Johnson, for Bloch & Co.' He then carefully wiped the white sheet with absorbent cotton and rotated it lengthwise, ninety degrees, to inscribe his invisible message with one of the match heads. Janowski wrote in German, using block letters, from a text that had been carefully prepared and checked by Johnny. A first attempt to have Janowski make a simultaneous carbon copy of the secret message failed, because it left too clear an indentation in the white sheet. So Johnny simply watched carefully as the prisoner placed the sheet on a plate of glass and wrote slowly, letter-by-letter. In English translation, it read: 'Landed all right on November 9th. Had to overcome difficulties with country police. Did not find suitable living quarters until now. Radio with me. Hope to begin radio sending on December 1st. Bobbi.' Janowski then addressed a white envelope to 'Dr. J.H. Nauckhoff, GREV. MAGNIGAN 17.B., *STOCKHOLM*.' After photostatic copies were made of the sheet and its envelope, and stamps applied, the letter was posted to inaugurate formally the double-agent operation. Presumably arrangements were made to get the communication past the Bermuda postal censors, who regularly tested letters for secret writing, though the RCMP file is silent on this point. 'The concealed message contained in this letter was to the effect that JANOWSKI had landed safely but had to overcome difficulties with local police,' said an RCMP summary report. 'This, it was hoped, would tend to allay suspicions the Germans might hold with regard to him due to stories having reached them through the breaches of censorship which already had occurred in this case.'

The Mounties also alerted U.S. postal censorship to the three mail-drop addresses, and over the course of the war American officials intercepted and examined at least thirty-eight pieces of correspondence, most of them bound for the Swedish address. FBI documents suggest some of these had been treated with invisible ink, though the outcome of the agency investigations has been deleted from the bureau file. Harvison also prepared sample sheets with secret writing and sent them to RCMP Sergeant S.H. Lett, at the Canadian Police College Laboratory in the Ottawa suburb of Rockcliffe. With help from the FBI, Lett determined that the chemical was quinine in about a 6 per cent solution –

hardly the exotic substance that Janowski had claimed. Quinine was rather a prosaic choice for the Abwehr, which had far more sophisticated options reserved for its top agents. (The Operation Pastorius saboteurs were also issued quinine-tipped matches.) A quinine message could be read by first washing the sheet with dilute sulphuric acid, then shining an ultraviolet light on the surface. The secret writing glowed in a yellowish white and was easily read. After several weeks, when Janowski's matches were already crumbling from the few times they had been used, Lett manufactured three more and even provided a quinine pencil to assure more even pressure on the paper. Ideally, Lett advised, the paper should be given a wash of dilute ammonia before posting. This would help protect the secret writing from the so-called universal developers used by postal censors and would overcome problems of too much quinine deposited, which could be readily detected by a censor's ultraviolet light even without the sulphuric-acid developer.

Some days after Janowski's covert greeting to the Abwehr had been mailed, senior officers in Ottawa examining the files and photostats from Montreal grew alarmed. The mail-drop address that had been scribbled in Janowski's diary before he left Germany was slightly different from the address he had inscribed on the envelope. For one, the diary said 'Dr. I.H. Nauckhoff,' but the 'I' had somehow become a 'J' on the envelope. The diary also listed the street as 'Magnigatan,' which was changed to 'Magnigan' on the envelope. Gagnon, rattled by the apparent slip when Ottawa drew it to his attention, insisted Janowski wrote his upper-case I's in a way that look like a J – though he did not explain why Janowski wrote a perfectly clear upper-case I in MAGNIGAN. And there was simply no good explanation for the spelling change in the street name. 'While this may have been purely accidental on the part of your prisoner, you will appreciate that it could very easily be an attempt on his part to notify his contacts that all was not well with him,' Assistant Commissioner Frederick Mead wrote from Ottawa. 'A very close check should be maintained for occurrences of this nature.' The game, it seemed, might already have been lost with the opening gambit. Only time would tell.

The next big hurdle for Harvison was to estabish radio contact using Janowski's puny 40-watt transmitter and receiver. This well-established Abwehr spy radio was known as an Afu, short for Agentenfunk or agent radio. The device, a compact thirty pounds, was specially developed for Abwehr chief Canaris before the war by the Telefunken Company to fit snugly inside a standard suitcase measuring 20 by 15 inches, 6 inches deep. The radio itself was durable, but had nowhere near the power for reliable transatlantic transmissions. Abwehr agents dropped into Britain were normally equipped with transmitters emitting between five and ten watts, even less on batteries, deliberately low to help avoid detection. Janowski's set was at least four times as powerful, but it also had an enormous distance to cover. Atmospheric conditions often interfered with the weak signals Afu sets mustered. British intelligence found the 5-watt and 10-watt models frequently inadequate for its double agents to communicate even across the English Channel. The 'Germans did not as a rule provide really sound equipment,' Masterman wrote in his 1945 summary of the double-cross system. 'Probably no German agent in the early days would have made contact without the technical assistance of our wireless experts.'

The Germans had established more powerful transmitters in South America that did manage to communicate effectively with Hamburg. Indeed, these South American transmissions inaugurated Canada's first signals-intelligence operation during the Second World War, through a small intercept station at Rockcliffe, near Ottawa, run by Captain Edward Drake of the Royal Canadian Corps of Signals. By late 1941, Drake's group had been able to intercept and decipher 740 German transmissions to and from more than 50 South American agents. The special advantage of the Rockcliffe station was its relative isolation from ambient local signals and electronic noise. The St James headquarters of the RCMP in Montreal, by contrast, was simply out of the question for radio, surrounded as it was by buildings and electrical wires that drowned or trapped weak signals. With just a week before the first scheduled transmission on 1 December, Harvison had to find a locale with few obstructions. It was also important for secrecy's sake to secure a location that was less of a thoroughfare for officers, reporters, clerks, and criminals than the St James Street offices.

A Constable d'Arcy of the RCMP reserve recommended to Harvison the home of his neighbours, a couple by the name of Le Riche who lived on the outskirts of Montreal. The house was surrounded by fields suitable for erecting aerials, and was believed to be a clean transmission point. The couple 'were not told the nature of the work being undertaken, but were advised that it was of extreme importance to this country and that it was necessary that it be kept most secret,' Harvison reported. On 28 November, the upper floor of the house was commandeered by the RCMP, and one room with a small window was established as the radio base. An aerial was erected, a recording system known as a Telecord installed to keep track of all messages, and a sophisticated receiver set up that was far more sensitive than the one Janowski had lugged ashore. The short-wave radio set itself consisted of three parts: a separate transmitter and receiver and a power pack set for 220 volts in Europe but readily alterable to North America's 110 volts. The transmitter operated within two short-wave ranges, selected by using a two-position switch, and could send only Morse code rather than voice. The receiver gave off only enough power for headphones and had a slightly narrower frequency range than the transmitter.

Harvison now assembled his double-agent team around Janowski. The radio man would be Gordon Southam, a Montreal printer by profession but also an amateur radio enthusiast for twenty years. A civilian, he had lent his radio expertise to the RCMP and other federal-government departments over many years and was regarded as trustworthy. Southam volunteered his time for the Janowski case, but the Mounties eventually paid him $4 a day for his services and reimbursed him for the used equipment he contributed to radio operations. Southam had some experience of amateur radio transmitters in pre-war England, and was aware of the great difficulties in contacting continental stations. The Afu set would be his most daunting long-distance challenge yet. Southam was also Janowski's understudy, scrutinizing the prisoner's Morse code rhythms and idiosyncracies – or 'fist' – for the day he might have to substitute because of illness, obstinacy, or even treachery.

Shortly before leaving for Canada, Janowski had been given a two-week intensive radio training session in a Berlin hotel, clocking in at about fifty words per minute. He already knew Morse code and the fundamentals of radio technology, partly through his Toronto training at the Radio College of Canada, paid for by his Canadian wife. Abwehr technicians in Berlin had also recorded his sending style on audio tape for comparison with any unusual signals purported to be from him during his actual mission. As a special precaution, he was given an innocuous signal that was to be slipped into his messages to alert his Abwehr masters that he was operating under control. Such signals, given to all Abwehr spies operating radios, were unique to each agent – perhaps a deliberate spelling mistake, a repeated letter that might be taken for a slip of the wrist, or even the absence of an agreed-upon typographical error. Janowski confessed his warning signal to the RCMP – Harvison's memoirs indicate he divulged more than one – though its precise nature has been deleted from the released Watchdog file. Southam would remain alert in case the prisoner tried to use it.

Southam would work closely with RCMP Corporal Ken Molyneaux, who was to become the radio code expert. Born at Ottawa in 1909, he joined the Mounties at Rockcliffe in 1932 and was posted soon after to Montreal. He had been promoted to full corporal just one year before Janowski's landing. Molyneaux carried out an intensive study of the coding system based on the instructions Janowski had brought, concealed on a microtext and discovered in the binding of his diary. Coding was time-consuming and complex. It was constructed in part by attaching a sequence of numbers to the letters in three Canadian company names: Rogers Majestic Limited, Trans-Canada Airlines Limited, and Imperial Airways Limited. The code, a widely used Abwehr type known as a 'book cipher,' also made use of two paperbacks. The first was a 196-page edition of *Mary Poppins* by P.L Travers, with a plain yellow cover. Measuring 4.5 inches by 7.75 inches, the book had been printed in Leipzig in 1937 as part of the Albatross Modern Continental Library. It warned: 'Copyrighted issue. Not to be introduced into the British Empire or the U.S.A.' The second volume was a 128-page collection of detective stories by J.S. Fletcher. The cover featured a stylized picture of a crook, and read: 'Fletcher Keeps the Night Lights Burning! – The Man in No. 3 – A Crime Club Book.' Bound in green and measuring 5.75 by 8.5 inches, it was published in London by W. Collins Sons Company Limited.

Janowski was to alert the receiving station which book – yellow or green – would be used for the message to follow. The code was then derived by substituting letters on particular pages, according to a date-based formula, for the letters of the message to be sent. The FBI went to some length to acquire its own copies of these two books, but could not locate the same editions. By the end of November, the bureau simply took photographs of every page of the paperbacks and turned them over to its Cryptographic Section for reference. The bureau, though, was already well familiar with book ciphers. William Sebold, an Abwehr agent sent to the United States in 1940, had immediately betrayed his mission to the FBI and was run as a double. Code-named Tramp, he sent reports to Hamburg by radio from Centerport, New York, using a code like Janowski's, except that his only reference book was the bestseller by Rachel Field, *All This and Heaven, Too.*

Janowski had also been equipped with a slide rule to transpose letters for additional code security. Individual transmissions, confined to either one of two agreed-upon frequencies, were limited to two hundred letters to help ensure the broadcast source would be difficult to trace with Allied direction-finding devices. Molyneaux and Janowski would each be handed copies of the German-language plain-text message to be sent to Hamburg, location of the Abwehr's main receiving station for the Western Hemisphere, and each would work out the coding on a mimeographed sheet containing a blocked-out diagram. Harvison would scan the separate results to ensure they matched before approving a Morse-code transmission. Molyneaux's remaining duty was to escort Janowski with two RCMP guards between the St James Street barracks and the Le Riche house. Johnny was the German-language expert. He was to examine the English-language texts provided by Harvison and ensure that Janowski's translations were accurate. Harvison oversaw the entire seven-person operation. The team's distinguishing feature was that almost all were amateurs – from Molyneaux, who had to give himself a crash course in coding, to Harvison, who had never run a double-agent case and had never received any MI5 training in double-cross techniques. Even Southam, who had immersed himself in radio for two decades, was a printer by trade. Among them, only Johnny had any experience of international espionage, and he was relegated to a relatively minor role.

The Abwehr had allotted Janowski two half-hour radio windows each day during which he was to try to establish contact with Hamburg. The first began at 4:30 a.m., the second at 6:30 p.m., both Central European Time, with first transmissions to begin on 1 December. Janowski was to broadcast his station call letters, changed daily according to a formula, for a five-minute period. He was then to listen five minutes for a reply, then transmit his call letters again, repeating the cycle until contact was established or the half-hour had lapsed. The first window was to be at the transmission frequency of 8137 kilocycles, the second at 13,395 kilocycles. This change in frequency was standard procedure for the Abwehr, whose radio experts were well aware that higher-frequency waves travel better in the day, lower frequencies better at night.

Harvison calculated that to conform to the first radio rendezvous, Janowski had to begin sending at 11:30 p.m. on 30 November local time to account for the five-hour difference with Hamburg. With Ottawa's approval, Harvison drew up a message to send if and when the stations made contact. It was essentially an abbreviated version of the message contained in the secret-ink letter from 25 November. In English translation, it read: 'Landed all right. Cleared temporary difficulty with country police. Now have suitable quarters.' Janowski was then to indicate which book, green or yellow, would be used for the next transmission and give a date. Like the letter to Stockholm, the message was meant to help neutralize any reports the Abwehr may have received about Janowski's capture.

The team launched the radio operation as scheduled, but during the first two windows nothing was received from Hamburg. Shortly before the second window on the afternoon of 1 December, Harvison took a telephone call from a Canadian navy signals specialist, Lieutenant C.W. Skarstedt. The German-speaking officer had interrogated Janowski once before and had become convinced that the Germans were fully aware of the capture because of press leaks. Skarstedt was now acting on an encyphered message cabled on 28 November from the Admiralty in London for more details of the device used in Berlin to record Janowski's Morse-code sending style, 'particularly method of use and technical composition.' After getting approval from senior RCMP officials, Skarstedt had arrived from Ottawa to arrange a second interrogation on this and other naval matters. Harvison arranged to bring Janowski back to RCMP headquarters later that afternoon for Skarstedt.

'Janowski now appears to have completely recovered from the nervous state in which he appeared at the previous interrogation, and his statements at times appeared carefully chosen and somewhat guarded,' Skarstedt later reported. The prisoner could offer almost no information about the recording device, just as he had had little to offer about

U-518's Schlussel M encyphering apparatus – a version of the famous Enigma machine – during Skarstedt's initial interrogation. One vital and unexpected piece of information did emerge, however. Janowski told Skarstedt that on 2 November German time had been altered by one hour. The claim was supported by Naval Intelligence, which had sent out a 2 November signal alerting all stations to the change. Janowski, however, had not bothered to advise Harvison of the revision. 'Before the undersigned arrived, the R.C.M.P. had been trying to contact at one hour too early, or according to the old German time,' Skarstedt told his superiors in Ottawa. Harvison duly adjusted transmission times.

Skarstedt's rough notes about the second Montreal interrogation, carefully expunged from his final report, also spoke of a 'brewing dissatisfaction' among the Mounties running the agent. 'It was further surmised, by remarks passed by the R.C.M.P. officers that they are not entirely in accord with the great publicity accorded "their" prisoner by outside sources,' he observed. In fact, five days before Skarstedt's visit the Mountie brass had decided not to forward any further interrogation reports to army, navy, or air force intelligence to help tighten security. That attitude, broadly alluded to in other RCMP documents, was somewhat ironic, given that Skarstedt had alerted Harvison's team to a potential flaw in their radio schedule. The Mounties' possessiveness was also contrary to the free inter-service exchange of ideas that helped make the British double-cross system so effective.

For more than two frustrating weeks, signals were sent twice daily from the Le Riche house with no contact made. From the outset, Harvison was keen simply to transmit blind, that is, to send a complete message without first establishing contact, in the hope that the Hamburg station would receive it anyway. Janowski had assured his captors that this would be normal procedure for an Abwehr field agent, and that failure to do so might arouse suspicion in Germany. Caution prevailed in Ottawa, however, and it was not until 16 December – after consultation with MI5 – that Harvison got approval for the blind message. The stand-by first message that had been ready since 1 December was discarded to focus instead on the radio problems. The transmission was sent in two parts, to keep each one under the maximum two hundred letters. At 11:40 p.m. Montreal time, the air waves crackled with the first information from agent Bobbi radioed back to the Abwehr. In translation, it read: 'I am sending QSY-1 and 2 since 1st Dec. Why do you not send with more power? Can not hear you. Very dangerous for me to transmit without knowing whether you are hearing me. I hear DFC well near QSY-1. If no contact soon say whether you are hearing me and if necessary give new instructions with QSY-1 over the DFC transmitter with the call WBR. WBR. Green book. I am always listening on QSY-1 and 2 and DFC. Letter written to Sweden on 25 Nov. Bobbi.'

QSY-1 and 2 was the standard international Morse Q-code abbreviation for the two radio windows and their separate frequencies. The letters DFC referred to the high-powered German Naval Control transmitter at Nauen, just west of Berlin, which could be heard at the Le Riche house near the prearranged receiving frequency of 13,500 kilocycles for QSY-1, which in Montreal was the afternoon window. Janowski was therefore suggesting that since he was unable to make contact directly with the Hamburg station, the Nauen station could be used instead to get a message across to him. Nauen was to use the call letters WBR so that Janowski would know the transmission was intended for him. The 'green book' was the paperback collection of crime stories, *The Man in No. 3*, which would be used to encode the first messages.

The afternoon following the transmission of the blind message, the team finally received a faint chirp from Hamburg, the call letters DCH repeated several times. Janowski immediately radioed back his own call letters for that day – WVA – to try to establish two-way contact, but to no avail. He then sent the blind message until well after the window had closed. Three more days passed until Hamburg was again heard, this time with the call letters GFK. 'Good morning, old boy,' Janowski replied in Q-code abbreviation. 'We are receiving you very weakly. Are you hearing us? Go ahead.' Still no contact, partly because of interference from a big American station. Through to the end of December, it was the same frustrating routine: anemic signals received from Hamburg giving only their call letters, and no acknowledgment of the clipped messages sent from Montreal. The blind message was not sent again.

Janowski's first feeble transmissions were in fact heard in the United States, though this was not unusual since radio waves were known to travel with less difficulty north–south than west–east. Receiving stations run by the U.S. Federal Communications Commission intercepted three of the transmissions, and the agency immediately turned over the material to FBI cryptanalysts in Washington. The first two signals were too garbled and fragmentary. But the third turned out to be Janowski's blind message, which was decoded and translated accurately. It was added to the FBI's rapidly expanding Janowski file. The new short-wave station was also heard by radio enthusiasts in the Montreal area, and word soon spread that the illegal transmissions might be from a German agent. 'We got calls at the office repeatedly, well on a few occasions, that there was a short-wave station in operation in Montreal,' Lawrence Conroy, the police reporter at the Montreal *Gazette*, later recalled. 'They said it was sent in code and no one could get it.' Conroy, who had seen Janowski several times at the St James Street headquarters, began to put two and two together: the agent was still alive, living at RCMP headquarters, and was likely being used as a double agent to make radio contact with the Abwehr. Censorship was still in effect, but Conroy kept detailed notes for the day when the story could finally be told.

The double-agent case was doomed if Janowski could make no contact with his Abwehr masters. By mid-December, Harvison and Southam were already hatching a plan to increase the power of the transmitter with an electronic 'booster.' This was tricky business. The signal had to be amplified only to the level that allowed it to cross the North Atlantic intelligibly. Too much power, and the messages would blast into Germany – a potential give-away that Janowski was operating under control. The plan was further complicated by atmospheric conditions. Power would have to be judiciously cranked up at times of intense electromagnetic interference and reduced when the air waves settled once more. The RCMP enlisted the help of Canada's Controller of Radio for daily briefings on transatlantic radio conditions, a task later turned over to the Canadian navy. To allay Abwehr suspicions, Harvison proposed that Janowski tell Hamburg that he had built a 'booster,' drawing on his radio training while in Canada in the early 1930s. Southam began constructing the new device on 22 December with about $47 worth of used parts – used, partly because wartime security controls made obtaining new parts a slow and difficult process. Power was increased in stages, eventually to lift the rating of Janowski's Afu to 238 watts, the maximum Southam dared used without popping the tubes. The signal strength was thus increased to between two and a half and almost six times former levels, depending on the atmospheric conditions.

Harvison also pressed for a new radio location. Commissioner Wood had never liked the exposed situation at the St James Street headquarters, and the problem had worsened as Janowski was transferred to the Le Riche residence twice a day. 'This man's presence in barracks causes discussion and curiosity among the personnel,' Harvison advised Gagnon on 9 December. 'So long as this man is seen around barracks there is little possibility of stopping discussion.' Johnny offered the use of his own small bungalow in the Town of Mount Royal, a suburb just north of Montreal. For perhaps $300, his unfinished basement with its nine-foot-high concrete walls could be adapted by installing a shower, toilet, and partitions separating the space into a bedroom, radio room, and guard room. The windows were far too small to permit escape, and entry could be had through the garage. There was also plenty of room in the yard for aerials. Southam had already spent a day at the location with a receiver and determined that the air waves were fairly clean. Johnny's wife Gerta, an excellent cook, could feed them all at 25 cents each per meal. Monthly room and board for the prisoner would run about $70. Janowski would never have to be moved, apart from a daily walk for exercise.

Wood had indicated that the transfer to any new location should await the conclusion of Harvison's seemingly endless interrogation. But Harvison noted that 'after starting to be truthful, [Janowski] had several lapses because of his fear that we would – to use an expression that he used many times – "pull all the worms from my nose and then hang me anyway". If his transfer follows immediately the completion of questioning, it seems probable that this fear will return. Having spent many hours daily with this man since his capture, I believe there is a decided possibility that in the event of his getting that impression he would refuse to make himself of any further use to us.' In view of Janowski's dread fear of execution, Harvison's caution seemed misplaced. More likely, the prisoner would do anything required when faced with a clear threat of death. In any case, Wood accepted Harvison's proposal and the team worked from 31 December to 4 January to establish the new location.

Harvison hired a construction company to erect a fifty-foot pole in the backyard and a twenty-foot pole attached to the bungalow's chimney. Between these were strung two separate lengths of wire, each appropriate to the frequencies of the two radio windows. A switch was rigged so that the same aerials could be used for either transmitting or receiving. The final bill for the renovations was $514.61, including a $14.18 heater to ward off the winter chill in the damp basement. Janowski was brought to his new home under guard on 5 January, Harvison pointing out to him that the bathroom door could not be locked and that the only exit from the bedroom was through the guard room. The biggest local security problem now became the neighbours, as Harvison noted in his memoirs. 'Johnny spoke with a strong German accent, as did his wife; and they had been regarded with some suspicion by their neighbours since moving into the district,' Harvison wrote. 'The neighbours were quick to notice strange goings and comings through Johnny's basement door. When these were followed by the erection of a radio tower, the neighbours felt sure that they had uncovered enemy plotting. Several of them visited our offices to report their suspicions.' The local police chief also received complaints, but was pacified by the assurance that the RCMP was testing some new top-secret radio equipment. He was asked to spread the word quietly through the neighbourhood.

The same night Janowski was moved into his new quarters, at 11:30 p.m., the team resumed short-wave broadcasts to Hamburg with their more powerful transmitter and precisely tuned aerials. Hopes were soon dashed. For the next week and a half, it was the same trying routine as at the Le Riche station. Janowski would call, and nothing was heard. On 10 January, they did catch faint signals from Hamburg, but it was clear the Abwehr operator could not pick up Montreal. All the while, Southam adjusted the apparatus, increasing the power slightly and changing the aerial wire. They even tried transmitting at a different time. Still nothing. Harvison then ordered a blind message sent: 'I have been sending on QSY one and two since December 1st. Since January 5th have found better quarters for radio. Must strengthen your signal ... very dangerous for me to transmit continuously without hearing you.' There was no question that the booster had increased the output substantially. Officials at MI5 had cabled RCMP in Ottawa that for the first time the signals were being picked up by short-wave receivers controlled by Britain's Government Code and Cypher School, the sophisticated signals-intelligence station at Bletchley Park. The blind message was also read several times between 10 and 14 January at the FBI's monitoring station at Clinton, Maryland, just south-east of Washington.

Then, at 1:35 p.m. on 14 January, weeks of persistent radio work paid off. Listening intently through the static crackle in the headphones, Southam picked up a brief Morse message from station AZE: QSA1 AR K, standard Q-code that meant 'Receiving your signals weakly. Go ahead.' Janowski, whose call letters that day were TSX, immediately tapped out: HI HI ROK VY FB DR OB QSA2 HR QTC2 QRV? K, which in Q-code meant 'Greetings. Greetings. Received OK. Very fine business dear old boy. Your signal is at strength 2. Have two messages. Are you ready for them? Go ahead.' There was no further contact, though, partly because Hamburg was transmitting about 30 kilocycles below the agreed level. The next afternoon, the contact was more secure. The Hamburg frequency setting was even more askew, by about 50 kilocycles, but both stations could now clearly hear one another. Southam took down the first full message, in German, from the Hamburg station. In broad translation, it read: 'Service message: from now on, additional traffic time is 15:00 to 15:30 Middle European Time, because conditions are better then.' Janowski acknowledged the message and said he would call again the next day. This brief short-wave exchange was also picked up by the FBI's monitoring station at South Natick, near Boston, and translated the same day in Washington. The agency immediately recognized it as Canada's new double agent.

The next morning, the extra transmission was made and from the outset the signals in both directions were strong. The new radio window had made all the difference. 'Thank God, at last,' Janowski transmitted in German. 'Have been sending since Dec. 1st on QSY one and two. Have found better quarters for radio and strengthened output on Jan. 5th ... Green book. Greetings to family.' Hamburg acknowledged the message, and responded: 'Very glad to receive traffic. Best wishes. For your own safety no traffic until Jan. 31. Calling you Feb. 1 15:00 Middle European Time.' Janowski acknowledged the signal, and messaged back that he would call again tomorrow – despite Hamburg's order to cease communications until 1 February. Both stations then signed off. The signals were so clear that the FBI easily read all of the traffic at both its South Natick and Clinton stations. 'I regard the instructions contained in the message received today as indicating that no suspicion is entertained regarding our prisoner,' an enthusiastic Harvison told Commissioner Wood. 'While a message may have been received even if they were suspicious, it seems most probable that in that event they would have maintained traffic daily. That they are concerned over the safety of the agent appears most encouraging.' Canada's first double-agent case appeared to be well and truly started.

Janowski was relieved. 'He was growing very discouraged and nervous and, earlier in the week repeated his fear that we would extract all information from him and then, in the event of contact not being successfully established, "Hang me anyway,"' Harvison observed. 'He appeared to be greatly pleased when contact was finally made and to be enthusiastic in planning future work.' In Germany, there would be celebration as well. Major Werner Trautmann, who ran the Abwehr's Hamburg listening post from an elegant stucco house on the outskirts of the city, was in charge of about 120 radio-men. Working round-the-clock in four-hour shifts, these highly trained experts would patiently sift through an avalanche of static for the barely audible Morse cheep-cheeps of their agents. The radio-men, stationed in the second floor of the house, would listen on two frequencies simultaneously – one fed into each earphone – for a newly dispatched agent's first call home, which sometimes took months. To encourage concentration, Trautmann gave a goose to the radio-man hearing an agent's first call. In Janowski's case, the lucky recipient was likely Bruno Kreis, the man who had trained him in Berlin.

RCMP Commissioner Stuart Wood was a Mountie's Mountie. He was the son of Zachary Taylor Wood, who built a career with the North-West Mounted Police, rising to become an assistant commissioner. (Zachary was a grandson of Zachary Taylor, a hero of the 1846–8 war with Mexico, which helped him win the U.S. presidency in 1848.) Born in 1889, Stuart came of age in Dawson City, Yukon, where his father was posted for thirteen years. He was sent to Upper Canada College in Toronto and the Royal Military College at Kingston, Ontario, before joining the RNWMP in 1912. Posted in the Yukon, British Columbia, Saskatchewan, and Ottawa, he was appointed commissioner in 1938 and saw the force through the tumultuous war years. One of his sons also joined the Mounties, and died in the line of duty after the war. Wood's strong jaw, clipped moustache, and determined eyebrows made him look every inch the dapper British officer, and in fact his British connections were strong. He had studied criminology at Scotland Yard, for example, and headed the RCMP's contingent in London to mark the coronation of George VI in 1938. So it was perhaps not surprising that he turned to the British for help in running the RCMP's first double agent.

Wood wanted an MI5 officer steeped in the double-cross system to supervise the initial stages of the Janowski operation, as Harvison had virtually no expertise beyond the local monitoring of Quebec Nazis. Stephenson's British Security Co-ordination in New York had only limited experience with double agents, and there were growing frictions between BSC and the FBI, so Wood appealed directly to Sir David Petrie, MI5's director general. Petrie consulted the Twenty Committee, which oversaw MI5's B1(a) section for double agents. Named for the Roman numerals XX, or 'double-cross,' the committee was an interdepartmental panel specializing in Britain's strategic-deception campaign against the Germans. The panel, chaired by Sir John Masterman of MI5, concurred with the suggestion to turn Janowski against his masters, although the rationale for the decision must remain obscure without access to British security files.

Masterman's group chose to dispatch Cyril Mills, one of Britain's more experienced double-cross case officers. Mills was one of about ten experts who ran the more than forty active double agents under section B1(a). He was in charge of six such agents, including Juan Pujol, the long-lived double recruited in April 1942 and known as Garbo. 'It was expected that I should be in Canada for three weeks and during my absence my agents would be "nursed" by other officers,' Mills later recalled. In the first week of December, he travelled to Prestwick, Scotland, to begin a harrowing flight overseas. 'It was from there, in the middle of the 1942 winter, that I began my first wartime crossing of the Atlantic in the bomb-bay of a Liberator,' Mills wrote in his published memoirs. 'We were in darkness all the way, smoking was not allowed and for five hours the temperature inside was thirty-five degrees below zero. When coming in to land at Montreal the aircraft stalled, as the result of ice on the tail plane, but we were saved by the skill of a brilliant pilot and landed safely two hours later when the ice had been shaken off. I was only one of twenty-three men who had been terrified, for we all knew what the trouble was.'

After briefing sessions with Wood and Harvison, Mills was given access to the prisoner at the St James Street headquarters of 'C' Division. This icy interrogation inaugurated a period of awkward tension between Mills and Harvison, not unlike the FBI-BSC dust-up over control of Dusko Popov. 'When he was first brought to me for interrogation he was accompanied by two RCMP constables, and when I asked them to leave the room they said they were not allowed to do so,' Mills remembered. 'After an argument with Harvison, the men left but only when I had given Harvison a receipt for the body. That done, I told Janowski he had ceased to exist. He now belonged to the British Intelligence Service and if he lied to me he would be given one warning but if he lied a second time I should take him to London where he would be hanged.

'His reply was that he would not lie because he was only a second rater and his mission was to set things up for four important agents who would follow him. He then said he would co-operate with me in the capture of these agents if I would spare his life. And I then knew I was dealing with one of the dirtiest four-letter men in the world, and told him that whether he liked it or not he would co-operate with me and would be given no guarantee of any kind.' Mills sized up the prisoner as a loyal, dissembling Nazi – clearly not the reluctant spy that Janowski claimed to be with Harvison. For the next ten days, the MI5 man interrogated the prisoner intensively for two or three hours each day. Mills regarded Harvison's own interrogation reports as naïve and unreliable, and he was determined to establish a baseline from which to measure Janowski's successive lies. This was according to the principle laid out by Masterman in his double-agent manual, *The Double-Cross System in the War of 1939 to 1945*. 'It was also necessary to obtain at the earliest possible opportunity an accurate and detailed account of the agent's life from his earliest year ... because any deviations from the truth would almost certainly be detected sooner or later,' Masterman observed. 'The greater the detail into which an agent goes, the more certainly will he trip himself up if he strays into falsehood.'

Mills's brittle and uncompromising method of questioning was also standard procedure as set out by the Twenty Committee. In Britain, newly captured Abwehr agents were placed in handcuffs and taken by military escort to Camp 020. The camp was in fact an MI5 interrogation centre at Latchmere House, a three-storey Victorian mansion on wooded grounds in the village of Ham Common, Surrey. Once used as an asylum for shell-shocked officers, the property was fitted with high-security perimeter fences and a one-storey cell block was added to the east wing. The bare interrogation rooms were on the mansion's first floor. New prisoners were strip-searched, put in prison garb and denied cigarettes, reading material, or even the most mundane conversation with guards. They were placed in solitary confinement for several days to help build anxiety about the future. 'The first interrogation was considered crucial,' says one authoritative account of Camp 020. 'The prisoner was brought before a board of four or five officers. He was marched in and remained standing at attention throughout an interrogation designed to impress upon him the omniscience and omnipotence of the British Secret Service; the hopelessness and isolation of his own position; and that the penalty for espionage was death and the only way he could help himself was to tell the truth.' All prisoners were advised that they were beyond the reach of civil authorities and could be executed at any moment without benefit of trial. The guards were also trained to torment their charges, treating them roughly and insinuating their coming execution. The fumbling, kid-glove treatment of Janowski in the hours and days after his landing near New Carlisle stood in sharp contrast to the psychologically brutal British approach. Mills was just trying to make the best of a botched job.

In laying claim to the prisoner, Mills also named him. The case would now be referred to as Watchdog, rather than the RCMP's loosely enforced 'Braulter et al.' 'I gave all my agents double-barrelled names which could be taken easily from the British Code Book and I took care to ensure no cover name could be identified in any way with the agent's name, nationality, background or even sex.' The RCMP continued to use the 'Braulter et al.' rubric for some filing purposes, but their prisoner was rechristened Watchdog within the rapidly mounting pile of correspondence.

Mills's planned three-week stay in Canada soon began to stretch beyond all intentions. Never having used a typewriter and lacking secretarial help, Mills was forced to slowly peck out his own reports and letters. Eventually, the Twenty Committee sent over a secretary, Pixie Verrall, to help with the growing workload. The RCMP's intelligence section, which at the outbreak of war was run by a half-dozen men from the Criminal Investigation Branch in Ottawa, had expanded rapidly over three years. The six had become ninety-eight by 1943, and the divisions rapidly added their own personnel so that Toronto and Montreal now had about twenty intelligence staff each. Few had any relevant training, so that the man from MI5 was suddenly a busy tutor. Word of Mills's arrival in Canada soon spread to the army, navy, and air force intelligence chiefs in Ottawa, who frequently asked for advice. 'I spent most of my time studying security in Canada and in the few places where it existed at all it was in a chaotic state and I made this known to Commissioner Wood and my London office,' Mills recalled. 'I made contact with, and friends of, the Canadian Naval, Military and Airforce Directors of Intelligence, none of whom had ... any training in Intelligence. They were always asking for help or guidance and I used to go see them in Ottawa every few days.'

The Twenty Committee soon decided that Mills would remain in Canada indefinitely, minding the Watchdog case and trying to raise security and intelligence standards through all the Canadian services. The RCMP began to advance him cash, $200 in the first month, to help with expenses. Masterman's committee agreed to the prolonged absence partly because Stephenson's troubled relations with the FBI and other American agencies were rapidly becoming a liability at British Security Co-ordination in New York. Mills would now become MI5's North American and Caribbean liaison officer – a role he could not perform from a United States base since that was regarded as MI6's exclusive jurisdiction. He would maintain his link with the double agent Juan Pujol by eventually running Moonbeam, one of Garbo's notional sub-agents, from Canada and adding yet another sub-agent, Moonbeam's purported cousin in Buffalo, New York. Neither person existed, but Mills was to gather North American intelligence that could safely be handed over to the Abwehr through Garbo to build credibility in the network. For security, Mills would tell no one in Canada about the double-cross operation he was running on the side.

Mills also took over the job of screening Europeans in North America who were seeking entry to the United Kingdom. 'Stephenson had been responsible for vetting all those who escaped from Europe in order to join their forces in Britain but his vetting was like an Irishman's net ... a lot of holes tied together with string. When this job was given to me I caught two men who were on their way to the U.K. and having interrogated them I got the names of two others who had sailed right through to England. The mission of one was to steal a Mosquito aircraft and fly it to Germany and he had already been posted to a Mosquito Squadron but as a result of my message to London he was arrested and as he was a citizen of an occupied country he was tried, found guilty and hanged.'

Among Mills's first Watchdog tasks was to supervise the writing of another secret-ink letter to Janowski's Swedish mail drop. The letter was sent on 21 December and presumably corrected the potentially dangerous typographical errors of the 25 November letter. (A copy has not survived in the RCMP's Watchdog file.) Mills also arranged the formation a Canadian version of the Twenty Committee, with representatives of the RCMP and the intelligence chiefs of the armed forces, to coordinate information fed back to the Abwehr by Watchdog. The group would vet facts about wartime production and defence that could safely be transmitted to Hamburg alongside half-truths and exaggerations. The RCMP, like the FBI, was primarily a police organization whose chief interest in double agentry lay in the capture of future saboteurs. Mills, however, wanted to broaden the operation to eventually include strategic objectives in concert with MI5's other double agents. In Britain, the Twenty Committee's greatest challenge lay in deceiving the Germans about the timing and location of the cross-Channel invasion of Europe, then eighteen months away. Ideally, Watchdog could help play a role, but only if he was kept credible for long enough. Harvison and Wood, on the other hand, had a narrower, more practical horizon: they were eager to pick up the Abwehr II men that Janowski would beckon ashore from their U-boats. Both approaches, however, meant deceiving Hamburg into thinking their agent was productive and legitimate.

On 19 January the Canadian committee met for the first time in Ottawa and worked out an administrative procedure whereby approved raw intelligence would be sent to Montreal for compilation and eventual transmission. 'It was agreed that the development of communications to and from Germany would take time, a minimum of three months, and therefore prudence was stressed, lest there be over-anxiety on the part of anyone to see results quickly,' an RCMP report noted. The vetting process was relatively straightforward. Harvison's Watchdog team would scour newspapers and the Wartime Information Board's publication *Canada at War* for tidbits of potential interest to the Abwehr. Into this mix they added unpublished information that any resident of Montreal would accumulate, such as the identity and location of local training camps. The 'intelligence' items were then categorized according to the agency from which approval was needed, that is, each of the three branches of the military, RCMP headquarters itself, and, in at least one instance, the FBI in Washington. Written approvals or vetos were returned to Montreal on standard forms, and the Watchdog team could then select from a body of sanctioned intelligence, as appropriate, for their radio messages.

Wartime production figures were generally exaggerated by about 20 per cent. Mills expressly forbade transmission of material that 'in any way anticipates future developments' of military hardware, technology, and movements. Harvison's memoirs claim his team had learned that the RCAF was planning to announce details of the new all-wood Mosquito bomber, designed and built by de Havilland at Toronto. Air-force officials were asked to withhold the announcement for a few weeks so that Watchdog could first tell the Abwehr, helping to build his credibility without damaging the war effort. 'Thus German Intelligence had all the information regarding the aircraft about two months before it was made public in Canada,' Harvison wrote. In fact, the Watchdog file shows that although the Abwehr did ask Janowski for details about the Mosquito bomber, which they already suspected was being built by de Havilland, they were never given any information about it.

The intelligence chiefs of the army, navy, and air force agreed to the release of virtually every proposed message that fell within the above guidelines, with some significant exceptions. The army's Colonel William (Jock) Murray vetoed information about a large order of skis, a new anti-tank gun, the manufacture of the new Ram tank at Windsor, Ontario, the weight of the new U.S. Mark 6 tank, and the winter training of U.S. troops near Winnipeg. Group Captain H.R. (Ronnie) Stewart of the RCAF suppressed an item about Bendix Injection Carburators being fitted to U.S. aircraft, about the routes Ferry Command bombers took to England, and a report of a shipment of deadly gas being sent to England. Lieutenant-Commander C. Herbert Little valiantly tried to quash widely available information about the construction of new frigates in Canada. He eventually acceded to the view that most Canadians already knew about these vessels from newspaper accounts and that other Allied double agents had already tipped the Abwehr about frigates. Little did stand firm, though, on holding back items about potential U-boat targets along the St Lawrence River. 'One of my main objectives is to keep enemy away from St. Lawrence for a number of reasons which you will appreciate,' he declared.

A proposed item on the kinds of aircraft aboard U.S. aircraft carriers went to the FBI for approval. Hoover deleted reference to the Douglas Devastator torpedo bombers, but otherwise gave the go-ahead. The FBI was simply returning a favour. On 31 March Canadian intelligence authorities had approved release of information about Canada's production of front-line aircraft, for use by a double agent named Max Rudloff whom the FBI was running. When Watchdog's masters asked him a similar question some weeks later, likely an effort to compare it with Rudloff's information, the RCMP team was careful to ensure the answers were similar but not identical. '[We] do not wish to possibly cause suspicion on the other side by having our answers too divergent or too closely aligned,' Mead had advised Group Captain Stewart. To ensure continuing coordination, the RCMP from 21 April onward regularly supplied the FBI with copies of Watchdog's radio traffic for their use in the Rudloff deception.

Just when the case had reached this crucial juncture, as contact with Hamburg was finally established, Harvison had to abandon his interminable interrogation of Janowski. From 5 January to 6 February he attended Court of King's Bench to assist in the prosecution of a conspiracy case involving the Engine Works and Trading Inc. Long hours spent in court, and with prosecutors at night preparing next-day evidence, left Harvison little time for Janowski, apart from the radio transmissions. This was contrary to the principle set out by Masterman in his manual of the double-cross system. 'It is also important that no case officer should be overburdened with too many cases,' he wrote. 'Probably in more than one instance cases have gone awry, or have failed to start at all, simply because the case officer was fully occupied at the moment by a crisis in one of his other cases. Experience seems to show that no officer should ever handle more than two cases of major importance at the same time, and ideally he should never have more than one.'

Harvison's long absences may in fact have been fortuitous, for they allowed Mills a freer hand at his own tough interrogation of Janowski.

By about mid-January, Mills felt he had let the prisoner run on at the mouth long enough. Janowski's account of his past collapsed under the weight of its own inconsistencies, not to mention the lies readily exposed by Mills's intimate knowledge of the Abwehr. Mills sent reports to Commissioner Wood detailing his findings, and urging that a hard line be taken with Janowski: either come clean or face the hangman's noose. The suggestion increased tensions with Harvison and Gagnon, his supportive boss in Montreal, who felt a gentler hand would coax the truth from the prisoner.

'The threat may lead to him concocting another "whitewash" story which would add further volumes of correspondence without accomplishing anything concrete,' Harvison said in opposing Mills's recommendation. 'There is a possibility, even if remote, that Watchdog would become convinced that we intend to handle him in "Gestapo" style in any event, and that he would refuse to proceed further ... I regard Watchdog as a thoroughly unscrupulous adventurer, possessing considerable physical courage, but entirely devoid of scruples or principles. In view of this and the fact that he was and is fighting for his own neck, it is not surprising that he should attempt to "whitewash" some of the dirtier spots of his own career. So long as the whitewash does not interfere with our main purpose in using this man it must be regarded as of secondary importance.' Ottawa diligently tried to find a compromise between the mutually exclusive approaches of Harvison and Mills. Assistant Commissioner Frederick Mead supported Mills, but with the proviso that in confronting Janowski he refrain from 'bulldozing' the prisoner. In fact, the Harvison-Mills head-butting was an inadvertent application of the classic good-cop, bad-cop interrogation technique. Janowski was well aware the bad-tempered MI5 visitor was ready to take over if Harvison failed to produce the desired results.

Soon another MI5-RCMP clash emerged. Janowski had been pressing Harvison for permission to complain to the Abwehr about the out-of-date Canadian currency he was given. 'Our visitor feels that as he is in the bad graces of the Party they may have given him these large bills in order to trap him and now, if he does not mention the fact, they will immediately become suspicious,' Gagnon told Wood. Harvison was sold on the idea, but Mills was adamantly opposed. The released RCMP documents in the Watchdog file have Mills's arguments deleted. But he may have been sceptical that the money was truly a give-away, since the Bank of Canada had already reported to the RCMP that thousands of the large-sized bills remained in circulation across the country. Even if the Gestapo had some sinister motive, they likely would have picked a more reliable method of betraying their victim. Especially troublesome was the implication that the Gestapo would risk a U-boat and thousands of dollars in difficult-to-obtain U.S. and Canadian currency to dispose of someone they disliked. The German secret police normally employed less inefficient methods, such as beatings, executions, and one-way trips to concentration camps. Perhaps Janowski's real motive in complaining about the currency was to signal his Abwehr masters that he was under control. At the very least, the information about the outdated currency would help the Abwehr better equip the next agent dispatched to Canadian shores.

As the scheduled 1 February resumption of transmissions approached, Gagnon and Harvison took advantage of Mills's temporary absence from Montreal. They sought and obtained permission from Wood to transmit a message that complained about the oversized dollar bills. (Wood appears to have been unaware of Mills's contrary view.) On the appointed morning, the two stations quickly made contact, but the Hamburg station was found to be using the wrong call letters, apparently forgetting that the 'green book' code was to be used. Janowski pointed this out, and Hamburg corrected its transmission. Soon the prepared message was tapped out, with Janowski offering some unsolicited information. 'Without selective service papers it is dangerous to travel and impossible to get work. National Registration card is not enough. Papers must be shown from last employer before getting work. Trying to obtain papers. Long bills out of circulation for years. Whose inefficiency is this? Have much news on hand. Listen for me daily at this hour. Will transmit when safe.' Such was the word-for-word repetition of the message formally approved by Ottawa. Then Janowski added 'Greetings to my folks' and concluded the transmission. Hamburg asked him to repeat the last part of the message, from word 23 forward, and Janowski complied. The contact was closed after about forty-five minutes on the air.

The intelligence Janowski now began to ship back to Hamburg was based on a lengthy questionnaire he had memorized during his training in Berlin. About half of the fifty or so questions had to do with the three branches of the armed forces, the remainder with industrial production and civil matters. 'Attempt to secure information about possible U-boat traps. To see especially how the river St. Lawrence is guarded up as far as Quebec City ... Where are convoys put together?' Janowski was especially urged to find out if Canada was developing rocket-powered aircraft. The Abwehr also wanted to know about morale among French Canadians, whether many Canadians wanted to become U.S. citizens, and the number of desertions in the armed forces. Janowski was also to determine 'how many Jews in government.'

On 3 February another morning contact was made, only with difficulty because someone in the Mount Royal neighbourhood was operating an electric motor that fouled the air waves. Hamburg advised Janowski that it was eliminating the 4:30 a.m. MEZ window (11:30 p.m. Montreal time) because of poor conditions. The Watchdog team then offered Hamburg a rosy picture of Canadian affairs. 'Food situation here very good. Rations of butter, sugar, tea very generous. No coupons in restaurants. War effort strongly supported by French Canadians against our general opinion. Non-English-speaking French Canadians enroll Free French. Canadian export for 42 up to $2,385,000,000. Since outbreak of war Canadian steel production increased 110 per cent.' On 5 February, Janowski passed on information about the locations of airforce training schools across Canada. The next day he offered production figures on military vehicles and other innocuous information readily obtained from Canadian newspapers. Production of rubber, tanks, and planes dominated the next contact on 9 February, in addition to the confident observation that 'all harbours, bridges and dock installations are well guarded by the RCMP.' The transmissions had now settled into a kind of morning routine, Hamburg accepting the information Janowski offered without putting any special or follow-up questions to him.

There was nothing routine, however, about the latest round of interrogations. Beginning 7 February, Harvison was finally free of the conspiracy trial and was feeling the pressure from Mills, who was insisting – with Mead's backing – that Watchdog be made to come clean on his story. Janowski was by now well aware that the RCMP had acquired some high-powered, knowledgeable help from MI5. The no-nonsense sessions with the stern Mr Mills had clearly rattled him. In addition, the Allies had captured thousands of prisoners since November in a powerful attack on French North Africa. Interviews with these POWs could soon begin to poke holes in the North African chapters of Janowski's convoluted story.

'On February 10th JANOWSKI apparently came to the conclusion that with the assistance of other Intelligence Services we had too great a knowledge of the German Intelligence Service for him to endeavour to continue with the story he had been given,' says an RCMP summary of the Watchdog case. Commissioner Wood was forced to alert Hoover at the FBI, Stephenson at BSC, and Petrie at MI5's Blenheim Palace that they should set aside Harvison's previous interrogation reports. 'This man is now in the process of giving a new version of his story which will force us to disregard much of the information previously supplied by him,' Wood wrote in letters on 15 February. Mills's role in Janowski's latest conversion was officially ignored, perhaps to play down the RCMP's earlier gullibility. 'By way of explanation of Watchdog's present conduct, it is reported to us that for some time he has been gaining confidence and has led himself to believe that he may be used as an agent on behalf of the Empire at some future date,' Wood advised. 'With this in mind he has now expressed a desire to give this "truthful version" of his history.'

FIVE

C'est la guerre

Cliff Harvison, whose ignorance of the Abwehr organization had allowed his prisoner to weave elaborate lies, struggled to save face now that Watchdog was singing like a canary. Mills had urged a hard line against Janowski, but Harvison portrayed this final confession as the product of his own velvet treatment of the prisoner. 'In my report of February 2nd, I expressed the opinion that Watchdog would, in the near future, voluntarily supply information regarding certain parts of his own career which he had considered it advisable to withhold during early questioning in order that he, personally, might be considered in a more favorable light,' he reported to Superintendent Gagnon on 10 February. 'During the past few days, such additional information have [sic] been volunteered by W.'

The first thing Janowski wanted to get off his chest was that he had secretly divorced his Canadian wife while in Germany. He had led his captors to believe the marriage was still alive, perhaps a limp attempt to save his skin by linking himself with a Canadian citizen. He had even attempted to get a message to her from his jail cell in New Carlisle, an act of desperation in circumstances he felt might end inside a noose. In fact, German authorities had granted him a divorce from Olive Quance in June 1940 once Janowski produced a letter from her indicating her own intention to file for divorce. This document, combined with their more than five years of separation and her enemy nationality, freed him from this mercenary mismatch. On 18 February 1941, he married a German woman from Aachen whose family owned a toiletries factory and associated retail outlets, all of which had been closed with the outbreak of war.

C'est la guerre

Among the articles Janowski had lugged ashore near New Carlisle was a pocket-size volume of French love poetry entitled *Toi et Moi*. The inside cover page was hand-inscribed: 'A Buddy, pour qu'il n'oublie pas sa petite femme – Michele – 15-9-42.' Janowski had initially told his captors that Buddy was one of his cover names, and that Michele was a woman he had lived with in Brussels. But he now admitted that Michele, a Roman Catholic, was in fact his wife and he pleaded for the return of the poetry volume. 'This request may be reasonable but on the other hand the prisoner does not strike me as the sentimental type,' Harvison noted cautiously. He sent the book to the laboratory at the Canadian Police College in Rockcliffe, where it was bombarded with X-rays, ultraviolet light, and parallel-ray light and carefully scrutinized under a microscope. No secret writing or anything else untoward was found, and the book was duly handed over to the prisoner.

Janowski's drippy sentimentality about this woman soon gave way to cold-blooded accounts of destruction, as he confessed to Harvison the true nature of his military career. He had previously claimed he was stationed with the Lehr Regiment at Brandenburg from May to October 1939. This unit was formed as the Lehr und Bau Kompanie zbv 800 (Special Duty, Training and Construction Company no. 800), intended to train sabotage and espionage agents for service in foreign countries. Drawing on volunteers and POWs from Allied nations, the unit grew rapidly to a battalion, then a regiment, dropping 'Bau' to become simply the Lehr Regiment Brandenburg in October 1940. Janowski had earlier claimed that like many others he was recruited for his knowledge of foreign countries and languages, but that his service with the unit did not necessarily imply espionage work. Some sections – including his – trained as storm troops only, he said.

Janowski now revealed that his connection with the new unit had lasted less than a month. The commander, Major Theodor von Hippel, was a friend of his father and had previously helped Janowski join the Pioneer (Engineers) Regiment at Brandenburg on 1 January 1939 – military service that would otherwise be forbidden because of his service in the French Foreign Legion. Five months later, von Hippel got him transferred to the Lehr und Bau Kompanie, where he was questioned intensively about his North African experience. At the end of May, he was sent to Abwehr headquarters in Berlin, located in a block of former residences on the Tirpitzufer, an elegant tree-lined street facing the Land-wehr Canal that bisected Berlin. He entered the office of Colonel Erwin von Lahousen, head of Abteilung II, the sabotage arm of the Abwehr, to find Lahousen and von Hippel awaiting his arrival.

The pair peppered Janowski with questions about his service in the French Foreign Legion, especially his knowledge of French Morocco and Arabic. 'LAHOUSEN stated that war was coming in the very near future and that it was desired to carry out certain sabotage activities in French Morocco,' Janowski now confessed to Harvison. Janowski's assignment was to include smuggling arms to Arab nationalists, promot-ing mutinies, arranging the sabotage of ships, and creating a secret net-work of Arabs who would destroy railways, bridges, tunnels, roads, and communications links at the outbreak of war. In this work, Janowski was to assist a German agent already in place named Langenheim, born of German parents in Spanish Morocco. Described as thirty-eight years old and speaking five languages, Langenheim was regarded as one of the most able agents in RSHA VI, the foreign-intelligence arm of the state security service, the Reich Security Administration.

Janowski, thus, became a willing saboteur within months of his join-ing the German military. Lahousen, the Austrian that Janowski had pre-viously tried to portray as a counter-intelligence chief, personally assigned him sabotage work in North Africa even before war was declared. The day after the Berlin meeting, Janowski travelled to his par-ents' Hamburg home, and there received a message advising him of the date of his departure via passenger ship. On the appointed day, Janowski turned up at the pier, where he was handed a German passport in the name of Willie Branton, the name he had adopted while in Canada. He was also issued 5000 British pounds, thousands of French francs and Spanish pesetas, and percussion caps. On arrival at Ceuta, the Spanish Moroccan port opposite Gibraltar, Janowski bought a used car to attempt open entry into French Morocco, but was turned away at the frontier.

Janowski ultimately contacted an Arab nationalist leader who led him to an isolated hamlet, Ketama, high on a plateau near a poorly patrolled section of the French Moroccan border. The tiny outpost was notorious for smuggling and gun-running and became Janowski's headquarters for the next four months. With Langenheim's help, he eventually recruited about 150 Arabs for a meticulously planned sabotage campaign. Janowski's fat wad of money bought cooperation and plenty of dynamite, which was stockpiled in four French Moroccan cities, including Casablanca. On 4 September 1939 – the day after Britain declared war on Germany – Arab agents working under the direction of Langenheim and Janowski blew up a fully loaded oil tanker and a small freighter in Casablanca harbour. The same day, a minor rebellion broke out in the 4th Regiment Tirailleur, leading to the execution of several mutineers. Janowski eventually made his way by plane and ship through Spain and Italy back to Berlin, where Lahousen – already fully aware of the Moroccan successes – congratulated him personally.

Watchdog, it turned out, was no ordinary soldier forced out of military service to become a reluctant, low-level spy. Instead, he was active in sabotage well before the war and placed in charge of training dozens of subversives. Janowski's November 1942 return to Canada now seemed to portend something far more serious than garden-variety espionage and basic logistical help for professional saboteurs. The Moroccan chapter of Janowski's espionage career, however, was just the start of his long service with the Abwehr – and the RCMP began the enormous task of reinterrogating the prisoner about his every previous claim.

'W. now appears to be making a clean-breast of those parts of his story which he previously attempted to hide,' Harvison reported on 10 February. 'Considerable confusion and loss of time is already being caused by the necessity of referring to the many reports received from various sources as well as those submitted by this office.' Harvison decided to start again from scratch, finally tackling a job that should have been completed more than two months earlier. Reconciling the tangle of contradictions from the previous reports would be far too time-consuming. With the help of a full-time stenographer, Harvison's next report would instead attempt to eliminate the dozens of discrepancies that had so annoyed Mills and severely undermined MI5's faith in the RCMP.

The biography of Janowski that emerged from this fresh interrogation was far more sinister, with close links to the earliest days of the Nazi Party. About 1922, at age nineteen, Janowski joined the Frei Korps Schmidt, a private semi-military organization created with the quiet blessing of the German government to build a large army in defiance of the 1918 armistice. The next year, he paid membership dues and signed a card to join the Nazi Party at Glatz. 'Duties were of a volunteer nature and included posting of propaganda placards, guarding against the removal of the placards by communists – and destroying communist posters – attending Nazi Party meetings and breaking up C.P. [Communist Party] meetings,' he told Harvison. The next year he moved with his parents to Wehlau, where he joined the militant branch of the party, the Sturm-Abteilung, and became a volunteer reporter for the local propaganda paper, the *Wehlauer Warte*. In 1925, the family moved to Koenigsberg, where Janowski signed up for flying lessons paid for by his father.

The Nazi Party was banned in 1925–6, and Janowski claimed to have let his connection lapse, though he did not formally resign membership. He took advanced pilot training at Berlin in 1926, and after a brief period stunt-flying with a local circus he took a job as a flight instructor in April 1927 with the Black Reichswehr. This was an illegal branch of the German armed forces, which were limited by the armistice to 100,000 men. Thousands of extra troops were recruited into the illicit branch, which included an air force – something Germany was also forbidden – paid for in part with funds from industrialists. Janowski trained pilots in unarmed aircraft equipped with movie cameras intended to instruct in the use of machine guns because of their mechanical action. Although a mere private in the official Reichswehr, Janowski rose to become a first lieutenant in April 1929 in the illegal air force.

For reasons never clearly explained, Janowski decided in February 1930 to come to Canada. He had studied flying with a Hellmuth Wiebe, who had come to Canada in 1928. Janowski now contacted Wiebe in Montreal, asking that he forward a letter to Germany saying a job was awaiting him in Canada so Canadian immigration officials would accept his landing. Arriving at Montreal by ship in May 1930, Janowski and a man from Munich he had befriended on board immediately contacted two fellow Germans in the city. In the summer of 1943, the RCMP contacted this mystery man from Munich, whose name is deleted from the Watchdog file. The man told the Mounties he and Janowski had visited two of Janowski's friends in Montreal, including one who worked in a local restaurant. This was clearly Wiebe, but Janowski later chose to deny this, saying he was unable to identify either of the two. It seemed that even this 'full' confession would also have its suspicious blank

106

spots as Janowski either tried to protect his friends or to hide the true nature of the meetings.

In the thick of the Great Depression, Janowski and his friend were advised by several Montreal employment agencies to head west for jobs. They got as far as Ottawa, where the Munich man's uncle worked at the Dominion Government Experimental Farm on the outskirts of the city. He advised the pair to travel to London, where there was supposedly plenty of work at farms in the surrounding countryside. In London, a local Jewish clothing merchant who also ran an employment service found Janowski a spot at a farm owned by a Jack McPherson in nearby Ailsa Craig. Janowski worked and boarded at the McPherson farm until April the following year, when he moved to London, doing odd jobs. To raise some much-needed cash, Janowski sold the revolver, rifle, and binoculars he had brought to Canada.

'Yes, I distinctly remember Janowski,' Bert Keen of Ailsa Craig told a newspaper reporter after the war. 'Back in 1930 I had a contract to lay some sidewalks in the village and Janowski worked two days for me. He was a good worker but very cocky, boasting that he came of a prominent German family. While he was around here Janowski had a tiff from Cpl. Syd Hall, now in the Veterans' Guard. I don't think it came to blows but Hall didn't like the way Janowski shot off his face about Germany and the last war.'

In early April of 1931, Janowski met Olive Blanche Quance, a rather plain-looking forty-four-year-old spinster. Quance had been born in Biddulph Township, not far from Exeter, Ontario, and having become a skilled milliner – a hatmaker – she moved to Toronto in 1918 to pursue her chosen field. By 1926 she had bought an existing millinery business on Broadview Avenue and soon prospered. Quance often visited friends in Ailsa Craig, not far from her birthplace, and while there one day ran into the twenty-six-year-old German immigrant. Janowski, clearly despairing of the hard labour on farms and enchanted by a spinster's wealth, turned on the charm when Quance returned on vacation that summer. Janowski played cello in a local orchestra, and in 1931 won first prize in a cello competition at the London Music Festival. He romanced Quance with his music and regaled her with inflated tales of his aviation past. Janowski proposed, and they were married in a small Presbyterian service in Toronto on 5 December 1931. The bride's mother was said to be uneasy about Janowski, predicting no good would come of the match.

About six weeks after their marriage, Janowski approached the *Toronto Star Weekly* for some self-sought publicity about his amazing and exemplary life. The newspaper published the results with photos on 23 January 1932. The interview he gave was a heady concoction of lies. He claimed to have been wounded in the German army during the Great War, at age fourteen; to have led an air circus throughout Europe for five years; and to have studied medicine for two years at the University of Berlin. For the next twenty-one months, Janowski bled his wife of cash, first enrolling in a six-month radio course at the Radio College of Canada on Yonge Street, said to cost an astonishing $3000 in tuition. He also apparently took language courses in English and Spanish, again paid for by Quance. 'She bought Janowski an expensive camera and he displayed a marked interest in public buildings in the city, photographing them and the viaducts and waterfront scenes repeatedly,' said one postwar newspaper account. 'Often he would leave home for days at a time without explanation. On his return he would fly into a rage when she asked him where he had been. Frequently, under the influence of liquor, he threatened to kill her.'

Many details of this sordid chapter in Janowski's life are impossible to verify, but there is little doubt the marriage gradually soured. Janowski had no hesitation in lying to his wife about his past – he told her, for instance, he had been placed in a cadet school at age six and had not lived at home much after that. In July 1932 he received a letter and some money from his mother, asking that he visit her in Hamburg as she had taken ill. Janowski did so, travelling by ship and staying about six weeks in Germany. 'He states that trip was made at the request of his mother and for personal and family reasons only and had no connection with the German Government, or the Nazi Party,' Harvison reported.

Once back in Canada, Janowski worked occasionally for the Majestic Radio Company of Toronto, repairing customers' radio sets that were sent to him. 'He also attempted to write and have published, stories, supposedly featuring his own adventures,' said one RCMP account of this period. 'It is understood that these manuscripts were submitted to True Stories Magazine, but none were accepted.' Years later, Quance accused him of philandering and of stealing from her business to augment the money she gave him. In the spring of 1933, he and his wife made several short motor trips to visit Detroit, Chicago, and Buffalo that Janowski claimed were for pleasure only. For reasons unrecorded, Janowski legally changed his surname to Branton by deed poll on 24 April 1933. 'Subject was an ardent Nazi, and when Hitler was first elected in Germany, he was very pleased and enthused,' said an RCMP officer who later interviewed Quance. 'He used to have a small lapel pin bearing the swastika. This was made of blue enamel.'

In August 1933 Janowski informed his crestfallen wife that he was leaving her. He 'apparently thought that his wife had more money than she actually did have, and upon him finding that the amount involved did not come up to his expectations, his ardour rapidly cooled off,' said an RCMP report. He sold her Chevrolet, and used some of the proceeds to buy a ticket from Montreal to Le Havre, France, aboard the SS *Ascania*, departing 22 September. (The RCMP could never verify his departure, despite repeated efforts.) Janowski said he decided not to return to his parents' home, as his father was unhappy with his son's aimless and drifting life. Instead, he went to Paris, squandered his last $250 on night clubs and alcohol, and in September joined the French Foreign Legion for the minimum five years. The RCMP were able to confirm this part of Janowski's story when they later obtained copies of correspondence he sent to Quance, including a Christmas card.

Trained for seven months in Algeria, Janowski was posted in March 1934 to Fez, in French Morocco, as part of the 3rd Regiment. Two months before his official discharge on 21 September 1938, Janowski was granted two months' leave in Rabat, then was issued civilian clothes and fare back to Germany. At the end of September, as he arrived at the German border station of Kehl, Janowski was taken into custody by the Gestapo, who had been alerted to Janowski by the French police. He was immediately imprisoned at the notorious Dachau concentration camp, along with four other German veterans of the Legion, for his traitorous behaviour. Thanks to the intervention of his father, who had joined the Nazi Party in 1933, Janowski was released provided he report monthly to the Gestapo over the next two years. Major Theodor von Hippel soon entered his life, and a few months later Janowski was back in North Africa helping Arab nationalists attack the very legion that had given him steady employment for five years.

On his return from the Arab sabotage operation, Janowski was sent to an officers training school at Jüterbog, about 50 kilometres south of Berlin. For about six months, he and three hundred others were taught the finer points of blowing up bridges, railways, and tanks. Promoted to sergeant, Janowski joined a company of about 150 men stationed at Arsbeck, near the border with the Netherlands. For the next month, the group trained for the invasion of the lowlands. Janowski was given charge of a squad of eleven men who were to wear Dutch greatcoats and helmets over their German uniforms and enter the Netherlands just before the invasion to prevent a key bridge from being destroyed by the Dutch army. Part of the training included surreptitious reconnaissance missions inside Holland in civilian clothes, as well as lessons in the Dutch language – such expressions as 'Lay down your arms,' and 'Surrender is your only hope.' The squad would be helped by two Dutch traitors who were to act as guides. Janowski said the mission was also intended as training for the time when the men would become agents in foreign countries, and for that reason they were taught how to manufacture their own explosives from readily obtained materials.

The invasion was set for 5:30 a.m. on 10 May 1940. About 1 a.m. that day, Janowski's squad proceeded by bicycle to the border, then by foot into Holland. But before they could reach the bridge, about 1.4 miles inside the border, they heard a terrific explosion at about 1:30 a.m. The Dutch had somehow been forewarned, and blew up the structure even before the invasion had begun. Janowski's unit proceeded to the location anyway, and lobbed grenades into a group of about two hundred Dutch troops, eventually taking sixty of them prisoner, while the remainder managed to flee. The group held the town until the arrival of the invading German army, then regrouped back inside Germany. Janowski's next assignment was to have his squad enter Belgium, again disguised in Belgian army uniforms, and seize three key locks that held back the sea at Nieuwpoort. The group took a bus part-way to their objective, then learned that an armistice had been signed, and so discarded their Belgian uniforms. But as they approached the locks, they came under fire from British soldiers trying to hold the position. Janowski's men eventually drove out the British and commandeered the locks, which they found were wired with enough dynamite to destroy them. The group held the position for thirty-eight hours, all the while suffering British artillery fire, before the German army relieved them.

The next stop was Le Havre, where Janowski's men guarded the water works and ammunition dump. Then on to Dunkirk in June, where the British evacuation was already in progress. Eventually, Janowski was attached to the Sonderstab Hollman, a unit whose duties included counter-intelligence work along the newly conquered English Channel coast. Janowski, now a sergeant-major, was placed in charge of a motor-cyle squad of seventy-five men. Their new mission included preparations for the invasion of Britain, using the same tactics as for Holland and Belgium, that is, enter the country disguised as British soldiers hours before the main invasion force. Janowski's group was given detailed instructions to seize three docks in Dover, and to hold them for the invading German army. But by October 1940 it was clear that Operation Sea Lion – Hitler's cross-Channel invasion – would not take place. The *ruse de guerre* in which commandos wore enemy uniforms in advance of an invasion worked well in the low countries, but the English Channel had proved an effective barrier. Janowski's squad was broken up. He joined Rommel's Afrika Corps in February 1941, but about three months later was posted to the German Armistice Commission in Casablanca because of his experience in French Morocco. In September he was transferred to Libya, until December, when he was again ordered to report to the Abwehr in Berlin.

A Captain Ernst Mueller now ordered Janowski to Brussels, where he was to set up a network of agents along the coast. On his way there, Janowski was asked to stop at Kiel, where a group of perhaps a dozen men were being trained for espionage work in Britain and North America. Mueller wanted to know whether they had sufficient knowledge of English for this work, and Janowski reported that all but one did not. After stopping at his parents' home in Hamburg, Janowski took up his new duties at Brussels in January 1942. His main challenge was to find French and Belgian agents who could be pressed into service through blackmail or bribery. Most were paid 15 marks a day, with bonuses of up to 5000 marks for especially valuable work. Among their assignments was the task of infiltrating a prisoner-of-war camp in Ghent to determine whether the British prisoners were plotting an escape. On each occasion, the Abwehr plant was uncovered. Janowski also identified a British agent with a radio set in Belgium. The work involved exposing resistance members as well, and many executions resulted from Janowski's thorough work. 'Janowski claims to have recruited and controlled 250 agents, mostly Belgians, who covered the whole of Belgium and Northern France, and had the task of investigating the bombing activities of Belgian patriots and tracking down the wireless sets, used to send information to England,' Lieutenant Wilfred Samuel had reported in November. Janowski may well have exaggerated his own role, but historians do regard the early anti-Resistance work of the Abwehr in France, Belgium, and Holland as one of the service's most successful operations.

On or about 6 August 1942, Janowski claimed, his brilliant espionage career came to a grinding halt. He attended a late-night drinking party, during which the conversation shifted to the subject of the Gestapo – and Janowski made some disparaging remarks that later extended to the Nazi Party itself. A Major Krazer, who had previously taken a violent dislike to Janowski, objected to the statements and had him confined to his room for ten days. (Harvison's published memoirs say that Janowski was placed in a concentration camp for associating with a woman who was part-Jewish, but there is not a shred of support for this claim in the Watchdog file.) At the end of this incarceration, a friend intervened and Janowski was ordered to Berlin, where he again found himself before Captain Ernst Mueller. 'He was informed that Major Krazer had submitted a report with regard to his [anti-Nazi] statements, that this report would ordinarily have been forwarded by the Abwehr to the Nazi Party, but in view of his good work [Abwehr chief] Admiral Canaris had temporarily withheld this action,' the RCMP report noted. 'He was told that providing he volunteered to then undertake espionage work in Canada the report would be permanently held.' The next day, Janowski accepted the mission. During his Berlin conversation with Mueller, Janowski claimed that Mueller and other officers appeared 'almost unbelievably ignorant' of Canadian affairs – the result, they said, of the arrest of Germans in Canada on whom the Abwehr had been depending for information. Six further conferences with his Abwehr masters confirmed this view, and Janowski was made to memorize a long questionnaire for his mission.

Janowski also claimed that his principal duty was to arrange for the eventual landing of saboteurs in Canada. Such a role fitted well with his espionage career, which had begun in 1939 as an organizer of saboteurs in North Africa. He had later been placed in charge of undercover agents in Holland, Belgium, and France – so that the extension of his activities to Canada, especially in view of his English-language abilities and knowledge of Canada, was no break with the past. Far from being a low-level agent, Janowski was likely the spearhead of a renewed North American sabotage campaign. Like all his 'confessions,' Janowski's claim that he had been blackmailed into the mission must be regarded with suspicion. He had been a loyal and active Nazi from the party's earliest days, and seemed to need little prodding to undertake Abwehr missions in foreign countries. The Canadian operation seemed rather to be the natural culmination of his training and experience.

Janowski was now given intensive individual instruction in radio transmitting and code-work by a Bruno Kreis, who would later become the reply-station operator when Bobbi was tapping out messages from Canada. The pair worked in a room at the Hotel Statt Dresden, in central Berlin. Janowski was already familiar with International Morse, logging in at fifty words per minute, so most of the two weeks of training was focused on learning the book cipher. He did practise transmissions from a remote location, and visited a laboratory where a record was made of his transmitting style. Next stop was the Baltic port of Kiel, where he was given about four days' training in identifying ships, estimating their tonnage and reading depth charts. On 6 September he was sent to his old headquarters in Brussels for instructions on using secret ink, then to Dieppe where he secured an automobile licence and two National Registration Certificates from two Canadian prisoners of war.

Janowski met his wife in Aachen, took her to his parents' home in Hamburg, then returned to Brussels, where he was given the two matches for secret writing as well as the three mail-drop addresses. Then it was back to Berlin, where he picked up his radio equipment, custom-made naval uniform, and wad of Canadian money, handed to him by Mueller. Canaris personally 'wished him luck on his new venture and assured him of his support,' Janowski told Harvison. On 25 September, fully trained and equipped, he went to Kiel with a Captain Weisshuhn who had assisted with the training in Berlin and Brussels. The next morning, Weisshuhn and a military band bid farewell to Janowski as he stepped nimbly down the ladder inside *U-518* to begin his dark adventure to Canada.

'He seemed to take a considerable pride ... in being superior to the saboteurs,' Lieutenant Wilfred Samuel of Canadian Naval Intelligence had written on 14 November after his first interrogation of Janowski. In fact, it was now clear that Janowski's very roots were in sabotage work and his Canadian mission was a return to those roots. But there were still nagging doubts at RCMP headquarters in Ottawa about whether Janowski had truly come clean. 'The story was still far from the complete truth and in fact we have no reason to accept his present story as being entirely accurate, though in many points it has been confirmed,' Corporal Richard Robertson, an RCMP intelligence officer, wrote in a review of the case. By finally exposing his Abwehr II past, Janowski appeared to be a more valuable double agent, since his training supported the claim that he was preparing the way for the landing of saboteurs in the spring. But on this point, too, Robertson questioned whether Janowski was 'not merely using this story as an inducement and a method of prolonging his life.' The claim that the German intelligence service was woefully ignorant of Canadian affairs seemed curious as well, since the RCMP had tracked the extensive pre-war activities of Nazis in Canada who would have been a mine of information for the Abwehr. To this, Janowski could only respond that inter-service rivalries sometimes prevented the free flow of intelligence within Germany.

The portrait of the prisoner clarified by this more-probing interrogation was that of a typical sociopath. For Janowski, clearly, people had no nobler purpose than to be manipulated for one's own ends. Lacking the ability to empathize with emotions in others, Janowski would cheerfully cheat, steal, and betray with no messy moral qualms to constrain him. His cold-blooded marriage to a naïve spinster was merely the means to gain access to her money. When her wealth began to wane and boredom took root, he dropped her like a dirty dishrag. A human chameleon, Janowski could swiftly change colours to suit the next role as he drifted through life with little direction or purpose. Lies welled up in him almost compulsively. Even before his wartime espionage, he freely lied to friends, acquaintances, and reporters about his past and his beliefs. The lies fed his arrogance, and his arrogance in turn helped to control those around him. Most mature personalities who came to know Janowski disliked him intensely. Even young Geraldine Annett could spot the phoniness behind his lizard smile, all tooth and no heart. Mills was revolted by Janowski within minutes of their first meeting. A former employer in the London, Ontario, area found him deliberately abrasive, perhaps to test his sinister ability to conjure useful emotions in others. Lieutenant Samuel of Naval Intelligence regarded him as a thoroughly disagreeable and habitual liar. Only Harvison, it seemed, found anything to like in Janowski. Despite his often tough stand, Harvison frequently defended his prisoner against the stern Mr Mills and against naysayers in the other intelligence services. Harvison, rather ambitious even as he passed his fortieth birthday, saw in Janowski a potential triumph for an already solid police career. As the days stretched into weeks, Harvison seemed almost to fall under the prisoner's spell.

The icy, penetrating light of this second interrogation had also exposed another unsettling aspect of Janowski's twisted personality. He was, it turned out, a dyed-in-the-wool Nazi from the very birth of the party in the early 1920s. Something about the party's mean-spirited analysis of Germany's troubles struck a resonant chord within Janowski's sociopathic nature. He was a loyal Nazi minion well before joining the illegal German air force, and was joyous at the triumph of Hitler in 1933. There was little spine to Janowski's soulless, self-absorbed life, save for his allegiance to National Socialism in the homeland. Janowski had few qualms about betraying people and beliefs, except for Nazis and Nazism, which became his only steadfast purpose. Any who failed to recognize these dangerous traits risked becoming his victims.

Harvison now presented his prisoner with a long list of Germans who had lived in Canada but who had returned to the fatherland before the war. Janowski eventually selected eighteen surnames that seemed familiar to him. With some difficulty the RCMP obtained photographs and descriptions of this group, and from these Janowski identified one man who occupied a high position in the intelligence arm of the Reich foreign ministry under Joachim von Ribbentrop. This officer, who had lived in Manitoba and British Columbia, was well known to the Mounties, having once tried to enlist in the RCMP. Sir David Petrie of MI5 was also quickly alerted to one aspect of Janowski's confession that had an immediate counter-intelligence interest. A Brussels prostitute identified only as Dolly was being trained to become an agent who would be sent to England with another agent posing as a magician. This woman – described as five-foot-seven, slim, brown hair, blue eyes, 'very good fig-

115

ure' – was apparently a favourite of the senior Abwehr officers in Brussels. Janowski reported that she had been shirking her radio training and still had not departed for England by the time he left Brussels in August 1942.

The British were also alerted to a resistance radio station that Janowski had discovered near Arras, in northern France near the Belgian border. 'The station and code were taken over and continued operation,' Janowski reported. 'British planes are said to have continued to come over once a week and throw off by parachute big tubes filled with explosives, cigarettes, propaganda material and candies. This was still in operation until August of 1942.' He also referred to a Belgian couple at Izeghem, near the French border, who operated a radio set and gave shelter to an English soldier who had escaped from Dunkirk. Once uncovered by Janowski in about April 1942, the Belgians were executed and the soldier taken to Berlin for some unspecified intelligence operation. Apart from these few details, Janowski said he could provide little else – no names, for example, and no inside view of any double-agent operations. Weeks later, Janowski was asked to examine fifty-eight photographs of German nationals residing in Haiti to identify any in the employ of the Abwehr. He said he did not recognize a single face.

Now that he had divulged the existence of wife no. 2, Janowski claimed he wanted to get her a message right away. Harvison readily agreed, and so the transmission of 12 February set aside intelligence gathering and focused on personal matters. 'Please to inform my wife to buy mortgage or to pay that mortgage of parents. What about my promotion promised to me? Have to change living quarters soon. Please to greet my wife and parents. Forgotten man?' Three days later, Watchdog resumed transmitting intelligence, but there was heavy interference. Bruno Kreis, the radio engineer who had trained Janowski and was now operating the reply station, alerted him that a new station with a slightly different frequency was to come on air the next day at an additional contact time to try to improve the connection.

The following morning, the regular 10 a.m. contact was made with the old station. But Janowski and Southam could tell immediately that the sender was not Kreis since the Morse lacked his distinctive touch or 'fist.' In any case, the contact could not be maintained. An hour later, the new station came on the air for some test transmissions. As intended, no messages were exchanged, but it was clear from the brief Morse contact call that Kreis himself was keying at the new station. On 20 February, after many test contacts, Kreis finally sent his first message from the experimental transmitter, which was apparently intended only to send messages to Canada. 'We are thankful for the messages received up to now. Question of promotion not settled yet but we are using all influence. Message to your wife transferred. Everything OK. Heartiest wishes from your wife. In question of bad bills, we have complained. All send best wishes. Please report reception of messages over old frequency.'

Janowski's spartan wardrobe, meanwhile, was looking tattered after just three months in Canada. Harvison applied for permission to buy about $100 worth of new clothes for his prisoner (about $1600 in today's currency). With Ottawa's approval, he placed an order with Henry Morgan & Co. in Montreal 'as the Superintendent of that concern is one of our R[eserve]/Constables and the matter could be handled throughout with the utmost secrecy.' The final bill came to $83.40, including $9 shoes, a $27.50 suit, handkerchiefs, pyjamas, and rubbers. A detailed description was kept on file and all the clothing was specially marked in the event Janowski bolted. A light blue thread, for instance, was sewn for about a quarter of an inch along the bottom seam of the inner breast pocket of the new jacket, unknown to Janowski. And the inner lining of the top right shoulder of his overcoat was marked in blue ink: 'Feb. 17/ 43 Braulter.'

The radio work continued apace, as Janowski offered a range of intelligence based on the questionnaire he had memorized in Berlin. 'Montreal has three airports, St. Hubert, Dorval and Cartierville,' he messaged on 22 February. 'Dorval huge new field used by air force ferry command and commercial company. St. Hubert is air force training station. Carterville for testing.' The next day: 'Many bombers on field at Dorval but fence too far out to get details. Ferry pilots plentiful in Montreal. Dorval certainly part of bombers ferrying service. Special police and air force guards.' All of this information was readily available to anyone reading local newspapers and government publications or living in the city. There followed an eight-day break in transmissions until 4 March, when a new station with an unfamiliar operator boomed in: 'Letter two from December twenty-first has been received. Very pleased that connection has been made. Letter one not received. Best wishes. Bruno.' These letters were the secret-ink messages to the Swedish address that had been posted on 25 November and 21 December. The first message, sent without the benefit of Cyril Mills's review, had contained the misspelling that RCMP headquarters was worried might have been a tip-off. Its apparent failure to arrive thus seemed to avert potential trouble. But just as this one headache vanished, another emerged to take its place.

Newspapers throughout Quebec carried a 5 March report of a speech by Onesime Gagnon, the Union Nationale member of the Quebec legislature for the Gaspé riding of Matane. Gagnon, once a federal Tory cabinet minister under Prime Minister R.B. Bennett, was now in Maurice Duplessis's opposition ranks in the Québec house – and was highly critical of defence measures against U-boats in the Gulf of St Lawrence. In a long legislature speech on 4 March, Gagnon made a clear reference to Janowski. 'Sur les entrefaits, la Sûreté [de Québec] a en mains des dossiers qui confirment ce que je dis – un espion allemand a été arrêté à New Carlisle. Il a été surpris en flagrant délit de donner des renseignements précieux sur la défense de S-Laurent.' (At this time, the Quebec Police Force has in hand certain files confirming what I say – a German spy was arrested at New Carlisle. He was caught as he was about to give out important information about the defence of the St Lawrence.) Although some radio news reports referred to parts of Gagnon's speech, his reference to the spy was carefully deleted, thanks to alert editors at radio stations and effective work by the air-wave censors. German news reports on short-wave radio, picked up in Canada the next day, did refer directly to Gagnon's speech. They had clearly monitored the Canadian broadcasts but were, of course, blind to Gagnon's espionage references. But because of a slip-up, the story about the New Carlisle spy did make its way into many newspapers, including *La Presse* and *La Patrie* of Montreal, *L'Action Catholique*, *L'Evénement-Journal* and the *Chronicle-Telegraph* of Quebec, *Le Droit* of Ottawa, and the British United Press wire service. All these news outlets had been warned back in November to suppress the story, but through some miscommunication with censorship the reference had leaked out.

Mills was livid. In Britain, newspapers were forbidden to publish any spy stories unless they were first vetted by government, a measure designed to safeguard MI5's massive double-cross system. Mills strongly suggested a similar vetting process for Canada in which the RCMP would review every proposed press report about spies. 'I am afraid this is entirely out of the question, as the number of such stories is too great,' Assistant Commissioner Mead wrote in rejecting Mills's proposal. 'Almost every newspaper and magazine contains them, and, apart from that it would mean parallel action in the United States where the number of such stories is multiplied many times.' Undaunted, Mills pressed his point and Mead finally agreed to ask the chief censor to issue a blanket order suppressing all spy stories. The censors were highly sceptical, however, especially in connection with the Watchdog case. 'In view of this unfortunate break and earlier published references, we feel that the possibility that this information has reached the enemy will have been greatly increased,' Wilfred Eggleston and F. Charpentier wrote to Mead on 13 April. 'Would you be good enough to advise us whether ... you can still reasonably assume that the enemy has not learned of the capture.' Mead could only respond that the RCMP for now was proceeding on the assumption that Germany had not yet been apprised of Janowski's capture.

Mills also suggested releasing a phony press story about how some German prisoners of war had escaped and that not all had been recaptured. Such an article would lend credence to Janowski's early message about trouble with the local police and make his current transmissions consistent with repeated stories about his initial capture. 'I do not think this is advisable,' Mead wrote back, gently dismissing the plan. 'It is to be remembered that we are not absolutely certain Germany is unaware of the capture in this particular case, although everything points to the fact that this is so. It seems to me, therefore, that if a further reference is made in the Press to the escape, it would merely draw attention to the improbability of our friend sending out messages uncontrolled, and consequently add to suspicion.'

Gagnon's ill-advised speech in the Quebec legislature had forced a security issue into the political arena and the federal government was under pressure to respond. The job was left to Angus Macdonald, the former Nova Scotia premier who since 1940 had been Canada's minister of national defence for naval services. On 10 March Macdonald made a veiled reference in the Commons to Gagnon's speech. 'There were also statements made about the presence of spies. Any reference to spies, to their arrest, or their operations, were helpful to the enemy, rather than to Canada.' The comments, carried in the *Ottawa Citizen* and other papers, served only to draw further attention to Gagnon's indiscretion. Commissioner Wood eventually decided not to press ahead with any prosecution of the offending Quebec newspapers, arguing that a court case would immediately expose the Watchdog operation. In the end, Mills and Mead agreed that 'nothing very much more can be done at the moment, except to watch the traffic very carefully.'

And watch they did. The St Lawrence shipping season would open in a few weeks, likely bringing more U-boats prowling close by Canadian shores. Janowski had said some of these submarines would carry as many as four saboteurs separately to Canadian shores, and he was the link to all of them. There was heightened expectation among the Watchdog team that the first real payoff to the double-cross would come within weeks – if the Abwehr still had confidence their man was free from Allied control. The first few messages seemed to indicate the game was still on. 'Closer description of selective service papers required. Greetings from all,' came an 11 March message from Hamburg, apparently over a new transmitter. 'At home everything OK. Mortgage and dowry understood as such. That cash belonging to your wife is to be put into real estate. Regards from wife and friends.' Two days later, an even more reassuring message: 'Send as little as possible and only most important ... For your own safety we will call the first five minutes in future. Answer only if your hear us.' This was a reversal of current procedure – Janowski normally spent the first five minutes calling out. A member of the relieved Watchdog team noted in the margin of the daily radio log that the message 'would appear to be a good indication that they are not suspicious that W is under supervision.'

His confidence renewed, Harvison now proposed a ruse to determine whether the Abwehr had a courier system through which they could spirit documents out of Canada. Watchdog had alerted his Abwehr masters to the importance of selective-service papers, told them he had obtained a set, and was now being asked for a detailed description. Harvison had Janowski transmit a rough description on 14 March, but the message ended with the coy observation that it was 'impossible to give details over air.' In the days that followed, it was clear Hamburg was not about to take the bait: there were no instructions on getting the material to Germany. Earlier in the month, Lieutenant-Commander Herbert Little, director of Naval Intelligence, had suggested a similar gambit. Janowski would make a notional trip to Quebec City and return to Montreal offering the Abwehr a chart of the defences surrounding the Fort of Quebec. No radio report could possibly convey the details of such a chart, so the Abwehr would be forced to expose any courier system. A version of this Plan B came into play when the Abwehr failed over the next week to ask for the selective-service papers. Watchdog messaged in late March that he planned a ten-day trip to Quebec City and east-coast ports and would be off the air throughout. Harvison's published memoirs inaccurately portray this intelligence-gathering journey as Hamburg's idea, but at no time did the Abwehr ask Janowski to leave Montreal.

It so happened that Little was in Halifax during this period on official business, and he took time out to gather information that any outsider – such as Janowski – might pick up. 'Noticed approximately 45 merchant ships at anchor,' he reported. 'As a rough guess I observed about 70 small war ships.' Such on-the-scene intelligence was vital to the double-cross game, as Masterman had noted. A 'double agent should, as far as possible, actually live the life and go through all the motions of a genuine agent,' Masterman observed in his double-cross manual. 'If he could not go a substitute was sent in his place. The agent on such a journey sought information exactly as a spy would, that is to say, with the most intense regard for his own safety, and in consequence he secured the sort of account which a genuine spy would have got.' In the RCMP's Watchdog case, however, that principle got overlooked – and it was left to the initiative of the chief of Naval Intelligence to fill the gap.

Watchdog's next message on 8 April claimed he had returned from a successful trip the previous evening and would soon begin to transmit the results. But the ruse about the Quebec chart had to be put off for weeks. The Watchdog team wanted to have a copy on hand before the transmission in case the Abwehr insisted on an immediate courier. Producing a credible chart, however, proved frustratingly difficult and in fact was never carried out. Over the next weeks, Janowski did tap out a variety of items purportedly gleaned from his east-coast trip. The messages also suggested that travel in the area was extremely difficult, as police constantly checked papers. This was partly to discourage the Abwehr from landing agents independent of their Montreal agent Bobbi.

Radio conditions, however, were extremely difficult throughout April and the German station ordered him off the air for the latter part of the month. 'Holiday appreciated,' Watchdog replied on 22 April. 'Is that for my personal safety. Sic. Sic. Or appreciation of my work. Sic. Sic. I wonder. Easter greetings to my wife and all my well-wishing friends.'

Communications resumed on 30 April with an unusual message from Germany that again renewed confidence among the Watchdog team that the case was still alive. 'Congratulations for your birthday [on 26 April] also in the name of your family. Everything is alright there. Highest recognition for your work. Decoration recommended. Easter leave also for your personal safety. Greetings transferred. Everybody proud of you. Best wishes and heartiest greetings. Chief.' The message, the thirteenth received so far, was supposedly from Admiral Wilhelm Canaris, chief of the Abwehr. Superintendent Gagnon in Montreal was now convinced that Germany had no inkling of Janowski's Allied supervision. If they did, he reasoned, they would either cut him off or continue communications to help save his life and secure some truthful – albeit controlled – information. The fact that Janowski had confessed his warning signal to the RCMP and had not used it meant that the Abwehr had no reason to fear for his safety. The only reason to communicate with a controlled agent would be to acquire information – but if that were so why cut off transmissions for ten days? Clearly, the Abwehr viewed Bobbi as a legitimate and successful agent and was limiting his transmissions to guard against discovery. Or so Gagnon reasoned.

Three days after the comforting greetings from Canaris, Harvison composed a message from Watchdog that he would come to regret. Janowski had claimed that among his duties in Canada was the identification of sympathetic Germans in Montreal who could be pressed into Abwehr service. (Harvison's memoirs say Janowski was supposed to contact members of the Canadian Fascist Party, though there is no support for this claim in the RCMP's Watchdog file.) The RCMP in Montreal already had at least ten people of German heritage under surveillance as having suspected enemy sympathies, and Harvison's plan was to extract possibly damning information from the Abwehr about their loyalties. The approach was in line with Harvison's original responsibility for the surveillance and arrest of Quebec Nazis and fascists. 'Contacted Germans holding important positions in war plants,' was Watchdog's message on 3 May. 'Some may be willing to work for us. Please check different organizations to ascertain if they know a man by the name of [deleted]. Was in Germany in 1939. Returned to Canada same year in spring. Is Austrian about 39 years old.' The request spoke eloquently of the dichotomy between the RCMP's narrower policing functions and the larger, strategic objectives of Britain's double-cross system. Harvison wanted to nab a suspected traitor; Mills wanted to preserve Janowski to help deceive an army. Harvison, unschooled in the subtleties of strategic deception, was prepared to risk the operation in the hope of making an arrest.

The trouble was, Harvison's bold move had been expressly forbidden by Assistant Commissioner Mead three days earlier. 'It is not deemed advisable to put over the information of contact with Germans holding important positions,' Mead had written to Montreal on 1 May. Harvison sheepishly replied on the day after transmission that the message to Germany had already been sent. He claimed Mead's letter had not been received in time and implied that he did not regard the message as requiring pre-approval from RCMP headquarters. Harvison then played down any perceived risks. 'Care was taken in framing the question to avoid giving details regarding the company, or location of [name deleted] which might possible [sic] be of assistance to other enemy agents,' Harvison wrote. 'I regret that this traffic has already been sent, but again suggest that it may serve several useful purposes and that no risk was involved.' He then boldly asked Mead to reconsider an earlier vetoed message that had Watchdog asking his Abwehr masters for more money.

Mead was clearly angry on learning about Harvison's unauthorized transmission. 'The matter ... was freely discussed with Mr. Mills. I did not like it; Inspector Drysdale did not like it and Mr. Mills did not like it,' he wrote. 'The chief reason of objection was, it was considered to be almost inconceivable that Germans holding important positions in war plants and possibly willing to work for Germany, would be available for contact by W. ... I do not agree with you when you say that no risk was involved.' As to the issue of money, Mead again categorically rejected Harvison's request. 'This matter was discussed with Mr. Mills also and his much greater experience in matters of this kind ought, of necessity, to be our guide. He was against such a request and I agree with him. W. had well over $5000.00 in bills and gold to use and I am quite sure you will agree with me that up to the present, W. has done nothing to indicate substantial amounts have been spent.'

Over the next two weeks, there was no Abwehr response to Watchdog's query about the thirty-nine-year-old Austrian. Instead, Hamburg began to pepper its agent with a string of specific queries. 'Said that Canadian chemists have discovered new explosive. Asked are description of results and specific weight. Detonation speed. External appearance and use,' said one coded message. Another: 'Report types, acreage, buildings, stories, number of employees, working hours, monthly production, for both Pratt and Whitney and Canadian Associated Aircraft.' And another: 'Where are Catalinas built? At Vickers Montreal or Boeing Victoria?' Finally, on 16 May, the Watchdog team got its answer to Harvison's vexing request for details about the Austrian's background: 'Work at all costs alone and do not look for any helpers as this would be dangerous. Your work is most valuable even if you have nothing to report for longer periods. Give only most important military information. For your sake only very little traffic necessary. The most important thing is that you remain undetected in order to be able to clarify the most urgent questions. Let us know about yourself by sending two letters spaced two weeks apart.'

The Watchdog team and RCMP headquarters in Ottawa had by now waited patiently for six months for word about Janowski's fellow saboteurs. A police operation, which Mills had valiantly tried to salvage as a strategic deception tool, was now stalled. 'Work at all costs alone,' was the troubling admonition from Hamburg, 'and do not look for helpers as this would be dangerous.' The shipping season in the St Lawrence was well under way, and spring was already two months along. If there were any truth to Janowski's claim about preparing the way for saboteurs in the spring, he surely would have been told by now the details of the agents to follow. Even more troubling was Janowski's claim that he was to contact local Germans. The message from the Abwehr suggested quite the opposite, that he was specifically to avoid seeking out 'helpers.' Did that veto also extend to the 'helpers' that were to be landed by U-boat? And why was Hamburg suddenly flooding the air waves with

124

specific intelligence requests, about war-plane production, submarine-detection devices, and military markings? The month of May, begun with reassuring praise for Watchdog from Admiral Canaris himself, now ended with grave suspicions that Janowski had somehow turned himself into a triple agent right under the noses of his captors.

SIX

Collapse

Long before the Watchdog case began to go sour – before the Quebec press leak, before the unauthorized message about local German war workers, before Hamburg's admonition against 'helpers' – Janowski began to plot his departure from Canada. Harvison's belated re-interrogation of his prisoner had finally extracted details about Abwehr counter-espionage operations in northern France, Belgium, and Holland. Janowski saw an opening. He now formulated a 'proposition' in the event the Watchdog case failed, and Harvison had him put it in writing for examination at RCMP headquarters. 'I would be willing and enthusiastic to work in Belgium and France,' Janowski wrote. 'I would have no difficulty in penetrating the German coastal defence line in Belgium and France, thus enabling me to provide the Allies with detailed information about strength of defence units and location of armaments. Thousands of lives could be saved by having this special information.'

Janowski went on to outline just how the mission could be accomplished. He would be parachuted behind enemy lines near Dunkirk in a German grey sapper uniform, equipped with a radio transmitter. In addition to broadcasting military intelligence back to the Allies, Janowski could also help eliminate all of the radio-equipped Abwehr agents he had recruited in towns along the Belgian and French coasts. 'I understand that you will hesitate to trust me, but what risk are you running if I am working on my own, as I do not need any connections on the continent,' Janowski argued. 'It would be a great personal satisfaction to me to be able to settle a certain argument with certain gentlemen in occupied Belgium.' This last comment was evidently a reference to Major

Krazer and colleagues, who allegedly had turned on Janowski after his ill-advised comments about the Gestapo and the Nazi Party during the drinking party the previous August.

Harvison was intrigued. 'W. in advancing his proposition claims that he has gone much too far with us to be able to double-cross us by using his plan as an escape scheme,' he advised his superiors. 'In the event of some accident – such as further press releases, bringing about the collapse of our present work, it might be considered.' As evidence of his good faith, Janowski created a neatly drawn chart of the coast along Belgium and France. The German coastal defence lines were sketched in roughly, and the map was dotted with the locations of more than four dozen Abwehr agents, distinguished between Abteilung I and III (espionage and counter-espionage), with a special lightning-bolt key indicating which were equipped with 14-watt radios.

The chart was accompanied by a list of the names, locations, and detailed descriptions of seven such agents, whose chief missions were to remain behind after the coming Allied invasion in order to radio military information ahead to the Abwehr. Janowski also provided details on defence plans to strangle any Allied invasion attempt. 'In the event of a breach of the coastal defences being effected the invading troops would be allowed through the breach in large numbers and would then be attacked on both flanks and in front by Panzer divisions and Artillery while the guns of the fortifications on either side of the breach could shell the rear.' On the face of it, Janowski's information seemed a rich trove – but the once-burned RCMP was now twice-shy. 'No comment is being made with regard to either of the reports ... as it is realized that you are in a much better position to judge of the accuracy of their contents,' Commissioner Wood wrote cautiously to MI5 in passing along a copy of the chart and its accompanying material.

The most curious aspect of Janowski's unlikely proposal to work for the Allies in Europe was its timing. The Watchdog operation was well under way: contact with Hamburg was firmly established and the first messages received suggested there was no Abwehr suspicion of him. The flurry of press leaks that plagued the RCMP were unknown to Janowski, who for obvious reasons was kept in the dark. And yet here he was already looking to his future prospects. In the weeks following, he would expand his bail-out proposal, naïvely suggesting that he could

become a European member of any international police force established by the United Nations after the war. RCMP headquarters in
Ottawa never paid much heed to these bizarre proposals, but the odd
timing did suggest that Janowski felt the Watchdog case was somehow
doomed. Why the pessimism when from what Janowski knew, everything seemed to be running smoothly? Or was there something he knew
that he wasn't telling?

As the weeks passed, the RCMP also grew more pessimistic. Harvison was occasionally behaving like a renegade, taking risky initiatives
without consultation with MI5 or RCMP headquarters. At times Harvison seemed overly protective of his prisoner, almost as if Janowski was
skilfully pulling his strings. Mills became more frustrated about control
of the case, and as early as April had put his concerns in writing to
Assistant Commissioner Mead. A top-level meeting was proposed to
smooth ruffled feathers and re-establish clear direction in the case. 'We
should have a discussion in Ottawa at which either Gagnon or Harvison
should be present as it is not our wish that there should be any misunder-
standing in regard to this matter of Watchdog,' Assistant Commissioner
Mead wrote to Mills. 'We here realize that your experience in matters
such as this is greater than our own and we naturally look to you for
advice and direction.' But Harvison's police instincts and impatience
continued to threaten the case. 'The present exchange of messages is of
little immediate value and of somewhat doubtful future value unless it is
to lead to the capture of further agents and protection against sabotage,'
Harvison wrote to his commanding officer in early May.

By mid-May, Commissioner Wood was weighing a suggestion that
Janowski simply ask the Abwehr outright when to expect the promised
saboteurs, thereby forcing an issue that had begun to fester. He reminded
Justice Minister Louis St Laurent in a 19 May letter that 'Watchdog's
primary object in coming to this country was to prepare for the reception
of a group of saboteurs to be dispatched from Germany in the spring of
1943 and it was remarkable, in the messages received from Germany, no
reference has been made up to now to further that proposal. This neglect
has caused us some concern and we have been giving consideration to
the transmission of messages with the object of inducing some sort of
reply from Germany indicative of the truth of Watchdog's contention.'
Wood then asked for St Laurent's view on whether Janowski should be

shipped off to MI5 in Britain for the remainder of the war if it became clear that no saboteurs were forthcoming and the RCMP decided to abandon the case. Sir David Petrie had extended the offer, as Janowski might have some value as a living reference library, especially with his knowledge of the Belgian and French coasts. 'I agree,' St Laurent wrote in the margin. Wood and Mead made their final decision on 9 June: Hamburg was to be confronted directly with the question of the spring saboteurs. They ordered the Watchdog team to draft a message to this effect for final approval by Ottawa.

Hopes for the Watchdog case were revived briefly on 23 June when Germany sent a long message requesting technical information about Allied defences against U-boats. 'Is there infra red ray apparatus used for U boat defense. What type of device is used for registering these rays. How are the American shortwave radioray detecting devices constructed for searching and detecting U boats from plane, ship or land. Information asked about wave length, range and accuracy of bearing.' Two days later, the enemy station added: 'Are there used oscilloscope tubes with a luminous screen and how?' The lengthy request stirred debate about whether the Abwehr would bother to ask a controlled agent for such sensitive, detailed intelligence. Surely the Allies would never permit the enemy any insights into recent developments in defences against U-boats – so the Abwehr must have believed its own agent was free to answer honestly. Otherwise, why expend resources on an obviously wasted effort? But the darker, more sceptical view prevailed at RCMP headquarters in Ottawa. 'Germany might be equally likely to place this question before a controlled agent in the hope that, amongst the information subsequently supplied to them by the controlling agency, there might be some truth which would assist them in compiling information upon anti-U-boat devices,' observed Assistant Commissioner Mead.

Sparks continued to fly between Mills and Harvison on how to conduct the Watchdog case in the interim. Harvison strongly favoured a message to Hamburg requesting permission to purchase a car and warning that the money would run out in a few months. The car would make Janowski appear better equipped to assist additional saboteurs, Harvison argued, and replenishing the money might help expose an Abwehr courier system in Canada. Mills objected, again arguing that the more than

$5000 that Janowski had brought to Canada would have adequately covered the expenses of a real agent for more than a year. A demand now would merely breed suspicion in Hamburg. Mills also argued that an agent would simply acquire a car without first seeking permission. This disagreement bubbled away for weeks. Officials in Ottawa patiently tried to find a compromise, but in the end had to side with Mills. 'As the matters ... are of a general technical nature with regard to the handling of agents, we must of necessity follow the advice of Mr. Mills,' Assistant Commissioner Mead told the team on 10 June. 'It would be folly not to do so.'

Heads butted as well over what to do about Hamburg's message on 16 May asking Janowski to send two letters spaced two weeks apart. The Watchdog team wanted to sidestep trouble and simply have Janowski claim to have sent the letters without in fact posting them. Their eventual failure to arrive could always be blamed on Allied ship sinkings at sea or on vigilant postal censors. Mills disagreed, urging that the team use the opportunity to augment the strategic deception. 'This matter is an extraordinary one and one where Mr. Mills has greater knowledge than we have,' Mead said in ruling that MI5's advice must prevail on this issue as well. On 7 May, the Watchdog team received a perplexing coded message from Germany that Harvison and Molyneaux could not completely decipher – until Mills stepped in. 'It seems very unfortunate that this matter has to be cleared up for us by Mr. Mills, whereas it could have been cleared up by your staff through the use of the code of which you are in possession,' Mead observed. Mills's repeated one-upmanship over Harvison stirred deep resentment.

Their most serious disagreement, however, arose over the precise wording of the message that was to force the issue of the saboteurs. Days were wasted as these two men sparred over vocabulary, phrasing, nuance, inflexion, and even sentence length. Mills initially drew up a relatively verbose message, not provided in the released Watchdog file, which Harvison showed to his prisoner. Janowski objected, saying it contained too much information and would readily expose him as a double. Not surprisingly, Harvison adopted Janowski's view on the matter and went to Ottawa to ask to have the message altered. 'I felt the sending of the message would possibly blow the case,' Harvison advised Mead. Harvison was simply told to work out a compromise with Mills, who was away on business but was to return the following week to Montreal. After a long discussion, Harvison and Mills finally found common ground. Two shorter messages would be sent, one dealing with the question of 'helpers,' the other with a money shortage. The product of their negotiations, arrived at more than a month after Mead had asked for a draft message, was forwarded to Ottawa and approved.

Meanwhile, a further press leak drove another nail into Watchdog's coffin. The *Daily Gleaner* in Fredericton, New Brunswick, published a front-page article in its 14 June edition, under the headline 'C.P.C. organized on St. Lawrence – German officer spotted in hotel by woman – Varied personnel on watch.' The story quoted the head of a civilian watcher group in Rimouski, Quebec, who praised a hotel-keeper's wife for spotting a spy at New Carlisle the year previous. 'The woman watched a stranger throw down a cigarette package. When it fell she picked it up and saw it was Belgian. Later, the man paid for his room with the large-sized Canadian dollar bills which went out of circulation years ago. The woman noticed these details, notified the police and the man was arrested. He led the police to his cache on the beach where he showed them his German uniform, a radio and handcuffs. He spoke French and English as well as German but he wasn't smart enough to outwit the people of this peninsula.' The story, although a badly garbled version of the facts, was the most complete account yet to find its way into print. The Abwehr would have no difficulty linking it with Janowski.

Army Intelligence officers in New Brunswick had been the first to spot the story, which they noted had been distributed by the *Toronto Star* news service. Censorship authorities investigated and informed Commissioner Wood that the article had been inadvertently released to the *Daily Gleaner* by a careless *Star* editor, who was aware of the publication ban, but that no other paper had received or published it. J. Alex Crocket of the *Daily Gleaner* pleaded ignorance, saying his editors simply assumed the *Star* had obtained permission for release. Fredericton RCMP determined that the paper did not reach the local internment camp, notorious as a back-channel of information to Germany, but may have been read by some German and Italian prisoners of war being treated at Victoria Public Hospital in the city. 'With this continued broadcasting of this case it would seem hopeless to think that the Huns will not find out about it,' Gagnon, the commanding officer in Montreal, noted in exasperation.

Commissioner Wood was even more pessimistic. 'As this is the 3rd time that a leakage of information concerning this case has occurred through the Press, we are naturally extremely doubtful that Germany has no knowledge that we are controlling their agent,' he wrote in late June. Inspector Alexander Drysdale, the RCMP intelligence officer at Ottawa headquarters, had warned back in November that the Mounties simply could not keep the media genie inside the bottle. His advice not to mount a double-agent case, rejected outright at the time, was proving to be prudent and sage. Harvison's published memoirs are again grossly misleading on this point. 'The fact that not one line appeared [in newspapers] until the lifting of censorship at the end of the war made it possible to continue our operation of this case, and reflects great credit on the press in general and, in particular, on those reporters who had the story,' he wrote. The Canadian media were indeed generally cooperative in the year following Janowski's capture, but for one reason or another the RCMP was vexed by repeated press leaks.

Janowski seemed aware that the case might soon be coming to a close and his contact with Germany cut for perhaps years. He was allowed to send a personal message on 13 July. 'Please send to my wife. Darling only to tell you that I love you very much and that I hope everybody is in good health as I am here. Soon the war will be over and Boni and Putzi reunited. Please write [that is, to the Abwehr station for eventual broadcast]. You are always in my thoughts. Boni.' The next day, Hamburg replied somewhat brusquely: 'Everything well at home. Full appreciation and everyone sends greetings.' Finally, on 19 July, Watchdog transmitted the first of the two messages that Harvison and Mills had hammered out. 'Concerning conversation about sending helpers. You asked me if I could prepare the way for people to follow in the spring. Could now use helpers. You have asked me questions from Halifax to Vancouver. Much information could be secured but I cannot cover all of this huge territory as well as be radio operator. Is help coming?' The second message was sent the next day. 'Please remember I have funds to do only until October. If helpers coming they should bring ample funds.' The die was now cast, and Germany's response over the next days and weeks would determine whether the Watchdog case was to be killed.

Janowski, though, was already certain that Hamburg was aware of his Allied control. On 20 July, the day after the first message asking whether 'help' was coming, Hamburg sent a personal message acknowledging the transmission: 'Thanks and greetings from home. All is well there. Bruno.' Janowski claimed to be perturbed when this seemingly innocuous message was decoded. 'JANOWSKI's reaction to the reply was that it was too formal and he felt had been prepared by his masters and not by his wife, thus indicating that they were well aware of the control being exercised over him,' said an RCMP summary of the case. Janowski's claim was unusual, in that the message was no more or less formal than the one he had received on 14 July. Was Janowski skittish now that the RCMP was finally checking his claim about 'spring saboteurs'? Was he trying to wind down a case he knew was doomed while he could still claim a small measure of credibility? After all, if Watchdog was shutting down anyway he might as well get some credit for appearing to help the RCMP. It just might help his plan to be parachuted back into Belgium.

As events thus hung in the balance, the RCMP was jolted by yet another press leak – this time from a wholly unexpected quarter. In its 29 July edition, the *Montreal Daily Star* reported on a meeting of Quebec police and fire chiefs at which Lieutenant-Colonel Léon Lambert, assistant director of the Quebec Provincial Police, gave a speech in praise of his officers. Lambert – the man who had first tipped the RCMP about the arrest of Janowski on 9 November – told the meeting that 'the work and vigilance of provincial police members were responsible for the capture of more than one spy.' RCMP Inspector Josaphat Brunet at the Montreal headquarters of 'C' Division was more than a little sarcastic in pointing out the censorship breach to Commissioner Wood the next day. 'While no details appear to have been given by Lt. Col. Lambert it is doubtful if enough spies have been landed by Germany in Canada for Germany to require details.' The article was brought to the attention of Justice Minister Louis St Laurent, but, because of the sensitive nature of federal-provincial relations, there was neither a formal investigation nor letters of complaint as there had been on all other leaks.

Early in the Watchdog case, there was general agreement that Harvison would interview Olive Quance – Janowski's long-suffering Canadian wife – to verify details of the prisoner's so-called confessions. But Harvison was notoriously tardy in attending to such critical investigative

133

details. Six months after his second round of interrogations, for example, Harvison had still not delivered a full and final report to RCMP headquarters. Senior officers in Ottawa had to pester him repeatedly to get paperwork delivered, and they stepped up the pressure in mid-August. Similarly, Harvison did not get around to visiting Quance in Toronto as he had promised.

In the meantime, postal censorship had intercepted a Red Cross letter to a woman in Germany from a man in Toronto. The wording of the letter, written in July and allegedly to the man's sister, seemed peculiar and was brought to the attention of the RCMP, who soon recognized the name of the letter-writer. It was the young man from Munich who had struck up a friendship with Janowski on the boat from Germany in 1930. Janowski had suggested that this man, who had also worked on a farm in the London, Ontario, area, was extremely disillusioned with conditions in Canada and had likely returned to Germany. In fact, the man had gone to Toronto and lived quietly without coming to the attention of the RCMP for twelve years. Like Quance, he would also have to be interviewed to check on aspects of Janowski's story.

Harvison was now expected to do both of the interviews in early August, but again found himself too busy. Two officers from the RCMP's 'O' Division headquarters in Toronto finally got the job done without fuss on 19 August. Quance was not told anything about Janowski's capture or return to Canada, and was led to believe the questioning was merely routine. Her version of events tallied well with Janowski's, especially on the troubling problem of the date of his departure from Canada. Janowski had claimed this was by boat in September 1933, but official records were silent. Quance produced correspondence and documents sent to her by Janowski that backed his claims to have joined the French Foreign Legion in Morocco in 1933. She also expanded on Janowski's relatively neutral description of their marriage by noting, for example, that he stole from her millinery business. 'Subject had a very suave and pleasant manner, and was inclined to exaggerate things to his own favour,' the Toronto report of the interview said. 'He apparently considered himself a ladies man, and apparently did considerable philandering.' Quance also indicated she was 'somewhat apprehensive' that Janowski might return to Canada.

The interview with the mystery man from Munich also generally supported Janowski's account of his first weeks in Canada. The Toronto officers concluded that the man had not had any contact with Janowski since moving to Toronto at Christmas of 1930, but that there was 'no doubt that this man is pro-German in his attitude. He stated that it was his intention to return to Germany at the conclusion of the present war.' His name was added to the RCMP list of Germans to watch.

Radio traffic with Hamburg, meanwhile, was humdrum and routine. Watchdog conveyed some low-level intelligence about frigate and Liberty ship construction, the Vought Corsair fighter, and a new Dupont explosive containing hexamine. Germany merely acknowledged receipt of the message about 'helpers,' then asked about markings on Canadian uniforms and 'which divisions in Canada are ready for action?' For almost three weeks, the enemy station ignored Janowski's direct pleas for helpers and money. By any yardstick, the Watchdog case was clearly moribund. The season was far too advanced for 'spring' saboteurs to be landed, and Hamburg was obviously dodging the question. For those in the RCMP who had undertaken the case for policing reasons rather than for strategic deception, the operation was now pointless. There could be no further arrests. For Mills and the Twenty Committee in Britain, Janowski's true colours as a triple had been clearly revealed. There could be no double-cross of the enemy.

On 11 August, Commissioner Wood ordered Harvison to escort the prisoner to Britain for the further use of MI5 and the Twenty Committee. 'A live spy, even if he cannot transmit messages, is always of some use as a book of reference; a dead spy is of no sort of use,' John Masterman had observed in his double-cross manual. Wood dismissed outright a suggestion that Southam, the radio understudy, carry on transmissions by mimicking Janowski's 'fist.' Watchdog would be silenced by deliberately cutting off his transmission in the middle of a message, so as to suggest that police had caught him *in flagrante delicto*. In a letter on 17 August, Wood explained his decision to the FBI's J. Edgar Hoover: 'The failure of the German authorities to open negotiations for the proposed future landing of saboteurs in this country and their apparent reluctance to answer our questions transmitted on July 19th last, together with the undue publicity unfortunately given to this case at various times and other circumstances have forced us to hold grave doubts as to its genuineness.'

Wood did not spell out exactly what he meant by 'other circumstances,' but Cyril Mills, the MI5 man whose shadow crosses every page in the Watchdog file, provided a clue shortly before his death in 1991. Mills, who had been in Canada since December for what he expected would be three-week mission, planned to return briefly to London in August. 'Before leaving, I drafted all the messages which were to be sent; Janowski translated into German which I approved and all he had to do under RCMP supervision was to put the messages into cross-word squares in which all the spaces were blanks,' Mills recalled. 'When I returned I asked to see the squares used and in the top left hand corner of one I saw S.O.S. which he had cleverly worked in via a couple of spelling mistakes which his minders had not noticed. I knew at once that his German masters would know he was working under our control and forbade the use of the radio. Harvison objected and I went to see Commissioner Wood who supported me ... [Janowski] was a loyal Nazi and he did not think he was risking his life when he gave the tip-off. He knew I was in England and appreciated the incompetency of his RCMP minders and the fact that he had made a fool of Harvison.' Mills's dating of Janowski's treachery is difficult to reconcile with the released file, since it implies a mid-to-late-August exposure of his illicit SOS to Hamburg, even though Wood appears to have decided by early August to shut down Watchdog. Unfortunately, the coding worksheets have not survived in the file to verify Mills's statement. The officially sanctioned history of British intelligence in the Second World War says only that the Watchdog case was shut down because Janowski was 'truculent and difficult to handle.'

Radio transmissions from Montreal concluded on 12 August with Watchdog's message no. 90, about the construction of the American Corsair fighter. That same day, Hamburg transmitted their message no. 68, which turned out to be a rather more fitting conclusion to the case: 'At your parents home all is well. Butzi [presumably his wife Putzi] and I are here sociably together. Heartiest greetings. Bruno.' The RCMP plan to cut a transmission dramatically in the middle of a message had to be abandoned as atmospheric conditions conspired against all contact. The radio set was kept active until 8 September, however, to monitor any of Hamburg's transmissions that managed to pierce the electronic din. The 'fist' of a new reply-station operator was heard on 7 September, but no messages of any substance were received. The Afu transmitter-receiver with its 'booster' was removed to an RCMP workshop at the St James Street headquarters. Janowski's slide-rule and code books, now dog-eared, were eventually packed up with most of Watchdog's other spy paraphernalia and sent to the RCMP museum at Regina for display when the war was over. The final sections of Harvison's second interrogation report, half a year overdue, were hastily completed and shipped by courier to MI5's Blenheim Palace headquarters. One more transmission from Hamburg was picked up by Captain Edward Drake's intercept station at Rockcliffe near Ottawa, but it too turned out to be insignificant when decoded.

Meanwhile, Southam the radio expert continued to monitor the air waves on his own time, with his own equipment, purely out of personal curiosity. Sure enough, his headphones caught the faint peeping of Hamburg's distinctive Morse, at the appropriate time and frequency. Southam jotted down messages received on 6, 9, and 11 October and passed them on to Corporal Molyneaux, Watchdog's coding expert. Altogether, eight post-Watchdog intercepts came into Molyneaux's hands. Try as he might, however, he could make no sense of them. 'Although the call letters and frequency were correct, the proper decoding key cannot be located,' Molyneaux said. 'It is possible that one or more groups are missing or the copy is incorrect. An effort will be made to break these codes but it is not known how long it will take.' Harvison had by now lost interest in the case and told Molyneaux not to bother. The code books and slide-rule were shipped to Regina, but had to be retrieved days later when Mills was informed about the intercepts and insisted that special efforts be made to decode the material. Molyneaux tried again but failed, noting only that the messages had been copied down accurately, but for some reason were unbreakable.

Harvison took a Trans-Canada airline flight to Halifax on 24 August to make final arrangements for Janowski's trip to Britain. The next day, he cleared the paperwork and inspected the brig on the military ship that was to give them passage. Two RCMP officers from Montreal arrived with the prisoner the same day on CN's Maritime Express, reporting to the embarkation commandant on Pier 20 at 7:30 p.m. Janowski was immediately taken to his cell. The ship steamed out of Halifax harbour two days later, and throughout the seven-day voyage Janowski was kept under guard by a sergeant and two privates. Harvison also visited the bare cell several times each day. On 2 September they arrived in England, where Janowski was received by local police officers and taken the same day to Camp 020, the interrogation centre run by the military for MI5 and the Twenty Committee in the village of Ham Common.

Janowski was assigned a cell, where he would remain until the end of the war, and an MI5 team began his third intensive interrogation. Harvison presented some documents in the case, including the two military railway passes that Janowski had brought ashore to augment his initial ruse. These were politely returned. Harvison did not remain to observe the procedure, instead taking some advanced police training at Special Branch of Scotland Yard in London. 'Later I visited Camp 020 and ascertained that the prisoner had arrived there in good health and appeared very willing to be cooperative,' Harvison later reported. 'While I was offered an opportunity to interview him at the camp, I gathered that at the time of my visit, he was under interrogation and it was considered preferable to leave him in the hands of the new interrogation officers. I did not see the prisoner again.'

Under the RCMP's arrangement with Sir David Petrie, MI5 was to use Janowski as a 'reference library' until the close of hostilities. It remained unclear who would deal with Janowski after the war, but the RCMP now moved to ensure they weren't stuck with him. 'In view of the fact that the prisoner co-operated with us to a considerable extent, there would have been no question of taking criminal action against him had he remained in this country,' Assistant Commissioner Mead wrote to Justice Minister Louis St Laurent on 7 September. 'I feel that the British Authorities should be informed that we have no desire to again take over the custody of this man and will leave his final disposition in their hands.' St Laurent agreed. Corporal Richard Robertson, an Ottawa intelligence officer, was asked to write a brief summary of the case. And in a final gesture to close the file, all of Janowski's money – $4994 in Canadian bills, $1.11 in change, and another $1000 in U.S. $20 gold pieces – was turned over to A.H. Mathieu, Canada's custodian of enemy property. The force would not even profit from the Watchdog case.

But the Watchdog file, in fact, was far from closed. For many months the Abwehr station dutifully continued its transmissions to Bobbi, which were picked up and carefully logged by the Allied receivers. For years after the war, as will be shown, Janowski kept in touch with his former RCMP minders in Canada. Watchdog's radio set with its special 'booster' was hauled out and used again in 1945 for another double agent operation, this a more successful venture that was kept hidden from the RCMP. And another U-boat spy, whose equipment and training offered fresh insights into the Watchdog case, arrived mysteriously one fall morning in 1944 on the Mounties' doorstep.

SEVEN

Operation Grete

On Sunday, 29 October 1944, Alfred Langbein placed a sheet of white paper on the writing table in his room and nervously composed a message that was to turn his quiet life upside down. He printed each tight, awkward letter of the two-sentence note, then signed his name, slightly losing control of the last 'n' in Langbein as he attemped a calligraphic flourish. He attached his National Registration Certificate, which gave his name as Alfred Haskins, and placed both pieces of paper in an envelope.

Langbein, small and mousy-looking, had tried to live in obscurity for the last thirteen months in this room at the home of Oscar Renaud and family, on St Andrew Street in Ottawa's Lower Town. He always paid his $45 monthly rent on time, and feigned a physical disability to cover the fact he did not have a job and wasn't looking for one. The Renauds knew he had some kind of income, enough that he once was able to give them a sizeable loan, but they weren't quite sure where the money came from. No matter. Mr Haskins, 41, was the ideal tenant: prompt with the rent, clean, law-abiding, pleasant, even sociable. His clothes were always well-tailored, expensive, and fashionable. Some days, he visited the staff at the Grand Hotel, where he had lived for a time, sometimes going on picnics to the countryside with them and their friends. He had even recently met a girlfriend, an Eva Rose. The pair often went out on the town together, Mr Haskins happily splashing money around. When he spoke English, his accent seemed odd – perhaps Dutch – but the Renauds were francophone and their own command of English wasn't nearly as strong as his. Any linguistic quirks were lost on them.

Beneath his calm exterior that Sunday in October, Langbein was in deep emotional turmoil. The next morning, he placed the fateful envelope in his pocket and walked over to No. 8 Temporary Building, a wooden structure hastily built near the Experimental Farm to handle the explosion in the number of wartime civil servants. He intended to hand the letter to the guard inside the entrance, but as he came up to the building he lost his nerve. For the next five or six hours, he ambled around the area trying to douse his fear. Langbein was quite familiar with the building. At least three acquaintances he had met through his friends at the Grand Hotel worked there, including a Miss Evelyn Hjorleifson whom he had visited in the spring, waiting for her in the lobby. The building was used exclusively for Canada's postal censors. But during this visit to Hjorleifson, Langbein noticed on the building directory that Naval Intelligence had offices there as well. He assumed incorrectly that it was their headquarters. The letter now weighing so heavily in his pocket was addressed to the commanding officer of Naval Intelligence, no name, but Langbein simply could not summon the nerve to deliver it. He was still thoroughly spooked by the end of the day as workers in No. 8 filed out of the entrance heading for home. He, too, returned wearily to his room.

The following morning, Langbein walked back to No. 8 with the envelope in his breast pocket. Again his nerve failed him. His thoughts dwelt on his family and on his own future, which surely would be lived out inside a dank prison cell. That prospect was far worse than any other fate he could imagine, even a bullet through the heart. For the second day, Langbein succumbed to cowardice. He shuffled back to Lower Town, overwhelmed by hopelessness and despair. His head that night was filled with imaginary trials, firing squads, iron bars, and cold stone walls. The next morning, he made up his mind a third time to hand over the letter. He turned up at No. 8 at about 10 a.m. – and again panicked. For the next four hours, he shambled about, trying desperately to screw up his courage. Shortly before 2 p.m., he decided he could delay no longer. Langbein waited outside the building entrance until about 2:30 p.m., when he was fairly certain that all the staff had returned from lunch. He slipped into the lobby and handed his letter to the duty guard, asking that it be given immediately to the officer in charge of Naval Intelligence or that someone from that branch come down to see him.

The startled guard telephoned Lieutenant Eric Yarrill in an office on the second floor. Briskly, Yarrill trod down to the lobby and found Langbein in what he described as a 'highly nervous state.' The stranger pushed the letter into his hand: 'Sir,' Yarrill read quickly, 'the enclosed Registration-card was given to me in April 1942 in the office of Kapt.z.See Menzel c.o. of Abw.I, Berlin, Tirpitzufer 86. Instead of giving myself up to the R.C.M.P. I come to you, because I want to give certain informations which concern naval matters. Alfred Langbein.' The accompanying registration card, made out to Alfred Haskins, 182 Younge St., Toronto, indicated it had been signed on 16 October 1940. Langbein told an astonished Yarrill that he had been landed by U-boat in Canada in early 1942 and was supposed to operate as an agent in Montreal and Halifax, but had instead come directly to Ottawa. 'His morale seems to have been badly shattered – apparently by the bombings of Hanover, where his people live,' Yarrill reported later that day. 'He expressed a desire to make a sworn statement in writing, and to get it over with as soon as possible.'

Yarrill immediately invited this unexpected visitor upstairs to a borrowed office. After a few minutes he picked up the telephone and ordered a car sent over to No. 8. The pair drove over to Cartier Square, where Naval Intelligence was actually headquartered. There Langbein was taken over by Lieutenant-Commander Wilfrid Samuel, the German-speaking intelligence officer who had helped break Janowski during the bumpy road trip from New Carlisle to Mont Joli. Samuel interviewed Langbein briefly about naval matters before determining that the case properly belonged to the RCMP. For the second time during the war, the navy had to concede a U-boat spy to the Mounties. Samuel alerted Superintendent Charles Rivett-Carnac of the intelligence section at RCMP headquarters, and over the next three days Langbein was allowed to compose a full statement about his background and mission to Canada. Presiding over these sessions was RCMP Sergeant Cecil Bayfield, who would play a key role in the September 1945 defection of Igor Gouzenko and the rolling-up of a Soviet spy ring in Canada; and Cyril Mills, the MI5 man originally posted to Canada to help with Watchdog. In contrast to the Janowski operation, Mills would be on the case from the outset.

On 2 November, the day after Langbein's surrender, Samuel sent a cyphered cable to the Admiralty in London and U.S. Naval Intelligence in Washington. He provided brief details, noting that Langbein claimed to have carried out no espionage since landing by U-boat along the Bay of Fundy in the spring of 1942. 'States has not used Portuguese and Swiss cover addresses and his wireless set remains buried near St Martins (N.B.) and has been living since August 1942 in Ottawa without employment on 6,000 dollars Canadian notes,' Samuel wrote. 'Suggestions & questions invited.'

Just before Langbein was to start dictating his statement to the RCMP, he was given the standard warning that he need not say anything, but that anything he did say could be used as evidence at his trial. Langbein then offered a meticulously detailed account, claiming to have lived in various parts of Canada from 1928 to 1932. During the war, he said, he was recruited into Abwehr I, the espionage arm of military intelligence, and carried out missions in Romania and Germany before being assigned to Canada. He had never intended carrying out any Canadian espionage, and lived on his Abwehr-provided money until recent events in Germany prompted his surrender.

One obvious check on his story was the buried radio set. Bayfield was detailed to escort Langbein by train back to New Brunswick, where they were to try to retrieve the apparatus. The RCMP file on Langbein, requested under the Access to Information Act, has mysteriously disappeared and Naval Intelligence files are silent on this New Brunswick trip. However, Eric H. Wilson, the son of RCMP Superintendent R.S.S. Wilson, published an article in 1974 recounting his father's memories of helping Bayfield locate the equipment. According to Wilson's account, Bayfield and Langbein met Wilson in Saint John, where the superintendent was stationed as commanding officer. Having learned that Langbein spent time in the hard-rock mining community of Flin Flon, Manitoba, Wilson asked the German whether he knew the red-light district in town where Wilson had once worked undercover. Langbein knew it well, and mentioned two madams, Blonde Annie and Swede Anne. 'This indication that the agent's story was truthful was confirmed a few minutes later when he identified the two madams in an old photo Dad located in a trunk in our attic,' the younger Wilson wrote. The trio then donned hunting gear to maintain secrecy, in case the RCMP decided to mount another double-agent case, and travelled by car to the St Martins area. They combed the ground for two days, but despite Langbein's best efforts the set could not be found.

Bayfield and Wilson then studied navigation charts of the area to find the right combination of buoys, reefs, and beach to match Langbein's memories of that distant night. On finding a likely landing spot, they arranged the use of a navy Fairmile torpedo boat, whose crew were told they were to help retrieve some top-secret American equipment that had been accidently dropped by an aircraft, Wilson wrote. As a snow quall blew up, Bayfield and Langbein were rowed ashore at the appropriate locale, although a buoy that had clanged at the first landing was nowhere to be seen or heard. The pair soon stumbled across a blanket that Langbein had lost more than two years earlier and a trench shovel he had tossed away. They dug under a large tree, and found the Afu and other items, all of them in good shape having been protected by two rubberized bags and a now-deteriorating canvas cover. Wilson returned to Saint John with the ship and dispatched an RCMP car to pick up Bayfield, Langbein, and the newly uncovered equipment. 'Unluckily, the storm continued and it was some time before the half-frozen pair saw the last of the landing point which had so occupied their attention,' Wilson wrote.

Bayfield returned Langbein to Ottawa, where Bayfield and Cyril Mills now carried out an intensive four-day interrogation beginning 19 November. Using Langbein's earlier statement as a baseline, the two men extracted further details and ironed out some discrepancies. It soon became clear to Mills that the prisoner was being straightforward and honest throughout, quite unlike Janowski. His many details of contact with the Abwehr, for example, corresponded well with the vast store of MI5 information about the service. Mills immediately ruled out a double-agent operation, as Langbein had grown stale after more than two years and was unlikely to revive credibly the interest of his Abwehr masters. But Langbein's life story was nevertheless highly instructive for the light it shed on some still-unexplained aspects of the Watchdog file.

Langbein was born an only child on 6 April 1903 to Willy and Elizabeth Langbein in Graenfenthal. The family moved to Sonderhausen, where Langbein went to school until age eight. There his father became an agent for an insurance company and was later transferred to Halle,

144

then to Hanover in 1914. Langbein remained in school until about 1920, lastly in a military academy. But with the end of the war, he forsook a career in the German armed forces for a job with a local firm that exported raw glass and chemicals. After a thirty-month apprenticeship, Langbein moved to Hamburg to work briefly for another export firm in 1923. Through his father's influence, he got a job as a steward's helper aboard a German merchant ship to help fulfil a dream to live abroad for a time. He wound up in Shanghai, working as a clerk for two trading companies with strong German connections. He later joined the municipal police force there as a special constable, while working on the side as a salesman for the local branch of the Manufacturers' Life Insurance Company, the Toronto-based firm.

Langbein returned to Hamburg in 1926, hoping to work in an export firm his father had founded. But the German economy was stagnant and again Langbein decided to go overseas. He applied for and received an immigrant visa to Canada, one of a special class reserved for those able to bring at least $100 into the country. The RCMP interrogation did not make clear why he chose Canada, though his Shanghai association with Manufacturers' Life likely played some part. While crossing the Atlantic, Langbein made the acquaintance of the wife of Alfred Barbe, a farmer in Pearce, Alberta. The ship arrived at Halifax in early April 1928, and the pair travelled first to Winnipeg, then Edmonton, and finally Pearce, where the Barbes gave him lodging while he scouted for employment. He first worked for a short time as a surveyor's chain man for the McLeod River Mining Company, then helped build the Canadian National railway line from Winnipeg to Flin Flon. After the line was completed, Langbein joined the Hudson's Bay Mining and Smelting Company, which operated the Flin Flon mine, as a member of a survey crew. Presumably it was during this period that he met the alluring Blonde Annie and Swede Anne.

In late 1931 he went to Winnipeg, occasionally writing freelance pieces for the *Winnipeg Free Press* and running down his small store of savings. Like thousands of Canadian men caught in the Great Depression, Langbein hitchhiked eastward for most of 1932, picking up odd jobs where he could. He ended up in Montreal, where two futile months were spent looking for work. In the end, Langbein got a job in the engine room of a merchant ship, which left Montreal in late 1932. He disembarked in Antwerp and eventually returned to his parents' home in Hanover, where he spent Christmas. All told, he had spent four years in Canada, but had little to show for it except his much-improved English.

Economic conditions were as bad in Germany as in Canada, and Willy Langbein's ailing export business was unable to support his son adequately. Hitler's rise to power in 1933, however, helped boost employment and by March 1934 Langbein had found work with a shale-oil company in the Hanover area. For the next five years, he improved his position with the firm, marrying Grete Rinne in late 1936. They had their first daughter, Karin, fifteen months later. Langbein's construction experience in Canada won him a better job in April 1939 building a five-kilometre section of Germany's Reichs-Autobahn. When Hitler invaded Poland in September, Langbein and his crew were ordered to build a camouflaged railway track into a munitions plant at Walsrode. They returned for a year to continue construction of the Auto-bahn. The crew got smaller as more men were conscripted into the military, but for some reason Langbein did not receive his call-up.

In about May 1940, Langbein had an unexpected and fateful meeting with an old school chum, Otto Homann, who claimed to be a kind of chiropractor. 'He was not a properly qualified doctor but professed to be able to diagnose complaints by looking in your eyes,' Langbein told his interrogators. Their short conversation was innocuous, but Langbein did mention he had lived for a time in Shanghai and Canada. Some days later, Homann, 44, set up another meeting with Langbein at the Hanover train station. 'During our conversation HOMANN expressed great interest in my travels to Canada and China and also in the fact that I spoke English to a certain extent,' Langbein recounted. 'I did not understand what HOMANN was getting at as he was vague and elusive and I therefore asked him to come down to business and tell me what the real purpose of this meeting was.' Homann hinted only that there might be an opportunity to go abroad and avoid military service.

Another meeting was arranged in Homann's house, where Langbein was introduced to a mysterious man from Bremen, Dr Nicolaus Bensmann. 'I really wondered whether or not these two men were working either for the British or the French and were trying to find out from me what was going on in [the secret munitions plant at] Walsrode which they knew I had visited.' The same vague promise was made of work abroad, perhaps in Bucharest, but no details were given. Langbein was asked point blank if he wanted the ill-defined job. He asked for time to think it over – and on his return home found that his military call-up papers had been delivered. This was enough to send him back into the arms of Homann and Bensmann, whom he knew could extricate him from military duty. Homann, also known as Dr H. Mueller, was heavy-set with a hooked nose. His real specialty was recruiting Abwehr spies in Holland. Bensmann, 46, was a chubby, short-sighted man who often nervously removed his glasses to fold and unfold the arms. Together, they formed an Abwehr recruiting team, seeking out men whose knowledge of foreign languages could be put to use for espionage. Langbein met them again in Bremen, where Bensmann was now in uniform. As it turned out, he worked for the Abwehr sub-post in Bremen, attached to the huge Hamburg post responsible for espionage in Britain and the Western Hemisphere.

Langbein was now offered a job as an Abwehr radio operator for an as-yet undisclosed mission. His code-name would be Max, his Abwehr agent number A 2024. All training and travel were to be provided by the Abwehr. Langbein immediately resigned his construction job and checked into a Bremen hotel on 19 July 1940 to begin his formal training in radio, of which he had no experience. He reported to the sixth floor of a building in the Bremen market, where the Abwehr sub-post had its main transmitter-receiver along with up to thirty transmitters used for training. From 10 a.m. to 5 p.m. each day for three months Langbein practised sending and receiving, sometimes taking his equipment out for field tests. About ten other men were being trained simultaneously, each with his own radio instructor. Langbein's teacher was a thirty-five-year-old man named Otto. Thin, stooped, and always smiling, Otto was a former radio salesman who managed to work his pupil up to a sending and receiving speed of fifteen or sixteen five-letter groups per minute.

For security reasons, the radio students were not to mingle, but Langbein – assigned the school's operational name Fred – got to know a few of them anyway. He told Bayfield and Mills that at least three were British subjects, two of them were brothers in training for an Egyptian mission. Two others were Belgians, who were to join a planned espionage mission to England. Langbein also told of a thirty-five-year-old fellow student by the name of Breuer, who would later travel by U-boat to a landing point off New Jersey. Breuer was a German citizen, but had lived and worked in New York City as a marine-engineering technician, building parts for American shipyards. His mission in America was to spy on the naval facilities at Newport News, Virginia, in association with another agent already on the scene by the name of Hartmann. Breuer was supplied a radio and secret writing materials; Hartmann, who had worked at the yard since 1938, had previously communicated only by secret writing to a mail drop in Portugal.

Langbein's training also included close study of oil fields in Polish Galicia and of refineries in Romania. In his last month he spent a day and a half at the Abwehr post in Brussels, where he was assigned a portable Afu and practised successful transmissions back to Bremen. His training complete, Langbein met with a Luftwaffe major named Ritter, who assigned him to Operation Lena. This was the Abwehr contribution to the coming invasion of England, code-name Operation Sea Lion, which Hitler had set for 15 September. The Abwehr had virtually no one in Britain in 1940 apart from Arthur Owens, or agent Johnny, whom the British were running as double agent Snow. Hitler had ordered invasion preparations to begin in July 1940 and there was scrambling among Abwehr posts to find dozens of agents for insertion.

'RITTER then said to me that he needed men to go to England to obtain information concerning Air Force matters such as aerodromes, searchlight and gun emplacements, numbers of aircraft,' Langbein told Mills and Bayfield. 'RITTER informed me that the idea was that I should be dropped by parachute in England in a region about 25 miles southeast of Bristol.' The mission – which Langbein believed involved as many as fifteen agents – was to be relatively short, perhaps six weeks' duration, at the end of which the Germans would already have successfully invaded Britain. At that point, Langbein was to stay behind enemy lines and transmit back military information about troop movements. He was given a British passport and identity card in the name of Alfred Merrell, two hundred one-pound Sterling notes, and a German army pistol with three rounds of ammunition. He was taught a substitution code, and told to use the password Llenloch to greet the Abwehr agent in England who was to meet him at the parachute drop. He was also provided this agent's address in London.

Langbein's wife was by now expecting her third child, and this would-be spy started to get cold feet. He visited his family in Hanover in early September 1940, mulling over his future. Leaving for Brussels in the midst of a night-time Allied air raid, he had a final meeting with senior Abwehr officials about Operation Lena. 'There and then I turned the whole project down and refused flatly to go to England,' he said. Most of his superiors took the refusal well, but did deny him priority train fare back to his Bremen sub-post, forcing him to spend several days in Brussels. That first night, 13 September, Langbein received a coded radio message that his son Jochen had been born. During this forced lay-over in Brussels, Langbein got to know one of the veteran pilots whose job it was to drop Abwehr agents into England by parachute. Oberleutnant Karl Edmund Gartenfeld, 40, had dropped many such agents by the time he met Langbein. 'On one occasion [he] told me that he considered his business of dropping parachute agents in England was the profession of a butcher,' Langbein recalled. Langbein soon hitched a ride back to Hanover in Gartenfeld's Heinkel III aircraft, painted black for its espionage missions.

Back in Bremen, Langbein spent several idle weeks examining Abwehr files for his own amusement. There he discovered, among other things, detailed panoramic air photographs of the south coast of England. These were likely part of the compendium *Informationsheft Grossbritannien*, produced by the Reich Security Agency in early 1940 to support Operation Sea Lion. The document, examined by the British after the war, was a rich trove of quite accurate intelligence about airfields, harbours, docks, warehouses, and oil tanks – a pinpoint guide for Luftwaffe bombers. The compendium also provided a detailed breakdown of the hierarchy of the British Secret Intelligence Service. In addition, Langbein reviewed a series of reports on repairs at the U.S. Naval Base of Newport News, obviously from Hartmann, and anti-torpedo defence measures on Allied ships. This tantalizing peek at Abwehr intelligence was by now somewhat academic for British intelligence, as four years had since passed and the June 1944 Normandy invasion was now history. Langbein also told how one of his Abwehr superiors was intent on gathering information about Hawaii, especially where aircraft could land at Honolulu and the beach at Waikiki. This nugget, which might have been vital in 1940, was now little more than a historical footnote.

Langbein's leisured sojourn in Bremen came to an end with another espionage mission for the Abwehr. He was now assigned to a Belgian fishing vessel sailing out of Blankenberge. The crew was to fish along the English Channel, as far north as Yarmouth, while Langbein would transmit by shortwave the positions of Allied vessels and aircraft flying overhead, as well as weather reports. He travelled to Antwerp to pick up his radio and to carry out some advanced training, then to Blankenberge to set up the equipment and aerial on the ship. The vessel was later moved to the Dutch harbour of Flushing (now Vlissingen), where Langbein lived ashore for a few days. One night there was an air raid and the boat sank – the only one in the harbour to meet that fate. The hull was raised and a hole was discovered below the water-line, indisputable evidence of sabotage. Suspicion soon fell on Langbein, but he managed to produce an alibi. Operation Yarmouth was cancelled.

Bensmann, the Bremen Abwehr recruiter, now had another more mercenary job in mind. Bensmann owned some refinery patent rights and was owed U.S.-dollar royalties by some Romanian oil companies. He planned to work from an office in Bucharest to find some way around Romanian currency restrictions, enriching himself while also earning some valuable foreign exchange for the Abwehr. Langbein was to help with Bensmann's business negotiations, but once in Bucharest was also asked by Korvetten-Kapitan Werner von Wettstein, the local Abwehr official, to act as a radio operator. He rigged up some aerials in his apartment and quickly established contact with Bremen, letting his neighbours know only that he was an amateur radio enthusiast. Von Wettstein's coded messages were primarily intelligence on movements of the Soviet Black Sea fleet, based on Abwehr agent reports from Constanta in Romania and Odessa in the Crimea. Langbein, however, grew deeply unhappy with his assignment. He often vocally disagreed with his boss, and in May 1941 concocted an excuse to return home. There he learned that von Wettstein had formally complained to Bremen officials about his 'sour face, general discontent and unmilitary bearing.' He was reprimanded severely and told he would not return to Bucharest. Thus ended Abwehr assignment no. 3.

For the next few months Langbein was stuck doing clerical work for the Bremen sub-post, but again got a keyhole peek at the breadth – and poverty – of Abwehr intelligence. 'In the course of my work at Nest.

Bremen I handled a good deal of information all concerning naval and merchant marine matters which the Abwehr had obtained from various sources,' Mills and Bayfield were told. 'When we passed information which came from agents to Berlin and received no comment on it it was assumed that it was good information, but there were a great many occasions on which Berlin commented that the information was bad. In fact most of the information which we obtained from or about England was bad.' Germany's intelligence analysts, Langbein's interrogation made clear, were not always readily duped by the vaunted British double-cross system.

In January 1942, Langbein was summoned from a visit to his home back to Bremen for instructions on his fourth Abwehr mission. His Bucharest nemesis, von Wettstein, had reminded Bremen officials about Langbein's background in Canada. For reasons that remain unclear, von Wettstein had a special personal interest in penetrating Canada and he and Langbein had sometimes discussed the possibilities. 'He told me that Canada was a country in which he was very interested on behalf of the Abwehr and even as far back as 1940 he had searched the Abwehr personal files,' Langbein recalled, 'and had even sent circulars to the offices of the Abwehr in an effort to obtain the names of men who had the necessary qualifications for going to Canada as agents.' Von Wettstein, it seems, had even contemplated going to Canada himself as an agent. In Bremen, Langbein was now closely questioned about his knowledge of the country, especially Montreal's harbour and the depth of the St Lawrence River. Abwehr officials, he learned, had already requisitioned a submarine to take an agent to Canada.

'It had for some time past been my hope that one day I should be able to return to Canada with my wife and family,' said Langbein, 'because neither my wife nor I, nor her parents nor mine, were in sympathy with the fact that my children would be forced from the age of six years upwards to wear the uniforms of the Hitler Jugend and the Hitler Maedchen.' Langbein now saw an opportunity to realize his personal plan, 'not in spite of the war but in fact because of it.' He readily agreed to accept any such mission to Canada, not, as he confided to his wife later, to spy but to hide out until after the war, when he could send for the family. Langbein assumed he could get work in Canada and would save the money that the Abwehr provided for the mission. With these savings, he would finance the trip across the Atlantic for his wife and children. Langbein told Bensmann, the Abwehr recruiter who set up the assignment, only that he wished to stay in Canada after the war and the completion of his mission. 'BENSMANN, on the assumption that Germany would win the war, had suggested that I should remain in Canada after the war and work as an undercover agent of the Abwehr there.' Langbein was still uneasy about the logistics of his family rejoining him at the end of the war. They finally agreed that Langbein's wife – an expert poultry breeder – would emigrate to Canada after the hostilities as a widow with children and they would marry again. This did not completely satisfy Langbein, since he had no intention of carrying out the work and the Abwehr might block her exit. There was also the remote possibility Germany might lose the war.

Langbein now began a refresher course under his radio tutor, Otto. Taking a break from his studies in February 1942, Langbein was sitting in a Bremen restaurant when he recognized a fellow radio student sitting at another table. They took in a movie together at which a newsreel showed a picture of a German submarine. 'This man asked me how I would like to make a trip like that and I said that I did not care for the idea very much but I was not sure that perhaps such a thing was not in store for me,' Langbein recalled. Later, over beer, the man mentioned he was slated to go to Canada by U-boat. Langbein did not know his name, but said he was about forty and was believed to be a former merchant who had owned his own business in Canada or the United States before the war. Langbein later learned that the man was to be sent to Canada after the U-boat captain reported Langbein's own safe arrival. 'I believe this man is now in Canada and that if he is he will do everything he can to harm Canada as he is a member of the Nazi party of old standing,' Langbein warned his captors.

Bensmann and Langbein travelled to Berlin for final instructions from Hermann Menzel, the top Abwehr official mentioned in the note Langbein handed in at No. 8 Temporary Building in Ottawa. At their meeting, Menzel asked whether Langbein had worn his moustache when living in Canada. He had, and Menzel ordered that it be shaved off. Once in Canada, his hair was to be cut as soon as possible to eliminate the distinctive German style. On landing, all the equipment and most of the funds were to be buried. Langbein was to find out what was topical in the area, such as the latest movie, so that he could carry on an innocuous conversation. He was to go to a church service on Sunday to get his ear accustomed to English by listening to the sermon. 'MENZEL then told me that he knew about my earlier activities with the Abwehr and although he was not unpleasant or vindictive he made it quite clear to me that I was being given another chance and that my previous three missions had been failures.' Such a warning could only have been effective against an agent whose loyalty was assumed, or against someone whose family remained under German jurisdiction.

Menzel preferred that the landing take place either on Cape Breton Island or somewhere along the North American coast between New York City and the top of the Bay of Fundy. Langbein ruled out any U.S. locale because he lacked knowledge of that country, so it was left to him to work out the final point with the submarine commander. Once the radio and other equipment was buried, Langbein was to establish himself in either Halifax – the preferred location – or Montreal, and about three months later to begin transmitting information about shipping, both merchant and naval. Abwehr receiving stations in Hamburg, Bremen, and Berlin would listen for him at the same time each night for one year, beginning on 1 September. 'MENZEL told me that if I ran into trouble of any kind ... I should write with secret ink which I should be given before departure to one or other of certain mail drops which I should also be given before departure.'

The questionnaire Langbein was made to memorize dealt almost exclusively with naval and merchant-ship matters. Of particular interest was pinning down the assembly point for North Atlantic convoys. 'We knew at that time that convoys assembled in the Gulf of St. Lawrence in the general area east, northeast and southeast of Anticosti Island, but we wanted the information in much greater detail,' Langbein said. The twelve questions also focused on coastal defence, convoy routes, Allied anti-submarine devices, changes in coastal light positions, and so on. 'In general, MENZEL made it clear to me that so far as obtaining information was concerned he wanted me to concentrate exclusively on the questions which he had given me.'

Menzel ordered some blank, forged National Registration Certificates brought into his office, and Langbein was asked what cover name he wanted to use. He decided to retain his own first name. For a surname he chose Haskins, after a man he had met while building the CNR line to Flin Flon. A few minutes later a clerk returned with one of the cards filled out, misspelling Toronto's Yonge Street as 'Younge St.,' and Langbein signed it without noticing the error. They agreed the mission would be dubbed Operation Grete, after the first name of Langbein's wife. Langbein declined lessons from Bensmann in Freemasonry, which were thought to be useful if he ever got in a jam, since he could then appeal to fellow Freemasons.

Langbein was now given elaborate instructions in secret writing, using a chemical Menzel claimed was newly developed and that Langbein would be one of the first to use. In fact, the substance was quinine – the same as that contained in Janowski's matchheads. Menzel produced a bottle labelled I.G. Farben, the notorious German chemical cartel, containing fifty quinine tablets. These were transferred to a Bayer Company of New York bottle, one of Farben's North American subsidiaries. Langbein was to dissolve the tablets in water and, using a matchstick or other similar instrument, was to write his secret message on white letter paper that was neither too glossy nor too absorbent. The secret writing was to be applied in block letters first, horizontally across the page in lines, vertically down the columns. A plate of glass was to provide support. The visible text was then written on the empty lines so that both texts were parallel but not overlapping. (Temporary pencil marks were to denote the vacant lines.) The entire sheet was also to be given a wash in a solution of soda dissolved in alcohol, then carefully dried and rubbed according to a set procedure. The visible texts were to be in English, addressed to Emelia, Emily, or Sir depending on the mail drop, and signed Mac or a last name beginning with Mac. He then diligently memorized the Abwehr mail drops – one in Lisbon, Portugal, the other in Davos-Platz, Switzerland – for he hoped to use them to communicate with his family.

Langbein now negotiated a financial package for his wife should he be killed on this mission, whether from an Allied depth charge rupturing the U-boat hull or by swinging at the end of a Canadian noose. The package included an Abwehr-paid life-insurance policy, a posthumous promotion to captain with its higher salary, all accumulated pay in addition to a military pension, and the standard military allowance given to families of serving captains. Through an oversight, Langbein was not asked to sign a standard Abwehr contract; in fact, he had never been required to swear allegiance to Hitler as were all members of the German armed forces. The meeting broke up and Langbein returned with Bensmann to Bremen, then to Hamburg to pick up his Afu radio and the novel that was to form the raw material for his substitution code. This was a paper-covered Methuen 'Sixpennies' edition of Jack London's *South Sea Tales*.

The substitution code and transmission procedures were similar to those of Janowski, though far less sophisticated. Langbein was restricted to one transmission a day, and his emergency code – to be used in the event he lost his *South Sea Tales*, for instance – was based on the name of his former employer, Manufacturers' Life Insurance Company, and on a fragment of doggerel:

Oh there was an old man by the name of Dirty Bill
Who lived way up on a garbage hill
He never had a wash and he never will.

Numbers were assigned in a sequence to the alphabet as it occurred in the company name and the doggerel. The numbers were then grouped in fives and transmitted. Langbein's 'fist' was already well known to Otto and other radio experts in Bremen and Hamburg who would be receiving his messages. He was also provided with a signal with which he could warn the Abwehr if he was being operated under Allied control. 'If I fell into the hands of the enemy and was made to operate my set for enemy benefit as, for instance by sending over fictitious information I was to begin my ham-chat with the group QSU? and then immediately say SR (meaning sorry) and then give the correct group QSA? The Morse group for A is . – and that representing U is . . – and it was therefore thought that I could quite easily make this mistake without arousing suspicion with people who would be monitoring my transmissions.' This tip-off could also be used at any point in a transmission, Langbein was told.

Langbein told his parents about the Canadian mission and the fact that he did not intend to carry it out. His father 'agreed that it was probably a better job than going to the Russian front with the Army and rotting there.' Langbein said his goodbyes to his wife and family, then went to

155

Paris on 20 April to await details about his U-boat embarkation. He travelled by train to the submarine pens at Lorient, examining the wad of money provided by the Abwehr. There were 140 American $50 bills, all used, for a total of $7000 U.S. He was also given about a dozen Canadian $1 bills. 'These Canadian bills were the old issue and we did not know at that time that new money had been issued in Canada,' he told his captors. 'The Canadian $1 bills were larger in size than those now in use.'

Langbein now reported to his submarine, *U-213*, commanded by Ahmelung von Vahrendorff. The 517-tonne Type VII boat, normally stationed at Brest, had been newly built that year and was among the first to be fitted with shafts for laying mines while submerged. The voyage to Canada was to be its third war cruise, though because some dockside loading apparatus had malfunctioned it would not carry mines on this trip. The captain had been the second watch officer aboard *U-47* under Gunther Prien, who on 14 October 1939 boldly attacked and sank the British battleship *Royal Oak* at its Orkney base in Scapa Flow. This legendary German victory was commemorated in the nickname of *U-213*, Stier von Scapa Flow. Its newest passenger was introduced to the crew as a naval lieutenant attached to the Ministry of Propaganda and People's Enlightenment, though all the officers knew the truth. Langbein loaded his radio set and other gear, traded his Paris-made naval lieutenant's uniform for a submariner's standard leather outfit, then spent the night ashore in a hotel. At 4 p.m. the next day, 25 April, Langbein embarked. Von Vahrendorff and he toasted the success of the mission with drinks below, then Langbein stood at attention with three others in the conning tower, the crew on the aft deck, as the commanding officer of Lorient gave *U-213* an official send-off. The diesel engines were started at 6:45 p.m. and the boat pulled away from the pier, bound for Canada.

For the next few hours, Langbein was assigned a life-jacket and breathing apparatus and shown how to use them. Instructions were also given in exiting the boat from the control room in an emergency and in operating the toilet, which became quite foul when the boat was submerged for any period. Langbein was also ordered to report to the officers' mess as his alarm station in case of a depth-charge attack. The submarine soon submerged for the perilous trip south-west across the Bay of Biscay, surfacing again just west of Cape Finisterre on the north-west corner of Spain. Shortly thereafter, *U-213* came under Allied attack and was forced to submerge. Almost everyone, including Langbein in the control room, scrambled to the forward torpedo room to help weigh down the bow in a crash dive. As they descended, between seven and ten depth charges exploded around the hull, rocking the boat and making the steel walls tremble and the lights flicker.

Langbein then gave an insider's account of the heart-thumping terror of an underwater attack on a frail hull. 'The man standing forward of the control room began to cry. Another man just inside the torpedo room was pounding his head against a chain. Several others lost control of their nerves. The W[ireless]. T[ransmitter]. man sobbed quite loudly. [Leutnant] KUELTZ [second watch officer] was rather vicious in trying to bring these men back to their senses. Von VAHRENDORFF was sitting in his bunk. At the time I could not see him, but after the attack was over I went into his screened-off room and saw that his automatic was on his desk. After I got to know him well enough, he told me that he would rather shoot himself than go through the agony of slowly dying in a damaged or sunk submarine.' *U-213* managed to escape unscathed, and surfaced the next morning to continue west past the Azores.

Langbein reported that the submarine was well provisioned and appeared to be in excellent shape for the voyage. The food was fresh and abundant, except for the bread, which rotted during the trip. Morale, though, was shaky – beginning with the captain. Von Vahrendorff, who had kidney problems and suffered from rheumatism, was clearly homesick and lonely for his wife. Although his service under Gunther Prien had helped boost his own naval career, von Vahrendorff belittled his former commander at Scapa Flow and detested the propaganda that had arisen from the incident. He disliked Nazism, partly because he was a devout churchgoer with deep religious convictions, and he sometimes sank into depression. 'He was extremely nervous and in moments of tension his skin would tighten over his cheekbones and the pupils of his eyes expand and contract rapidly,' Langbein recalled. 'I had never seen anything like it.'

Kueltz was a strict disciplinarian and would not allow the crew – mostly Baltic and North Sea fishermen – to display personal items outside their bunks. The radio-man blithely ignored the order and placed a picture of his mother in his work area. After a first warning was dismissed, Kueltz threw the picture to the floor and a shouting match erupted. Von Vahrendorff gave the man a severe dressing down and promised a military tribunal on return to France. The crew backed the radio-man and mounted a sullen work-to-rule campaign, carrying out orders slowly and belligerently. One of them wilfully drained all the fluid from an instrument. When the perpetrator would not come forward, von Vahrendorff cut off the ten-minute smoking privilege each crew member was entitled to in the conning tower when the boat cruised on the surface. Another officer – already moody – received a coded radio message about the birth of his son, which soon depressed him severely.

The weather was dismal. 'Continuous heavy seas are costing a lot of fuel, an inconvenience which must, however, be put up with in view of the task,' von Vahrendorff noted in his war diary on 3 May. Somewhere in the mid-Atlantic they sighted a convoy and submerged for attack. Several times, the ping of the Asdic sub-detection sonar devices could be heard inside the hull, but the convoy was soon lost to them after several course changes. A fellow U-boat returning to base was later encountered in North American coastal waters. Langbein spent most of his time writing, befitting his purported role of propaganda specialist. The Abwehr had suggested a possible landing on Cape Breton Island, but Langbein now ruled this out as it would have meant finding some means of making a further sea-crossing of the Canso Strait to the Nova Scotia mainland. After he and von Vahrendorff closely examined the chart – a British Admiralty issue as the Germans had not yet developed their own for these waters – they agreed on the jagged New Brunswick shore near St Martins. The chart showed a shore road a few miles inland and a rail line running north from St Martins into Sussex. As they nudged closer to the North American coast, a Halifax radio beam and coastal lights helped with their navigation.

'I intend to put into Fundy Bay to-night for the execution of the task, as I have to reckon with the deterioration in the weather and the prevailing currents make navigation too difficult in a fog,' von Vahrendorff typed in the 12 May entry of his war diary. 'Execution of task makes heavy demands on fuel ... Intend to run in by night, to lie on the bottom by day, then carry out the disembarkation by night and, with a view to the possibility of bagging a steamer off Saint John, to put out to sea again.' Von Vahrendorff used the loudspeakers to alert the crew to the imminent penetration of enemy waters, and on the night of 12 May they cruised silently into the Bay of Fundy. The boat passed along the main channel between New Brunswick's Grand Manan Island, on the port, and Nova Scotia's Long Island to starboard. 'All lights as in peacetime,' the commander observed. 'A few small coastal vessels, all carrying navigation lights. Visibility is getting still worse ... Off Saint John, a powerful searchlight sweeps the sea in an erratic fashion. According to expectations there were no signs of any patrols. Searchlight makes several sweeps in our direction, but that may be pure coincidence.' *U-213* was nudged to a point about two miles from the St Martins Light, and at about 6:30 a.m. local time the boat submerged and lay on the bottom at fifty metres to await the next nightfall. The powerful Fundy currents swept alongside the hull, turning the boat as it lay in wait.

Von Vahrendorff ordered the ship to periscope depth at mid-day, but the weather was so bad that visibility was nil. At 10:30 p.m. the boat surfaced and the diesels were started to recharge the batteries. The crew prepared a rubber boat in the forward torpedo room, then used the submarine's compressor to inflate it. Langbein, meanwhile, doffed his submariner uniform and put on civvies, a somewhat tattered brown suit, trench coat, grey felt hat, shoes, a shirt, and underwear. All had been made in the United States and were used, having been acquired by the Abwehr from Germans returning from America. Langbein turned over his military identification tag; in return, he was given an infantry shovel, a blanket, the radio equipment, the wad of money, and his National Registration Certificate. Langbein now noticed the misspelling of 'Younge St.,' but decided not to mention it. For a keepsake, he also gave von Vahrendorff the German army pistol he had been given in 1940 for Operation Lena. And he asked that some letters written during the voyage be posted to his family.

Kueltz, the second watch officer, and two seamen now climbed aboard the rubber boat and cast off with Langbein at twenty minutes past midnight, on 14 May. The faint clanging of a bouy was heard on the right, at the mouth of the Big Salmon River, and the shoreline that eventually hove into view was jagged and steep. High above, the rushing wind whistled through the tree branches. They pulled in a north-easterly direction, peering along the water's edge for a friendlier landing spot. Kueltz settled on a patch of boulder-strewn beach at the base of a

250-foot-high wooded gully that led to the cliff heights. The site was about one and a quarter miles south-west of the mouth of the Big Salmon River. With some difficulty, they beached the boat. One seaman remained behind while the other carried the radio and Kueltz blazed a trail up the steep gully. For an hour they stumbled ahead, losing the blanket at one point, dragging the radio with a rope, until they reached a patch of level ground. Here the sailors bid their farewells and Langbein was left to fend for himself in Canada, his new home.

Von Vahrendorff began to grow uneasy when the inflatable and crew still had not returned after one hour. Visibility was poor and a westward current pressed steadily against the hull, the main motor holding the submarine steady. After two hours and forty minutes, a prearranged light signal was given, but still no inflatable. Finally, four hours and ten minutes after setting out, Kueltz and his crew reappeared from the gloom and were quickly brought aboard. *U-213* now headed southwest along the coastline until it was opposite Saint John at daybreak, then submerged and lay safely on the bottom. The next night, von Vahrendorff surfaced again and sent a coded radio message to U-boat command: 'Have carried out task.' The run home was hampered by thick fog and no Allied merchant shipping was attacked. Two months later, on 21 July 1942, the boat was destroyed with all hands after an Allied attack near the Azores while on its next North Atlantic voyage.

Langbein pushed the suitcase containing the radio set ahead of him a few yards in the dark, then dug a shallow hole with the trenching tool, put the suitcase in and covered it with loose dirt. He did not mark the spot and did not bury the money, contrary to instructions. He tossed the shovel down the gulley, then curled up under a spreading tree and slept without a blanket. At dawn – Langbein thought it was between 7 a.m. and 8 a.m., though he did not have a watch – he began walking inland across some boggy bush until he came upon an abandoned logging road surrounded by tree stumps. This led to the gravel shore road, and he headed left towards St Martins. Two and a half hours later, he arrived on the outskirts of town, where he met a black youth who appeared to be a farmer's son. He asked the lad where the train station was, but got only a puzzled look. Langbein continued and entered the first establishment he saw, McLeod's store. He bought a new hat, leaving his old one with the salesgirl to discard, some cigarettes, soap, and other toiletries. He tendered some of the oversized Canadian dollar bills and the salesgirl accepted them without comment. He also learned that, despite the chart, there was no rail line into the village. That explained the black youth's puzzlement.

Carrying on down the road towards Saint John, Langbein was stopped by a man looking for a light. The pair sat by the side of the road, and Langbein mentioned he had been looking for work as a cook at one of the lumber camps near the Salmon River but was now headed towards Saint John. The man advised trying to hitch a ride on one of the frequent logging trucks. Langbein walked on, now turning north on the road towards Sussex, when another man in a lumber truck offered him a lift. The fellow was delivering supplies to a bridge repair crew nearby, but was headed back to Saint John afterward, so Langbein tagged along for the return journey. Langbein said he had slept in the bush and caught cold, which explained his dirty trench coat and helped to discourage excessive conversation, since he pretended to be able only to whisper. It was a ruse he would keep up for four or five days.

Once in Saint John, at about 1 p.m., Langbein checked in to the Lord Chamberlain Hotel across from the train station and visited a barbershop to rid himself of his distinctive German haircut, as Menzel had advised. While there, he donated some change to two women canvassing for the Red Cross. Their receipt, made out to Alfred Haskins of Edmonton, Alberta, added to his precious store of Canadian identification. The next stop was a second-hand clothing shop, where he purchased a cheap black suitcase, a cheap wristwatch, underwear, shirt, pullover, handkerchief, and socks – all paid for with a $50 U.S. bill. He split the 10 per cent exchange premium with the shop-owner, a Jew as Langbein was careful to note. Early the next morning, he bought a train ticket to Montreal via Moncton, and arrived the following morning to settle down to a quiet new life in Canada.

Langbein went straight to St Catherine Street West where, he knew from his former visit, there were inexpensive rooms. He found one for $1 a day at No. 156. For the next month, he saw movies, bought books, ate in various restaurants, and patronized many expensive shops. Langbein's penchant for classy clothes and other high-end goods stemmed solely from his need to cash $50 U.S. bills regularly. He had done this at local banks for a time, but got spooked when a teller asked him for some identification. He produced his Red Cross donation receipt from Saint John, which was accepted, but decided never again to take the same risk. During his stay in Montreal, Langbein learned with dismay that it was impossible to get work without Canadian selective-service papers, so he abandoned his plan to look for work in the mines of Quebec and northern Ontario.

On 18 June Langbein visited a shop to buy two pipes for $10 and tendered a $50 U.S. bill. The clerk was unable to make change, and a young man who was buying cigarettes in the store offered to take Langbein to a place where he could exchange the bill. 'He looked and acted like a pimp,' Langbein recalled. 'He was.' He led him along a side street off St Catherine Street East, to a bawdy house where the madam fetched him $50 in small Canadian bills, keeping the exchange premium for herself. She offered him a beer and as he was quaffing, the city police raided the house and arrested about twenty people, including Langbein. He spent most of the night at the central police station, until the desk sergeant advised him that he could go home only if he posted $50 bail and promised to appear in court the following morning at 10 a.m. Langbein turned over his newly acquired Canadian money and left. He immediately packed his bags and caught the 8:20 a.m. train to Ottawa. Harvison, who played no part in the Langbein case, gave a brief account of this episode in his memoirs. His version had Langbein cleverly claiming to be a married man who was desperate to keep the arrest from his wife, and had the knowing desk sergeant proposing a way out of the dilemma with a wink and a nod. These were clearly Harvison's inventions, having no support whatsoever in the Langbein file. Langbein's French-Canadian landlords were the beneficiaries of the belongings he was forced to leave behind in Montreal, among them a Hudson's Bay blanket and the U.S.-made brown suit brought over from Germany.

The train pulled into Ottawa at 11:35 a.m., and Langbein had the cab driver take him to an inexpensive, clean hotel – which turned out to be the Grand Hotel on Sussex Street, his new home for the next fourteen months. He initially took room No. 5 at $2.50 a day, but later switched to cheaper rooms. 'I worried considerably over the position I was in and, to put it quite bluntly, was very scared and the night after I arrived in Ottawa, I seriously considered surrendering myself to the R.C.M.Police or any other suitable authority and spent considerable time consulting the phone book to decide the most suitable authority to approach,' Langbein told Mills and Bayfield. 'However, I thought the matter over very carefully and after a day or two decided against taking such action as I wanted to retain my freedom.' From an Allied intelligence standpoint, this was an unfortunate decision, as Langbein's information became more stale and useless with every passing week. For the next six months, he left each morning at 9 a.m. and returned at 5 p.m. to create the impression of a full-time job. In fact, he went to movies, attended sporting events, bought and read books on political economy, and walked endlessly around town. Langbein also bought a ping-pong table and installed it in his room, where he had frequent matches with an RCAF flight lieutenant who was a neighbour.

This routine wore on Langbein, and his health slipped, so he sold the ping-pong table and let everyone believe he was now unable to work. He stayed all day in his room reading, rousing himself now and then for a meal. By the spring of 1943, he had made friends with several of the Grand Hotel staff. Often the cook and others would join him for a game of cards in his room. Langbein now started to go out occasionally with these people. While out on the town with the hotel owner's sister-in-law and her soldier friend, Langbein got a scare that shook him badly. The soldier had acted oddly and Langbein later asked the sister-in-law why. 'She stated that he had told her that he thought I was a spy and he was going to have me arrested,' Langbein reported. 'Without saying very much I convinced her that such a thought was ridiculous.' He now sought anonymity again, this time by moving to the French-Canadian quarter in Lower Town. He took up residence at the Renaud home on 19 August 1943.

Langbein again adopted a reclusive lifestyle, buying expensive clothing and going out to movies. By the spring of 1944 he was lonely for companionship and started seeing his friends at the Grand Hotel again. On a Sunday in late April, he joined some of these acquaintances for a 'picnic' near Buckingham, Quebec, though there was still snow on the ground. Tired of wearing his money belt, and certain that he would return in the summer to the spot, Langbein stuffed $2000 U.S. into a pop bottle and buried the money in the snow at the base of a rock. That August, lonely for female companionship, he got a girlfriend – Eva Rose – and began spending lots of cash on her entertainment. By September he found it necessary to replenish his funds and twice took a bus back to Buckingham, but on each occasion could not locate the damn pop bottle.

Langbein told his captors that his decision to surrender had everything to do with his conscience, not his depleted funds. 'I took the view that no one man's ideas or any philosophy of government had the right to inflict suffering and punishment as had been done on occupied countries or on Germany itself.' He claimed that after the Normandy invasion, the vicious policies of the Nazis in occupied Europe became clear. For good measure, Langbein added ten more specific reasons for his decision, such as 'the indiscriminate use of V-1 and V-2 weapons against Britain and my personal fear of retaliation in kind.' In his condemnation of Nazism and such Reich ministers as Himmler and Goebbels, Langbein oddly did not once mention Hitler. He was adamant that he had never intended to carry out his mission and did not attempt to communicate with the Abwehr in any way. After Mills and Bayfield finished their interrogation on 22 November, Langbein was turned over to Samuel, the Naval Intelligence officer, on the 28th. Like Janowski, Langbein was an intelligence disappointment as he had virtually no naval background and only a layman's understanding of the interior of a U-boat. He was packed off to an internment camp near Fredericton to wait out the remainder of the war.

Viewed against the recruitment, training, and modest Abwehr career of Langbein, Janowski's mission to Canada takes on a much larger significance. Bobbi was clearly the third or fourth such U-boat agent dispatched to Canada in 1942, at the height of Doenitz's Operation Drumbeat against the North American coast. Langbein, likely the first, was a wash-out from the moment he set foot on the wave-battered boulders of New Brunswick's Fundy shore. During his interrogation, he alerted the RCMP to another agent he had trained beside in Bremen who was to be dispatched shortly by submarine to the Canadian coast. This man, Langbein warned, was a devout Nazi who would diligently carry out his espionage mission. Janowski had also tipped the RCMP to an Abwehr agent, supplied with plenty of Canadian currency, who was landed in the spring of 1942 by U-boat. From conversations with Abwehr officials, Janowski gathered that the man sent just one letter back to a mail-drop address before inexplicably falling silent. It is possible Langbein and Janowski were referring to the same person, although Janowski indicated that the man he had heard about was a saboteur, while Langbein's associate was from Abteilung I, an espionage agent. Von Wettstein had told Langbein that the Abwehr was searching for suitable agents for Canada as far back as 1940 because the penetration of the country was a priority. Yet when action was finally taken in 1942, two or three agents had been swallowed up forever. Abwehr officials clearly did not want the same to happen to Janowski.

Langbein had a poor work record in the Third Reich. He flatly refused to accept a role in Operation Lena, in which the Abwehr desperately scrambled to carry out Hitler's orders for a pre-invasion drop of agents into Britain. Operation Yarmouth was abandoned when his fishing-boat base was sabotaged and suspicions fell on him. Langbein butted heads with his boss in Bucharest and was recalled to Bremen for insubordination. His mission to Canada, Operation Grete, was assigned on the strength of his English-language ability and knowledge of the country rather than his anemic track record. Janowski, at least on the face of it, was an agent of a far higher order. He had worked diligently for the Nazis in the early 1920s and remained personally loyal to the Fuehrer throughout his life. He enlisted as a simple soldier even before the war, in contrast to Langbein, who joined the Abwehr in 1940 only to escape regular military service. Although Janowski's service in the French Foreign Legion was a blemish, at least the experience was turned to his advantage when he carried out successful Abwehr II sabotage missions in Morocco. Janowski also led several pre-invasion undercover operations in Belgium and Holland, each efficiently concluded. And he was a member of one of the Abwehr's most effective counter-espionage campaigns, in northern France and Belgium. Over several years, Janowski had proved himself skilful, enthusiastic, and loyal. Clearly, the Abwehr had chosen its latest agent to Canada with much greater care than it had its first, Langbein. Admiral Wilhelm Canaris himself had personally bid Janowski good hunting in North America.

Janowski was also better prepared. Unlike Langbein, he was instructed to wear a naval uniform on landing in case he was captured, thus enabling him to claim rights as a prisoner of war. Langbein had two mail-drop addresses; Janowski was given three. Langbein had just one paperback novel for his radio substitution code; Janowski had two. Janowski's secret-writing matchheads were more sophisticated and convenient than Langbein's bottle of quinine tablets and do-it-yourself instructions. Even their questionnaires were distinctive: Langbein's focused solely on shipping, while Janowski was to supply a wide range of intelligence, from rocket-powered planes to Jews in government. Langbein was confined to intelligence-gathering; Janowski's supervisory and sabotage background was harnessed for an operation to prepare the way for other Abwehr II agents. Langbein, who had only Abwehr-supplied radio training, was assigned one transmission time each day; Janowski, a radio expert for twelve years, began with two. Langbein was to use secret writing only as an emergency backup; for Janowski, the letters were to be a more integral part of his mission. Both were unwittingly supplied with oversized Canadian bills, which only Langbein managed to spend without raising suspicions. But Janowski was supplied with a broader range of money, from Canadian and American currency to gold coins, while Langbein was forever trying to change his $50 U.S. bills. Whatever Janowski's personal shortcomings, some of which are reviewed in the next chapter, his service record, training, and background made him a credible candidate for a mission designed finally to give the Abwehr a foothold in Canada.

EIGHT

Autopsy

Janowski was the first and only Abwehr spy captured in Canada while on a wartime mission from Germany. For years, the RCMP and other police forces had warned Canadians to be alert against Nazi espionage agents, especially on the East Coast where U-boats could silently approach isolated coves and inlets under the cloak of night. In the tiny Gaspé community of New Carlisle, the public-education campaigns had paid off handsomely: civilians, with the help of the local police, trapped a spy less than twelve hours after he set foot on Canadian soil. The initial police work may have been shaky, but the Annett family behaved admirably and with bravery. Janowski was armed with a pistol and had little hesitation about pulling the trigger, as his missions in Holland and Belgium had shown. Young Earle, unarmed and slightly lame, took calculated risks in tailing the mysterious visitor to extract incriminating information. Word of the dramatic capture electrified the Gaspé peninsula and north shore of New Brunswick, where fishermen, housewives, and schoolboys had often imagined spotting one of Hitler's dark emissaries. And despite the admonition about loose lips sinking ships, the gripping news trickled from neighbour to neighbour, passed among servicemen travelling the trains, and slipped along telephone lines from hamlet to big city. A dangerous U-boat spy had been caught and perhaps thousands of lives saved: this was a moment of high drama in the life of a small community. And inevitably, within hours of Janowski's capture, thoughts turned to rewards, citations, decorations, medals, and letters of commendation. Taking credit, in fact, soon became a kind of cottage industry.

Harvison had travelled to Ottawa within a month of the capture to brief Commissioner Wood on the case, and they agreed immediately that a reward should be paid to Earle Annett Sr. Although several members of the family had been involved in the capture, Harvison and Wood likely reasoned that the father would be in the best position to apportion the credit. On 19 November 1942 Wood wrote to Louis St Laurent recommending that the elder Annett be paid $500 cash. 'While admittedly this is a large amount of money, a much greater sum would have been expended in tracing and apprehending JANOWSKI had he been successful in leaving New Carlisle before Police authorities got track of him,' Wood wrote. St Laurent thought this far too generous and cut the amount to $300, asking that Wood draft two letters of thanks for his signature, one in English to Annett, the other in French to Léon Casgrain, Quebec's attorney-general, responsible for the Quebec Provincial Police. The RCMP botched the Annett letter, however, and it arrived in New Carlisle addressed to Earl Annetts of the Maison Blanche, the rival hotel down the road. On 22 December Annett wrote back to the minister pointing out the mistake. 'I would greatly appreciate having you make the alteration as your letter will in due time become a family heirloom,' he said. 'All members of my family were more or less instrumental in capturing the individual.' An embarrassed Wood had another correctly addressed letter drawn up for St Laurent's signature, and it was exchanged with Annett for the first one. In the meantime, RCMP Sergeant Chapados and QPP Constable Duchesneau turned up at Annett's hotel on 18 December to hand over an envelope containing the $300 in cash, insisting on a receipt signed in duplicate.

Annett Sr used a small portion of the money to buy the scrubby patch of coast four miles west of New Carlisle where Janowski had stepped ashore that bleak November night. He reckoned it would become a historic site when the full story became known, and though badly eroded it has remained in the Annett family to this day. No plaque or monument marks the spot. Just how the rest of the reward money was spent remains a mystery. The surviving Annett sisters today say they were never told about any reward, and that no money was ever distributed among family members. Earle Jr, the person most directly responsible for the capture, apparently nursed a long-standing grievance about the whole affair, contacting St Laurent's office in mid-1944 to inquire about some recognition. He was politely brushed off. 'He is not a Policeman and therefore could not be recommended for the Police Medal ... and, at the present time, you know the Government's policy is that they are not disposed to recommend any further honors for civilians until the close of the present war,' Wood wrote to the minister's office.

Duchesneau, the officer made to witness the payment of all that cash to Annett Sr, also felt slighted. St Laurent's letter to Casgrain, a fellow Quebec Liberal, referred in general terms to the excellent cooperation in the case between the provincial police and RCMP, but failed to mentioned Duchesneau by name. James Ralston, the minister of national defence, had telephoned Lieutenant-Colonel Léon Lambert, the assistant director of the Quebec Provincial Police, to ask that Lambert convey his personal thanks to Duchesneau. Lambert also recommended a promotion for the constable, and received RCMP assurances that Duchesneau would be considered for a special commendation. The Mounties may have dragged their feet on the matter, recalling that Duchesneau had lost vital evidence, allowed Janowski to put on his naval uniform, and been initially lax about security. When no medal was forthcoming by the end of December 1942, noses quickly got out of joint. 'Do you not believe that he should, as well as ANNETT, receive a part of the $6,000.00 seized from this German and that we have given you back?' Lambert argued testily in a 30 December letter to RCMP Superintendent Gagnon in Montreal. Then, as many were to do in the years following, Lambert greatly exaggerated the role of his own man. 'After all DUCHESNEAU is surely the only one responsible for the arrest of the spy, since ANNETT only gave the description of a person which he believed to be a passer of counterfeit money.'

Gagnon, however, simply ignored the letter, assuming that the question of a reward had been settled by headquarters. Six months later, Lambert sent another letter impatiently asking about the matter – and when there was still no response, he spoke about it obliquely in public. In July 1943, he told a meeting of police and fire chiefs that his men were responsible for the arrest of more than one German spy. The press report about the speech, as shown earlier, contributed to the decision to shut down Watchdog. On 30 October, almost one year after the capture, the secretary of state finally approved the award of the King's Police and Fire Services Medal to Duchesneau. The announcement in the *Canada*

Gazette on Christmas Day did not refer to Janowski, but *L'Action Catholique* breached censorship when it reported that 'it is believed that Detective Duchesneau was decorated for his courage and presence of mind when arresting a German spy.' Other newspapers began pressing for permission to publish the full story, but censorship authorities managed to douse the fire.

The matter did not end there. The RCMP had turned the medal over to the office of Quebec's attorney-general with a reminder that the case was still considered highly secret so there should be no publicity. The message became garbled, however, and Lambert was given to understand that the medal was not to be handed over to Duchesneau until censorship on the case was lifted. The medal sat in a desk drawer in Quebec City for more than a year until a bureaucrat in the secretary of state's office noticed that no receipt from Duchesneau was on file. To everyone's embarrassment, it was discovered that the unfortunate constable had still not got his decoration more than two years after the capture. In the meantime, the Quebec Liberal government had been defeated by Maurice Duplessis's Union Nationale and the issue was soon shamelessly exploited for political gain. On 15 May 1945 Duplessis reminded the Quebec legislative assembly that 'Duchesneau had been appointed by a National Union Government, and that it had been due to his ability that the spy had been arrested,' the *Montreal Gazette* reported. 'Mr. Duplessis reproached Mr. Casgrain and ex-premier [Joseph-Adelard] Godbout for not having the good idea of making public the courageous conduct of Duchesneau, but perhaps that was because the detective had been appointed by the National Union government.' The premier then resurrected bizarre accusations that Ottawa had deliberately allowed U-boats to approach the Quebec coast during the war to ruin the Port of Quebec and promote the use of out-of-province harbours.

The RCMP were pursued by another would-be hero. A certain J.A. Beaudoin, an RCAF man stationed at Gaspé, had arrived by train in New Carlisle the very morning that young Earle Annett was tailing his German suspect. Beaudoin told his superiors that on arrival he had spoken with a taxi driver who had alerted him to the strange visitor. 'Beaudoin's suspicions were aroused; he instructed the taxi driver to board the train and report to the train patrol, a member of the shore patrol,' says the RCAF account, which was sent to the RCMP within two weeks of the capture. A Mountie investigation determined that the taxi driver worked for the Maison Blanche hotel and that Annett Jr had apparently discussed the affair with the taxi driver and Beaudoin. 'Mr. Annett appeared at a loss to know what to do, in view of the fact that the Service Police on the train had stated he was powerless to act,' a follow-up report noted. 'ACl Beaudoin further stated that it was he who suggested that Mr. Annett get in touch with the civil detective who later made the arrest.' The Mounties soon concluded that if Beaudoin's story was true, it was all talk and no action: no reward for the RCAF. The RCMP also turned aside other supposed claimants. They included the Le Riche couple, who were given $35 cash for the temporary use of their house in Montreal but no letter of commendation, as this was deemed a security risk; and P.P. Johnston, the retired banker at the Carlisle, who assured the Mounties he had been instrumental in collaring the spy. 'I personally was the only one that had an interview, of any length, with this man before his arrest,' Johnston wrote. 'My plan was to telephone your Sgt. St. Pierre, Campbellton, who knew me personally, giving, of course, full particulars ... As I considered the case an important one I had no intention of handing it over to the Provincial Police.'

With the end of the war in Europe on 9 May 1945, the press again demanded permission finally to publish their blockbuster stories about the German spy captured in New Carlisle. Commissioner Wood steadfastly insisted on continued suppression of the facts, citing a cable from British intelligence to the effect that 'the story of Watchdog's arrest and his use as a double agent should not be given publicity because of possible precedents in the United Kingdom, and because of suspicion which would be cast on other cases. They suggested that the matter be left secret for a space of three months until the German Secret Service was mopped up in Europe.' Wood noted that 'this particular man is being used as a valuable "reference library" in connection with the identification and tracing of members of the enemy's espionage organization on the continent.' But the commissioner made little headway with censorship authorities, who were sceptical about any security claims with Germany now prostrate. Chief censor R.W. Baldwin agreed to suppress the fact that Watchdog had been transferred to England, but would only request – not order – newspapers to delay publication about the arrest for a further three months. The Canadian Press wire service and several newspapers refused Baldwin's entreaty, so he ordered the arrest story to be released at 9:30 a.m. EDT on Monday, 14 May. Authorities believed the RCMP's attempt at a double-cross had not become known to the press, since none of the stories that had been submitted throughout the war contained such information, so the story was regarded as little more than a routine release.

The afternoon edition of the *Toronto Daily Star* that day broke the story in a big, splashy spread. Coverage included a first-person account by young Earle Annett along with pictures of the landing spot and many of the New Carlisle personalities connected with the arrest – including a grinning Léone Poereen, who had served Janowski his ham-and-egg breakfast. A few days later, the paper would resurrect its 1932 *Star Weekly* profile of Janowski and his new bride. The British United Press in Quebec City also released a generally accurate account, which made its way into several afternoon dailies, including the *Ottawa Evening Journal*. The *Montreal Standard* held its big story, headlined 'No medals for Werner,' for its weekend editions. Reporter Lawrence Earl had travelled to New Carlisle to gather first-hand descriptions and penned a full, reasonably accurate and entertaining narrative.

The most widely published account was that of Jack Brayley, a Canadian Press wire-service reporter based in Ottawa. Almost fifty years after the event, a senior CP executive regarded the spy story as one of the most memorable in Brayley's career, which included a long stint as CP's Halifax bureau chief and regular commentator on the CBC. Brayley's version, published in the *Ottawa Citizen*, *Montreal Star*, *Montreal Herald*, and many afternoon newspapers, in fact was garbled and fanciful. He claimed some old-style $2 Canadian bills had given the spy away, when every other report correctly indicated they were $1 bills. Without citing sources, Brayley said the spy had landed at Métis Beach, Quebec, on 6 November in a rubber dinghy – none of which was true. Brayley appeared to rely on the initial unreliable interrogations by naval officers and the Quebec Provincial Police, where other reporters had extracted more accurate versions of the arrest directly from the RCMP and other sources.

The *Montreal Star*, not to be outdone on its own turf, published a spy story on 15 May that claimed the RCMP had captured at least a dozen

German agents in Quebec. Police reporter Larry O'Brien claimed that seven of these were saboteurs or wireless agents investigated by Montreal RCMP, and six were held for periods at the St James Street headquarters. Among the Nazi spy rings smashed were one that operated from a home on Laval Avenue and another from an east-end beauty parlor. O'Brien also referred to a Toronto spy ring led by a Canadian man who had been trained by the Abwehr in Munich. O'Brien offered virtually no details on any of these supposed cases. The story was not so much journalism as the gathering up of every half-baked rumour that had floated through the *Montreal Star* newsroom during the previous five years. Harvison cited the piece as 'an excellent example of the sort of tripe that we can expect from the newspapers ... O'Brien is a cub reporter with a vivid imagination and as you will see from the article, without experience or judgment.'

The real scoop belonged to an obscure police reporter at the *Montreal Gazette*, Larry Conroy. Born in Montreal in 1907, Conroy was educated at McGill University, then embarked on a career that stretched almost four decades at three Montreal dailies, specializing in crime stories. By the outbreak of war, he was highly regarded by colleagues, having a wide range of contacts and sources inside the RCMP and municipal police force. In the paper's morning edition of 15 May, Conroy's story about the spy took a unique slant: 'Held in Montreal for months, the spy cooperated in the broadcast of his "reports" to Germany and even assisted, it is learned, in attempts to entice others [sic] espionage agents, saboteurs, and counter-espionage agents into Canada where they would fall into the Royal Canadian Mounted Police trap. The success of this plan is not yet known ... In those dark hours of the war it was another searchlight pointing the way to final victory.' Conroy had pierced to the heart of the Watchdog case. Although some details were slightly in error, he had correctly identified Canada's first double-cross operation, including information about its primary goal. The article was preceded by a testy editor's note railing against inconsistent censorship rules and claiming that much of the story had been prepared more than two years earlier.

Conroy's story hit the RCMP like an artillery shell. Group Captain H.R. Stewart, chief of air-force intelligence, called Commissioner Wood the day the article appeared to speak on behalf of his colleagues in Army and Navy Intelligence. All agreed, he told Wood, that the Mounties were to blame for this major press leak on a sensitive security matter that everyone had worked so hard to keep secret. 'The circumstances ... have placed this Force in a very embarrassing position,' Wood wrote to St Laurent, 'amounting to a breach of faith with the British Military Intelligence; has [sic] jeopardized the activities of the British Secret Service in tracing and arresting members of the German espionage and sabotage organizations on the continent and in England, and resulted in bitter criticism of this Force by other Government Departments.' The mess was turned over to Robert Forsyth, a senior counsel in the Justice Department, who was to determine whether the *Gazette* should be prosecuted. On investigation, he determined that sloppy communication between the censor and the newspaper had allowed the article to slip through, and concluded that no charges were warranted. 'The Commissioner is very jealous of the reputation of his Force and he fears that there is some suspicion that this information was communicated to the reporter by a member of the Force,' Forsyth noted in a 25 May memorandum. 'He states there is no truth whatsoever in this but he feels that the Armed Forces will not be satisfied with the evidence which he has to this effect ... It would appear that the whole matter ... simmers down to a dog-fight between the various Forces and the R.C.M.P. as to where responsibility lies for the information which has thus leaked out.'

Wood ordered Vernon Kemp, the RCMP director of criminal investigation, to travel to Montreal the day after Conroy's article appeared to determine for himself how the leak had occurred. On arrival, Kemp put Conroy, Harvison, and Southam, the radio operator, under oath. He dissected the story into its basic assertions to try to separate facts that were known generally by the press from those unique to Conroy's version. It soon became clear that the reporter, who visited the St James Street headquarters daily, was highly observant and adept at making connections between supposedly unconnected facts. The *Gazette* got calls about an unauthorized short-wave radio in the vicinity, so Conroy assumed there was a connection with the Gaspé spy. He surmised from RCMP chatter and other sources that Harvison had gone overseas, and correctly assumed he was returning the spy to England.

Kemp asked Conroy point-blank whether he had obtained any information directly from anyone inside the RCMP. 'No, but several times I would ask people what was going on – it is more negative, such as: "We cannot tell you, I am busy," ' Conroy said. 'That solidified my idea that the man was here and was being used. Even if I could not use it at the time it appeared to me that if the case was closed I might hear something, but instead of that each time I asked I was told "We cannot say anything, you will find out after the war." ' Conroy also indicated that he had gleaned some general operational details from FBI spy stories that had surfaced in the U.S. press. Harvison later testified that the mistakes in Conroy's story – for example, that a stand-in had tapped out all Janowski's messages – indicated that the reporter had used his imagination rather than an RCMP source to flesh out details. Kemp concluded that no Mountie, including Harvison, had deliberately conveyed information. Rather, Conroy was simply a shrewd reporter who had woven a generally accurate story from a few scattered threads.

The *Gazette* was also taken to task by the censors, who regarded the article as a brazen act of defiance. Their accusations prompted a feisty rebuttal from *Gazette* managing editor George Carpenter, clearly fed up after spending more than five years on a short leash. 'We work for our news here at The Gazette and do not depend upon news breaks being placed in our laps by the authorities,' he wrote to chief censor R.W. Baldwin. 'We have a police reporter who has more ability in the matter of digging into crime cases than 90 per cent of the policemen of this country ... We are known throughout the province as a paper which works for its news and dares to print it.' Carpenter then acknowledged he had defied a censor who, on 10 May, had forbidden publication of Conroy's story. 'Examining the situation as I might I could not see where security would be involved in any way, under conditions existing at that time, by publication of the story. It looked like a tendency to carry censorship into a period beyond that for which censorship was imposed ... Frankly, as much as we might like some of you lads personally, we do not want you forever on our necks.'

In Ottawa, Mountie intelligence officers drew up a master list of RCMP employees – most of them in Montreal and Ottawa – who knew the general outlines of the Watchdog case. They came up with an astonishing fifty names, a number that by itself spoke volumes about lax security. But Harvison was quick to point out that many people in armed-forces intelligence, as well as some Quebec politicians, also knew details of the operation. Superintendent Charles Rivett-Carnac, senior intelligence officer in Ottawa, also noted that the chief censor might himself have tipped the press to the double-cross angle by quietly informing key editors at the Canadian Press and other outlets about the security reasons for withholding the story.

Wood was keenly aware that Kemp's inquiry and these other arguments would never satisfy the RCMP's critics, who suspected a Mountie whitewash. So he pressed St Laurent to appoint a judicial inquiry, headed by someone independent of the Force, who would hold hearings into this unprecedented collision between state and press. The minister finally acceded to the request, and got cabinet approval on 29 May for a lesser departmental inquiry under the Inquiries Act. To head the formal investigation, St Laurent picked Forsyth, the Justice Department lawyer who had already recommended against prosecution of the *Gazette*. His task was 'to ascertain the person or persons responsible for divulging' the information about the use made of Janowski after his capture that was contained in Conroy's article. Hearings were set to begin on 5 June at the RCMP's St James Street headquarters in Montreal. Technically, the sessions were not *in camera* though the date, time, and place were never advertised, so that anyone not invited would have no opportunity to attend. Only the RCMP and the military were advised in advance of the sittings.

Just four witnesses testified in Montreal: Harvison, Conroy, *Gazette* editor Alex Morrison, and censorship official Ephram Bertrand. Kemp and Forsyth each took turns at questioning. The substance of the testimony was similar to that given during Kemp's investigation, though with much more detail. Conroy confirmed that the censors had inadvertently tipped him to the fact that British intelligence was using the spy. But he told Forsyth and Kemp that most of his story was based on inference, assumption, and surmise. Conroy had no particular 'source' for his article; rather, it was a clever and intelligent fusion of scattered observations. Towards the end of the day Cyril Mills – never formally identified, and referred to only as 'Mr. Mills' – was called upon to give evidence, but declined. 'I have had no contact with any of these people at all,' he told Forsyth. 'I just worked with Inspector Harvison on this job.'

The inquiry next moved on 8 June to Ottawa, where armed-forces intelligence was to be provided an opportunity to present their views.

Three military-intelligence officers turned up, including Group Captain H.R. Stewart and Lieutenant-Commander W. Wallace. 'It appeared to me that Group Captain Stewart and Commander Wallace were considerably exercised over this incident, to a degree which appeared to me quite unwarranted,' Kemp later reported. 'Group Captain Stewart had some remarks to pass regarding the number of Mounted Policemen in Montreal who would be aware of the fact that the spy was in custody and under control.' However, no one volunteered to testify officially and the inquiry was adjourned.

Forsyth's report issued twelve days later exonerated the RCMP and all other government departments and agencies, pinning the so-called leak directly on Conroy's educated guesses. 'I have come to the conclusion that that part of the article written by Conroy, which was not common knowledge, is merely a shrewd surmise by him,' Forsyth concluded. 'His surmise was founded upon public reports of the use sometimes made of spies and from information which came into his possession from sources outside those entrusted with the information.' Commander Eric Brand, now in command of Naval Intelligence, remained sceptical. 'Reading the [press] cuttings below alone, and knowing something of their accuracy, I cannot possibly agree with the conclusions reached by Mr Forsyth K.C.,' he scribbled in the margin of a Justice Department memorandum. Forsyth's conclusions, which closely followed those of the RCMP, were clearly no balm for the enmity between the Mounties and Canada's military-intelligence agencies. St Laurent ordered Forsyth's report to remain secret because it contained details of the double-agent operation, and so it remained for almost five decades.

The Canadian Press and other news outlets obediently refrained from pursuing or printing the double-cross elements of Conroy's story, in an agreement with the censors to withhold the information for three months following the end of the war in Europe. The Allies were to use that time to 'mop up' the German secret service without the interference of news leaks identifying whom they were using to ferret out Nazi spies and collaborators. As the three-month anniversary approached in early August, Canadian Press editors submitted another Jack Brayley story from Ottawa, this one highlighting the RCMP double-cross. Baldwin, the chief censor, alerted the Mounties but cautioned that there were no longer any legal or moral grounds to suppress the story. Still smarting from accusations about lax security, the RCMP brass were not about to be blamed for the next round of press reports. Deputy Commissioner Mead urged Baldwin to submit the matter to the Joint Intelligence Committee, with Group Captain Stewart as chairman. Baldwin declined and the story was approved for release on 9 August.

Brayley's piece was a confused mishmash of fact and fancy. He stuck to his initial claim that an oversized $2 bill, rather than a $1 bill, had served to betray Janowski. He also borrowed several erroneous elements from Conroy's story, including the assertion that an operator who had studied Janowski's 'fist' sat in for him. The prisoner was assigned the wrong age, twenty-seven instead of thirty-eight at the time of the landing. And basking in the glow of Allied victory, Brayley launched the first wave of media reports that erroneously claimed the RCMP operation had been a smashing success. 'It is reported that they were able to put under quiet watch a score of agents in Canada and the United States,' he wrote. 'By allowing these agents their apparent freedom they were able to hide the fact from German intelligence headquarters that Janowski was operating under Canadian directorship. But in cases where dangerous agents or dangerous plans were available, arrests were made.' Conroy had been careful to note in his earlier story that the success of the operation was not known, but Brayley had no such hesitation. Janowski was currently attached to the Allied Commission on War Crimes, Brayley assured, and was helping to hunt down Nazi agents who had betrayed the European resistance.

In late August, the RCMP issued its own version of events in the form of a two-page news release. The summary, prepared for the Wartime Information Board, was an accurate if bland account of Janowski's arrest. But it was mum on the double-cross except for the confirmation that the prisoner was taken to Montreal 'and used for counter-espionage purposes.' The Mounties also advised the board that 'no serious acts of sabotage had occurred in Canada which may be traced to enemy origin,' suggesting that the Watchdog case had in fact produced results. In the meantime, the *Toronto Star* did some admirable legwork in probing Janowski's past life in Canada. Reporter James Nicol tracked down some of the spy's former employers and associates, including people in and around London who had witnessed the whirlwind romance with Olive

Quance. Quance herself had gone into hiding at a friend's place in London and refused to talk with the press. Murdoch Martyn, a Toronto lawyer given the messy task of securing a divorce for Quance, would say little. 'My client's life has been almost wrecked by this man, though actually we are not prepared to admit that he is her husband.' In fact, Quance remained married to Janowski under Canadian law and Martyn would later require help from the RCMP and the Canadian embassy in Paris to launch legal action.

Watchdog was the first Canadian-run double agent, but was neither the first nor the only double-cross mounted against the German intelligence service on Canadian soil. The first, code-named Springbok, began when Abwehr agent Hans Christian von Kotze offered his services to British intelligence while posted in Rio de Janeiro. Von Kotze had arrived in Brazil on 9 June 1941 by air under the alias Hans Sievert, a representative of the Reich's Ministry of Economics and travelling on a diplomatic passport. In his mid-thirties, von Kotze was of noble ancestry, handsome, and well travelled in France, the United States, and South Africa, where he apparently had enjoyed a successful business career. Fluent in English, French, and Portuguese, he was also a notorious womanizer said to have seduced the wife of the British Security Co-ordination officer who was helping to run him.

For six months, von Kotze languished in casinos, bars, and night clubs in Rio, Sao Paulo, and Buenos Aires acting as an Abwehr courier and intelligence gatherer. He worked with Werner Waltemath, an Abwehr agent who had been his travelling companion when he first arrived in Brazil. Waltemath's primary task was to build an effective radio transmitter in Sao Paulo from parts purchased locally. In November 1941 von Kotze obtained a Brazilian passport bearing the name Johann von Huges. Using his connections and substantial supply of Abwehr money, he was issued a British visa, intending to travel to South Africa as part of his agreement with Berlin. On the advice of British intelligence, however, he persuaded the Abwehr to send him to Toronto instead to open an espionage window on Canada.

Von Kotze planned to relay his radio messages to the Abwehr via Waltemath, using a standard book cypher like that of Janowski and Langbein, based on a novel called *The Martyrdom of Man*. Waltemath received von Kotze's first secret-ink letter in February 1942, and soon others followed indicating that 'John von Huges,' as he was called, had found a job at the Toronto advertising firm of Vickers and Benson Limited. Von Kotze maintained a steady stream of correspondence with Waltemath and others in South America, at one point sending photographs of U.S. and Canadian aircraft and a government report on Canadian military strength. Just as the FBI kept British intelligence in the dark about Tricycle, Hoover was apparently left out of the loop on Springbok.

Von Kotze's radio connection was a failure, however, as no contact could be established directly with Germany or indirectly with Sao Paulo. In July and August 1942 von Kotze's letters insisted that more funds be sent to Toronto, but German intelligence in Brazil cut him off, perhaps suspecting that Allied spy-masters were peering over his shoulder. The Abwehr revived the Toronto connection in January and February 1943 – just as the Watchdog/Bobbi case was getting under way – and letters again were exchanged between Waltemath and von Kotze. (The Watchdog file shows that Cyril Mills made at least one trip to Toronto in 1943, suggesting he helped to direct the Springbok case as well.) The mail link remained shaky, though, and Waltemath was finally arrested by Sao Paulo police on 1 June and charged with espionage. British Security Co-ordination concocted a phony arrest of John von Huges in Toronto and the Springbok file, named for von Kotze's South African background, was closed.

The official history of British intelligence during the Second World War calls the Springbok case 'unproductive,' but Harvison's memoirs suggest von Kotze played a useful role in a bold counter-sabotage deception. The Mounties had arrested many of the members of the Canadian Fascist Party in Quebec, including leader Adrian Arcand, within a year of the declaration of war, but a shadowy organization survived, which the RCMP had only partially penetrated. Harvison claimed that Janowski had instructions to seek assistance from the party (although the Watchdog file does not support this contention), so the RCMP seized the opportunity to plant a mole. Johnny, the German who helped with the Watchdog translations, took on the role of newly landed agent and established himself as a dictatorial leader of the group. Johnny insisted on limiting membership and forbade sabotage, the better to surprise the enemy the day Hitler ordered a great uprising in North America. 'From then until the end of the war, the Force, through Johnny, controlled the activities of the Fascist Party in the Province of Quebec,' Harvison wrote.

In early 1944, the idled Quebec Fascists were becoming restless and began openly to challenge Johnny's veto on sabotage. To keep the lid on the pot, the RCMP brought in a turned German agent from Toronto – 'a tall, blond autocratic-looking individual' – to pose as the Nazi spymaster for North America. The agent was to meet with three high-ranking Quebec party members in Montreal and order them to put aside all thoughts of sabotage. Harvison did not name this 'phoney feuhrer,' but clearly it was von Kotze, brought back into play after the collapse of the South American assignment. In a small suite at Montreal's Windsor Hotel, von Kotze clicked his heels, saluted smartly with a Heil Hitler, and haughtily chastised the men for their disobedience. 'I am told that you and your associates are eager to get on with the business of sabotage,' Harvison quotes him as saying. 'This is nonsense. We are not playing a game of fireworks. We are fighting a war, and you will follow orders just as soldiers in the field must follow orders. When the time comes, you will get your orders. Until then there must be no nonsense.' Von Kotze reminded the trio that the great uprising would one day come, but until then no sabotage was permitted. He strode out of the room, the brief performance apparently swallowed whole, and Johnny's authority was restored.

The most successful double-cross agents in Canada during the war were, in fact, inventions of Cyril Mills's fertile imagination. In coming to Canada in late 1942, Mills had to turn over the massive Garbo deception to his colleagues in MI5. Garbo, as will be recalled, was the British cover name for Juan Pujol, an energetic and brilliant Spaniard who had been recruited by the Abwehr but offered himself as a double agent to the British. After being rebuffed at the British embassies in Madrid and Lisbon, Pujol was finally accepted by British intelligence in early 1942 and flown to Plymouth on 25 April to begin his new life as a double. He was met by Mills, who identified himself as Mr Grey, and by May the Garbo team sent the first controlled messages to the Abwehr. Mills ran the case from the outset, dubbing his agent Garbo because Pujol turned out to be 'the best actor in the world.' The operation eventually grew to include a network of seven agents reporting to Garbo – Arabel to the Abwehr – and nineteen sub-agents under them. These twenty-six people existed only on paper, most of their 'reports' being channelled to the Abwehr through Garbo.

Among Garbo's seven main notional agents was No. 5, later code-named Moonbeam by MI5, supposedly a Venezuelan student based in Scotland who was sent on Abwehr missions to Wales, the south coast of England, and the Isle of Wight. Mills had been transferred to Canada in December 1942, and sometime in 1943 MI5 decided to 'transfer' Moonbeam as well. The Abwehr readily agreed to the suggestion from Garbo, who forwarded to Germany a sample of Moonbeam's handwriting – actually a message scribbled by Mills. The flow of secret-ink letters began in the fall of 1943, just after the collapse of Watchdog. Indeed, Canadian intelligence historian Wesley Wark has suggested the British may have pressured the Mounties to shut down Watchdog so as not to place at risk this latest twist on the Garbo deception – or indeed the whole double-agent game, the extent of which was likely unknown to the RCMP. In any case, Moonbeam soon claimed to have secured several Canadian collaborators, and for good measure to have added a cousin in Buffalo, New York, to his espionage network. Mills claimed he withheld all information about Garbo's Canadian network from the RCMP, though he apparently did alert the FBI.

All Moonbeam's communications were by secret ink, but in late 1944 the Abwehr sent an Afu with agent No. 4 – MI5 code-name Chamillus – who escaped to Canada after coming under suspicion in Britain. Chamillus, of course, did not exist. Through Garbo, this notional agent was given a high-grade Abwehr radio cypher, and complex security precautions, which proved of some value to the Allies. Chamillus made radio contact with a Madrid station in January 1945 and continued two-way communications with Madrid and Garbo in London until mid-April, when Germany began to disintegrate. This radio connection was without doubt behind Mills's request to the RCMP in early March 1945 to borrow the radio 'booster' that Southam had built for the Watchdog transmissions. Harvison arranged for Mills to pick it up from the RCMP workshop in the St James Street headquarters in Montreal, where the device had lain dormant for about eighteen months. Mills apparently needed the booster to overcome severe atmospheric conditions that spring. His Moonbeam-Chamillus ruse appears to have been a success. The official history of British wartime intelligence notes that, with the fatherland in flames, the 'Abwehr's final orders were that Moonbeam and his associates should divide any remaining funds between them, and take all necessary precautions for their own safety.'

For ten months in 1942–3, virtually every scrap of Watchdog paper – memos, letters, radio transcripts, lab reports, photographs, coding sheets – was sent to Corporal Richard Robertson, an RCMP intelligence officer in Ottawa. Beginning with Janowski's capture and until his deportation to England, Robertson was asked to maintain a file watch, quietly assessing each new development objectively without becoming entangled in day-to-day operations. Born in Liverpool in 1909, Robertson emigrated to Canada at age nineteen and in 1932 joined the Mounties at Rockcliffe. He was successively posted to seven communities in New Brunswick before transferring in 1941 to Ottawa, where he was soon promoted to corporal. Robertson was a natural sceptic and meticulous – personality traits essential to the espionage game. His immediate boss was Inspector Alexander Drysdale, the intelligence officer who had argued so vehemently against running Janowski as a double. Days after Watchdog was shut down, Drysdale asked Robertson to write a summary of the case based on his close reading of the file. Robertson's thirty-one-page analysis landed on Drysdale's desk on 1 October, raising some unsettling questions and offering some unorthodox answers.

Janowski's bizarre behaviour on arrival in New Carlisle made no sense whatsoever, Robertson argued. 'Either JANOWSKI not actually wishing to give himself up, deliberately drew attention to himself in order that his apprehension might follow well knowing that if he co-operated with his captors his life would not be endangered, or he is as stupid and ignorant as he would have us believe his masters of the Abwehr to be,' he wrote. Robertson rejected Janowski's claim that he had been deliberately supplied with bad money by his enemies in Germany in order to entrap him. In fact, there was one explanation that could account for the 'trail so plain that his arrest even amongst the most ignorant of people could not have helped but follow,' Robertson wrote. 'It is that JANOWSKI was sent to this country with full instructions to bring about his own arrest, thus becoming a mouth-piece for the information we would have to supply to Germany in order to competently carry out a double agent case and form a source of wrong information for the Allied Nations. This explanation is not altogether substantiated by the information supplied by JANOWSKI for so far it does not appear to indicate deception from a strategic point of view. However, it does appear to be the only theory which would explain the otherwise crassly stupid acts which led to his arrest.'

FBI analysts had earlier noted that the behaviour of the wave of Abwehr agents sent overseas in 1942 suggested a profound system-wide incompetence. The 'Abwehr organization seems to be extremely careless with respect to small details when they send an agent abroad,' a 24 November 1942 agency summary concluded. 'These blunders are so obvious that they readily lead towards the apprehension of the agent. From them it would appear that the German Intelligence organization is either extremely ignorant or extremely careless.' At least one espionage historian has even argued that Admiral Wilhelm Canaris was so disillusioned with Hitler that he deliberately undermined some Abwehr intelligence operations to hasten the demise of the Nazis. How else to explain such apparent stupidity? For his part, Robertson was struggling to find a kind of middle ground between gross incompetence and deliberate failure – the view that Janowski perhaps intended to set himself up as a triple agent from the outset.

Although Robertson's was an extreme view, other RCMP post-mortems also suspected triple-agent treachery during the operation's earliest stages. The press leaks that began within a week of Janowski's capture were enough to convince some that the case had been blown from the beginning. Four months after Robertson's report, Drysdale speculated that the letter Janowski sent in December 1942 tipped the Abwehr. 'They may have considered that had the letter in question been despatched in the ordinary way, it would never have reached Sweden and, since it did, the conclusion that its receipt was facilitated would engender suspicion, if not absolute certainty,' he wrote on 9 February 1944. Commissioner Wood later questioned the *en clair* content of the Swedish letters, suspecting that Janowski's wording may have alerted the enemy to his capture. Two accounts in the early 1980s by authors with access to RCMP or British intelligence sources suggested that Janowski's transmitter itself was the tip-off. John Sawatsky argued in *Men in the Shadows* that the Abwehr intended that the set's weak broadcasts be relayed by U-boats in mid-Atlantic. Nazi spy-masters became suspicious when the signals were heard directly in Germany. In fact, U-boats were never used for this purpose; the rigid, twice-daily radio schedule was an impossibility at sea and would have exposed the submarines to potential Allied attacks. The U-Waffe had far more onerous responsibilities than acting as a messenger for the Abwehr. William Stevenson suggested in *Intrepid's Last Case* that Janowski's intended radio contact was another agent based in North America, and that Harvison – unaware of this arrangement – unwisely cranked up the radio power, giving away the game. Operation Grete helps to undermine this analysis, however, since Langbein was clearly supposed to broadcast to Hamburg directly. The 40-watt sets supplied to Langbein and Janowski were indeed underpowered, but so were the sets dropped with every German agent in Britain. The Abwehr did this deliberately to reduce the chances of Allied detection. The RCMP had Janowski explain the power increase by saying he had constructed a 'booster,' which fitted credibly with his technical background in radio.

All these explanations for the collapse of Watchdog, whatever their individual weaknesses, did have one thing in common: all agreed that relatively early in the case the RCMP's first double agent had managed to transform himself into an Abwehr triple. Mills may well have spotted a cryptic SOS from Janowski in one of the final radio transmissions from Montreal. But there were plenty of earlier opportunities for a well-trained and highly motivated agent to insert a surreptitious message into an otherwise innocuous broadcast. Janowski had several fall-back stories if his first lies after arrest were found out; doubtless, he had fallbacks in the event he was forced to divulge his wireless security check. His radio traffic has a suspiciously large number of family messages, for example, any one of which might have been a pre-arranged signal. Or he may have been supplied with a 'negative' security check whereby a deliberate error – such as the misspelling of the fifth word or the insertion of X as the twentieth character – would assure the Abwehr receiving station that all was well with the agent. A captured spy using such a system was better able to keep the wireless security check from his captors, since the controlled messages would read as if they were normal, yet the Abwehr would recognize their normality as a clear signal of trouble.

185

'There were variations of subtlety on this theme,' recalled Ronald Reed, an MI5 radio expert during the Second World War. 'If an agent was under control he might add – or omit – an X or a full stop or something small. It was difficult to know whether an agent was telling the truth about this. There were precedents to be consulted in previous cases, but the Germans (sensibly) did not seem to follow any consistent pattern – sometimes a sign was to be put in and sometimes omitted – and occasionally the agent couldn't remember his instructions properly.' The fact that all the information in the Watchdog case was one-way, and that Janowski's spring saboteurs never appeared as promised, strongly suggest that the Abwehr was stringing the RCMP along from the very first transmissions, perhaps to acquire controlled information, perhaps to assist an agent in trouble, perhaps to tie down Allied intelligence resources. And perhaps the SOS that Mills had spotted late in the case was an Abwehr tip-off not to Janowski's Allied control but rather to the fact the RCMP had finally realized he was a triple agent. Oddly, the Abwehr continued to transmit radio messages to Bobbi in Montreal for more than six months after his transmitter had fallen silent. Mills later suggested this was merely an Abwehr administrative oversight – officers had simply forgotten to tell the radio operator to cease attempts at contact.

Abwehr files seized after the war shed almost no light on the Watchdog case. In 1946, U.S. naval-intelligence officers sifting through the records at the Abwehr's Bremen post came across a green file folder containing nine documents about some of Bobbi's radio messages from early 1943. But the reports were verbatim decrypts with no analysis or commentary. U.S. Naval Intelligence, already aware of the Watchdog case, did note that all the reports were forwarded to the Abwehr's Brussels post, 'which coincides with the information furnished by the subject on his apprehension to the effect that he had been trained and was responsible to the Abwehr-Stelle in Brussels.' The navy gave the file to the FBI in Washington, which in turn forwarded a copy to the RCMP in Ottawa in June 1946. Apart from confirming one minor aspect of Janowski's story, however, the captured documents offered no real insights into the case.

In the wilderness of mirrors, as CIA spy-master Jim Angleton aptly called the espionage game, there are few certainties. Reality is illusion, fact is falsehood, loyalty is treachery. And so it was with the Abwehr's wartime operations against Canada. Janowski had arrived on the Gaspé shores in a period when Allied intelligence was virtually blind to coded U-boat radio traffic. Britain's Government Code and Cypher School struggled unsuccessfully between February and December 1942 to unravel the latest version of U-boat Enigma. In the meantime, there was no way to determine what spies were being landed where as Doenitz sent scores of submarines to North American coasts. This was the same eleven-month period in which Langbein landed near St Martins, along the Bay of Fundy. Other U-boat spies may well have set foot on Canadian soil during these months, as Langbein, Janowski, and other prisoners of war had intimated. Postal censorship and Britain's Radio Security Service did not intercept messages from any of these supposed agents, but there was simply no way to know for certain whether they operated successfully.

Nor is there any certainty about the value of Watchdog's service to either the Abwehr or the Allies. Janowski's message to Hamburg complaining about the oversized Canadian currency may have had a practical impact. A pair of Abwehr spies who landed by U-boat in Maine in November 1944 were provided with ninety-nine chip diamonds in addition to American currency – just in case the United States had changed the size of its bills. The diamonds could then be sold for the new-style currency. Mills has argued that the line of questioning from Hamburg, both in the radio contacts and in Janowski's master questionnaire, revealed some of the enemy's blind spots and larger intentions. 'Until [the Abwehr was] given the tip-off J was asked many interesting questions which showed where German knowledge was weak and everything I learned this way was given to the Chiefs of Staff in London,' Mills wrote. 'Definitely not a waste of time.' But Masterman has argued that the Twenty Committee failed to make full use of such information. And two British historians with official access to MI5 files concluded that Janowski's 'traffic had yielded no useful intelligence.'

Even less susceptible of resolution is Watchdog's role in code-breaking. Messages from double agents often acted like a barium meal: once received by the Abwehr station, they were frequently re-encoded in a higher-grade cypher for transmission to Berlin. British intelligence could often break the internal cypher because it already knew the text of the double-cross message, and could trace its passage through the system – just as a medical technician traces barium through the gut. Janowski's messages may have assisted in this sophisticated operation, but British intelligence files are simply not available for confirmation. Although Harvison's inept interrogation of his prisoner wasted much time and effort, more reliable information became available once Mills had yanked Janowski's chain. Just how this intelligence added to the Allies' portrait of the Abwehr, or how it helped root out German agents and collaborators after D-Day, remains unknown.

As to the question of Abwehr ineptitude, it became fashionable in the postwar press to ridicule the German intelligence agencies as bumbling and naïve. 'Dumbo comes to Gaspe: Stupid spy betrays self by using old-style currency,' was a typical headline, this one from the *Montreal Star*, as reports of Janowski's arrest became public in 1945. The 'Hitlerite intelligence system was operated by fools and amateurs,' declared a May 1945 editorial in the *Ottawa Citizen*. Yet John Masterman, the British intelligence chief whose double-cross system tied the Abwehr up in knots, made no such claim four months later. The 'Germans were at least our equals in all the arts connected with espionage and counterespionage,' Masterman wrote. 'In short there is no reason whatever to attribute our success and German failure to our superior wisdom or our greater ability or our better practical handling of the agents.' Another student of the Abwehr, Ladislas Farago, had similar respect for the service. 'The Canaris organization was certainly not as good as its apologists now claim,' Farago wrote in 1971, 'but neither was it as abysmally bad. It managed to sustain a respectable surveillance of the United States and the British Isles under exasperatingly difficult conditions.'

German intelligence analysts were not necessarily duped by all the phoney information proferred through the British double-cross system. As Langbein himself had told Mills, Berlin in 1942 recognized that much of the intelligence received from or about England was bogus. The most prominent historian of Nazi espionage, David Kahn, has noted that many of the German evaluating agencies were highly sceptical of agent reports. Masterman believed the very nature of war, rather than any innate superiority, helped assure an Allied intelligence victory. In 'time of war espionage in an enemy country is doomed to failure because the dice are hopelessly loaded against the spy ... Suspicion is rife, and is aroused at once by the least interest shown in military or semi-military undertakings; security checks abound and identity documents must be proof against examination; the transmission of any information presents almost insuperable difficulties.' Kahn arrived at a similar conclusion: 'The cards are stacked against the spy in wartime,' he wrote. 'Spy hysteria makes every member of the public into a counterespionage agent.'

Robertson's tantalizing suggestion that Janowski sought to bring about his own capture to become a triple agent is, on balance, highly improbable. Although the Abwehr planted one or two triple agents during the war, neither side had the sophistication nor inclination for such rarified Byzantine intrigue. Rather, Janowski was a relatively experienced and well-trained agent whose chief failing was arrogance. He was a loyal Nazi, confident of Hitler's ultimate triumph and of his own success by association. Janowski succumbed to the carelessness of conceit on that chilly autumn day at the Carlisle Hotel. Hubris sabotaged his own sabotage mission. 'He was a cock-sure type and I think he may have persuaded his masters that having lived in Canada and being able to speak English well he would have no difficulty in taking care of himself,' Mills put it. By the same token, Janowski's profound loyalty to Nazi Germany helped salvage the botched operation by focusing his efforts on tipping the Abwehr that his information was controlled.

The RCMP, by contrast, suffered not so much from arrogance as rigidity. Like the FBI, the Mounties were imbued with a policing ethos that was inappropriate for the gossamer games of espionage. British intelligence had moved beyond mere counter-espionage to the heights of strategic deception, thanks in part to the wartime recruitment of supple minds from law, business, journalism, and academia. In contrast, Mountie counter-intelligence continued to be run by cops trained to catch crooks. Like J. Edgar Hoover, RCMP planners had little patience with the double-cross game unless it led directly to the arrest of other agents. An internal RCMP history of the intelligence service made the same judgment. 'The fact was that internal security was still seen as a minor although necessary responsibility of the Force,' Carl Betke and S.W. Horrall wrote in *Canada's Security Service: An Historical Outline, 1864–1966*, referring to the outbreak of war. 'Most members still regarded intelligence work as something of an aberration. It did not offer opportunities for advancement, or a rewarding career. The members who did the security investigations in the field still saw themselves as primarily policemen, not intelligence officers.' This fundamental weakness in the RCMP's security and intelligence arm, badly exposed by the Watchdog case, was not to be rectified until 1983, when the service was stripped of intelligence duties and the job was finally handed to a civilian agency.

The British may also bear some measure of responsibility for the collapse of Watchdog. MI5's Colonel Walter Wren, who rushed to Montreal soon after Janowski's capture, persuasively argued in favour of a double-agent operation without adequately considering the inexperience of the RCMP's intelligence arm. Mills's own recollections emphasized his tight control of the case, which, if true, raises questions about whether any of the Watchdog missteps were Harvison's or in fact his own. Mills's claim that the case was rock solid until he temporarily left Canada and Janowski managed an SOS is at odds with the RCMP Watchdog file. The documents show that the case began to unravel long before Mills's August 1943 flight back to Prestwick. At the same time, the file makes clear that Mills had limited control over day-to-day operations, despite the fact Mountie brass generally sided with him in major disputes with Harvison. At the very least, the British were naïve to believe that the RCMP could launch a sophisticated double-cross in the first place, and that poorly trained officers could effectively manage the operation.

Janowski's life after Canada slid into a long, pathetic decline. He remained caged in his cell at Camp 020 until the end of the war. Having broken no British laws, he was transferred on Mills's advice to No. 5 Civilian Internment Camp at Truppen-Uebungsplatz, in the British zone of Germany, on 2 July 1945. Mills has confirmed that Janowski did no work for the Allied Commission on War Crimes or any similar group, apart from the use made of his interrogations from Ham Common. The Abwehr had apparently failed to deposit Janowski's army pay with his family and wife while he was on the Canadian mission. He began to press the skeletal postwar German government for compensation, at one point seeking a declaration from the RCMP that they had never been in receipt of his Wehrsold (army pay).

Released on 22 March 1947, Janowski got a divorce that April from his second wife – Michele, or Putzi – who had been unfaithful throughout her husband's captivity. His weight – a healthy 160 pounds on the shores of the Baie des Chaleurs – had dropped to 106 pounds by the autumn of 1947 with the severe postwar food shortages. On his release, Janowski was employed as a buyer for a textile factory near Hamburg. But the plant, owned by a friend, was shut down by December 1947. His father died on 28 October that same year, and mother and son eked out a miserable existence on an inadequate pension. Janowski apparently worked for a local circus during 1948, even as Mills was reviving his family's British circus, but by October was again jobless. He set himself up as a foreign-language instructor and translator in the late 1940s and married a third time, to a Gerda Ullman. By 1963, Janowski was employed by the German navy in some undisclosed capacity, and registered as a resident of Flensburg, near the Danish border, on 18 February 1965. He died on 22 February 1978, while on a trip to Benisa Alicante, Spain.

In 1947, with his world collapsing around him, Janowski wrote a personal note to Gordon Southam, the amateur radio enthusiast in Montreal who had sat tensely through every Watchdog transmission to Germany. 'More than 4 years have past since I left you. Let me thank you and your friends for the undeserved kind treatment I have received during the time I had to spend in Montreal,' he wrote in rickety English. 'Forgive me for not having been always honest and true. But you and your friends Ken [Molyneaux] and Slim [Harvison] understand that in times of war it was the ... duty of all of us to serve and stick to an oath. It was not only a fight for my life, but also a fight for my people and my country – a total war, which was not fought only by fire-arms but with our brains too, presupposition being an actor, a good actor with tough nerves and a bit of heart.' Janowski had adopted many personae throughout his deceitful life: Boni, Buddy, Branton, Bobbi, Billy, Bernhardt. But as Mills had perceived from the very first encounter, at Janowski's core was a steadfast loyalty to Nazi Germany. His patriotic oath justified every lie. A thickly spun web of deceit protected the lone principle of an otherwise unprincipled man.

Janowski stayed in touch with the RCMP as well. In 1947 and 1948, he obtained affidavits from two Germans who claimed that he had been sent ill-prepared on the Canadian mission because of political friction with the Nazi security service, or SD. One of these was from a Major

Josef Brinkhaus, who claimed to have heard rumours of friction between Janowski and the SD while serving in the same unit. The second was from someone who failed to declare his connection, if any, to the unit or the SD and clearly had been coached in his statement by Janowski. 'Janowski chose and had to leave too hastily for Canada, only to be arrested there a few hours after his landing because of insufficient preparations,' the statement said in translation. 'The greatest amount of the bank notes he had with him were out of currency ever since 1936.' Neither assertion was accurate: Janowski was relatively well prepared and well trained, and most of his money was perfectly negotiable.

Copies and translations of the two affidavits were forwarded to the RCMP, along with a request for certification about the arrest at New Carlisle, so that Janowski could claim his Wehrsold from 1942 to 1947 as a politically persecuted German. He also tossed in a suggestion that he might someday work for the RCMP's 'anti-Bolshevist' squad. Commissioner Wood ignored the latter request, but did send a declaration confirming the arrest and lack of army pay. A covering RCMP letter to British intelligence, who were asked to forward Wood's declaration, indicated a continuing scepticism about Janowski, the man who had so completely fooled his captors. 'We have only JANOWSKI'S word and that of the two men who have supplied statements on his behalf to show that he was forced to accept an espionage mission to this country,' Assistant Commissioner L.H. Nicholson wrote on 7 April 1949. 'As you will appreciate this is a story which would very naturally be put up by a captured enemy agent.'

The press finally got wind of the strange tale of Alfred Langbein, the reluctant Abwehr spy, in March 1952 when New Brunswick MP Dan Riley made reference to the case in the House of Commons. With the cat out of the bag, the RCMP on 13 March released a fairly accurate account to Ottawa reporters without disclosing the spy's German name. It quickly became 'the story of a playboy spy whom no Canadian apparently seriously questioned or suspected,' in a widely used Canadian Press report. The Mounties claimed Langbein 'poured a wealth of information about Germany into their files' – doubtful, since his insider's view of the Abwehr was already two and a half years stale by the time of the Mills-Bayfield interrogation. Indeed, exactly six months before Langbein's surrender the Abwehr had been dissolved as incompetent and its remnants absorbed into a competing Nazi intelligence agency. The Ottawa *Evening Citizen* interviewed the proprietor of the Grand Hotel, where Langbein had stayed. Alonzo Delorme insisted his former guest was no playboy. 'He was a nice, pleasant sort of fellow and he looked and acted like anything but a German spy,' Delorme told a reporter. 'While he stayed at my hotel he never did much drinking. He was quiet mannered and spoke with what I took to be an English accent. He once mentioned to me that he worked in some office on Wellington Street, and I naturally took it for granted that he did.' Delorme was much impressed with Langbein's expensive luggage – purchased so he could safely tender those $50 American bills and get some much-needed Canadian cash as change. 'Haskins was always ready to exchange a smile and a greeting with me and members of my hotel staff, but at the same time he appeared to be worrying constantly.' The RCMP said Langbein had been sent back to his wife in Germany after the war.

Harvison's career in the RCMP marched steadily upward, seemingly unaffected by the Watchdog fiasco. Despite the amateurish interrogation of Janowski, Harvison was called on to help handle the case of Igor Gouzenko, the Soviet cypher clerk who defected while posted at the Ottawa embassy. Harvison, newly transferred to Winnipeg from Montreal, was ordered to Ottawa in September 1945 to study the Gouzenko file so he would be able to interrogate intelligently if there were arrests in the case. After three months of study and no arrests, Harvison returned to Winnipeg, but was recalled to Ottawa again in February 1946 when a series of thirteen arrests was finally made. At the Rockcliffe police college, Harvison carried out interrogations of the Montreal suspects connected with the Gouzenko revelations, though he appears to have had only a minor role in the overall investigation. In 1953 Harvison was promoted to assistant commissioner, initially in charge of operations and criminal investigation, but in 1955 became director of security and intelligence, a posting that lasted about a year. While in charge, Harvison had to discipline James Morrison, an RCMP intelligence officer caught stealing money from the force. Harvison ordered Morrison, a profligate, to repay the money within a week – prompting the officer to betray an RCMP double agent named Gideon to the Soviets in exchange for cash. Gideon soon disappeared in Moscow, a victim of treachery and Harvison's clumsy handling of a security matter. Promotions to British

Columbia and Ottawa followed, and on 1 October 1960 Harvison became the eleventh commissioner of the Royal Canadian Mounted Police.

As part of his semi-diplomatic role, Harvison visited Germany in early 1963. He gave a speech at a 25 March meeting of the International Press Institute in Hamburg, an account of his remarks appearing in local newspapers the next morning. Later that day, Harvison got an unexpected telephone call from his old nemesis, Werner Alfred Waldemar von Janowski, now calling himself Billy Branton and soon to celebrate his fifty-ninth birthday. Janowski had seen Harvison's name in the newspapers and now proposed a meeting. Would the commissioner agree to a rendezvous the next day in Hamburg? Janowski worked for the German navy in Flensburg and needed permission to travel the ninety miles south to Hamburg, but would apply immediately. Harvison agreed but the meeting never happened. Instead, Harvison received a telegram the next day: 'Cannot see you after all STOP Only wanted your pardon for causing trouble during last war STOP All the best. Bill.'

Young Earle Annett, stuck on the home front because of a game leg, became an instant celebrity once the news of Janowski's capture became public. His first-person account in the 14 May 1945 edition of the *Toronto Daily Star* was just the beginning. In late September that year he was portrayed as the dashing hero in a syndicated colour comic strip called 'True Comics,' which ran in newspapers across North America. This romanticized but generally accurate version of Janowski's capture was reprinted in the spring of 1946 as one of several stories in a comic book entitled *Real Heroes: True Stories in Comics – Thrilling Stories About Real People* (March–April, no. 13). The ten-panel full-colour story, entitled 'Spy Catcher,' showed a concerned Annett glancing at the departing spy and thinking, 'It all adds up – the money, the bus, and the foreign matchbox. I mustn't let him get away.' Annett was unaware of the reprint until the day he turned up at a girlfriend's house and her excited mother asked him for an autograph. 'Unless you were in uniform you couldn't get a girl to go out with you, it was as simple as that,' his childhood friend René Lévesque had observed. Annett had neatly circumvented that iron law of wartime relationships.

Earle Annett Sr sold the Carlisle Hotel in 1947 and retired with his family to Kelly House, a rambling residence in town. Young Annett married the girl next door, Pansy Chisholm, in April 1949 and soon moved with her to Percé to run the South Beach Hotel. Pansy apparently grew homesick and unhappy with the non-stop life of a hotelier. They sold the hotel and returned to New Carlisle, where Earle joined the gin company DeKuipers as a sales representative, covering the Gaspé Peninsula and the north shore of New Brunswick. They soon had three children, the last born in 1958. In the late 1950s, Earle Jr was a guest on CBC's 'Front Page Challenge.' During the televised appearance, he tugged at one earlobe – a secret signal that meant 'hello' to all his friends and family back in New Carlisle. Earle Sr died in 1960, and his son moved the family to Montreal the following year to take a job at Seagrams. He was posted in 1963 to Halifax, where he helped develop a best-selling blend of Captain Morgan's rum for Maritime tastes. In the mid-1970s, Annett became ill with cancer and returned briefly to New Carlisle for a final visit. He died in hospital at nearby Maria in August 1977, at age fifty-four. Among the huge crowd at his funeral in New Carlisle was Quebec Premier René Lévesque – apparently the first time Lévesque had ever set foot in the town's Anglican church.

Mills ended his long wartime sojourn in Canada in September 1945, when he took a boat to England to be demobilized and begin the daunting task of resurrecting his family circus. While Mills was at sea, Igor Gouzenko stepped out of the Soviet embassy with his sheaf of top-secret documents – and MI5's point man in Ottawa missed the biggest spy scandal ever to break in Canada. Mills likely had had an influence on the case anyway. Since December 1942 he had been a window on Canadian security for MI5 and MI6, and his reports were alarming. Canada's intelligence services were in a desperate state, he warned, beginning with the RCMP (witness its clumsy handling of the Watchdog case) and extending through the three armed forces. Mills's repeated warnings perhaps help to explain the speed with which British intelligence officers arrived in Ottawa to ensure Gouzenko would be in capable hands.

Although Mills severed his formal association with MI5 in 1945, he continued quietly to provide intelligence services just as he had done in his de Havilland Hornet in the 1930s. Peter Wright exposed Mills in his 1987 tell-all memoir of a career inside MI5, *Spycatcher*. The agency had rented a house in London in the midst of some Soviet diplomatic buildings in order to eavesdrop electronically on the enemy. Mills agreed to be installed as a tenant in the house in the late 1950s, and for years MI5 transferred radio-detection equipment to the residence inside brightly coloured Mills circus trucks. Mills, who had kept silent about even his official wartime service, was outraged by Wright's indiscretion. But he was never shy about recounting the incompetence of Canadian wartime intelligence officers, especially Harvison, over drinks at the Special Services Club in London. Harvison's meteoric rise to the top of the RCMP left him shaking his head in disbelief. His war stories over the decades helped cement Canada's junior status in the world of Western intelligence.

The full official record of the Watchdog case remained safely locked away for almost half a century in the RCMP-CSIS central registry. Magazine writers, newspaper reporters, scriptwriters, movie producers, and would-be authors pestered the RCMP for access to the material over the years, but in every instance they were politely turned away. RCMP officials approved the release only of inaccurate newspaper clippings, which conveniently tended to praise the wartime vigilance of Canada's men in scarlet. *Maclean's* magazine thought it had pierced the veil with a September 1949 article by Colonel William Waldie Murray, purporting to recount the inside story of wartime counter-intelligence. Murray, head of army intelligence, was indeed privy to much of the Watchdog material, but his article was a gross distortion of a few facts and unabashed invention of many others. The 'man on the beach was part of what was perhaps the most dramatic chapter of the intelligence story,' Murray wrote. 'Call him Hans Schmidt, which could be his real name, although we were never certain that we actually learned it.' The capture in New Carlisle, Murray assured, was due entirely to the sharp eye of an RCAF officer on the train. And thanks to the quick-witted Intelligence Corps, the spy was made to betray his German masters. Harvison's own memoirs, as has been shown repeatedly, were similarly distorting when it came to the Watchdog case. But with the RCMP file safely locked up for all time, there was never any danger of contradiction. National-security matters, after all, were best left to the experts. Harvison died in 1968, doubtless secure in the knowledge that his memoirs would stand as the only authoritative record of the Watchdog case available to the public.

The RCMP maintains a small museum in Regina to display artefacts from more than one hundred years of policing. Days after Janowski's capture in 1942, senior officers were already pondering the shipment of his personal effects and spy paraphernalia to Regina. Most of the items arrived at the museum in a sealed box in the fall of 1943, as Janowski was being shipped to Britain. In the fall of 1945, the RCMP arranged a public display of the Janowski material. A printed card in the case read: 'Effects of Lieut. Werner Alfred Waldmar Von Janowski – German Army – Landed from German Submarine near New Carlyle, Quebec – November 9th, 1942.' Harvison, who had asked for the Janowski file shortly after returning from Hamburg in 1963, noted the spelling mistake in New Carlisle and found the caption far too sketchy. He immediately ordered another card created, and dictated the new caption. Harvison's brief summary was dutifully attached to the open lid of the radio set inside the display case at the Regina museum: 'In December, 1942 the Security and Intelligence Directorate of the Force was successful in making radio contact with the spy's control station in Hamburg, Germany. From then until November, 1943 messages were exchanged daily with Hamburg as part of a deception plan, which proved successful.' More freight, it seemed, from the cargo of lies.

Sources

Note: In about a dozen instances, I have inserted the names 'Cyril Mills,' 'Mills,' and 'Watchdog' into direct quotations taken from the RCMP's Watchdog file. These names were generally excised from the file as it was processed under the Access to Information Act, though the reviewer let them stand on several documents. My insertions of these names were based on context, and were checked by letter counts and in some instances by comparing the documents with uncensored copies contained in Naval Intelligence and FBI files.

Chapter 1: Broken Boats, Broken Bodies

Gordon Hardy kindly submitted to interviews from his home in Ingonish, Nova Scotia, on 15 Dec. 1992, 3 Dec. 1993, and 1 June and 5 July 1994 to discuss his experiences aboard the *Lord Strathcona* and *Rose Castle*. Some useful background on Hardy came from Mike Parker, *Running the Gauntlet: An Oral History of Canadian Merchant Seamen in World War II* (Halifax: Nimbus 1994), 108–13. Other background on the attacks at Bell Island, as well as the assault by *U-69*, came from Michael L. Hadley, *U-Boats Against Canada: German Submarines in Canadian Waters* (Kingston and Montreal: McGill-Queen's University Press 1985), esp. 137–42 and chap. 5; and from Steve Neary, *The Enemy on Our Doorstep: The German Attacks at Bell Island, Newfoundland, 1942* (St John's, Nfld.: Jesperson Press 1994). A copy of the war diary of *U-518* was obtained from W.A.B. Douglas, Director of History, National Defence Headquarters, Ottawa. Mr Douglas kindly provided explanatory notes about U-boat navigation as well. Robert Dietz of Halifax helped with translation. Most material on the transatlantic voyage of *U-518* was extracted from the Canadian

Sources

Naval Intelligence interrogations of Janowski, contained in RG 24 83–84/167 vol. 306 S-1487-J-2, obtained under the Access to Information Act from the National Archives of Canada. The section on the *PLM-27* is based on interviews with Pierre Simard from his home in Halifax on 5 May and 4 July 1994 and on background from Parker, *Running the Gauntlet*, 113–18. Information on the Allied attack on *U-518*, and on the German-language broadcast, came from the Canadian Naval Intelligence interrogation, cited above.

Chapter 2: The Stranger in Room 11

René Lévesque's reminiscences are from his autobiography, *Memoirs*, trans. Philip Stratford (Toronto: McClelland and Stewart 1986), esp. chaps 8–12. The Annett sisters – Marguerite Beebe, of New Carlisle, and Geraldine Langham, of Bay Minette, Ala. – offered reminiscences about Lévesque, and about Janowski's three days in New Carlisle, during interviews on 24 April, 30 May, and 22 August 1994 (Marguerite) and June 1994 and 4 October 1994 (Geraldine). Dorothy Sheehan of Saint John, NB, who was the Annetts' neighbour in 1942, offered similar observations in an interview on 15 October 1994. Simone Loubert of Carleton, Que., also consented to an interview on 23 January 1995. Sections on Janowski's landing are from the Canadian Naval Intelligence file, cited above, and from the RCMP's 3000-page Watchdog file, obtained from the Canadian Security Intelligence Service under the Access to Information Act. The RCMP and Naval Intelligence files are the primary sources from which much of the narrative in the remaining chapters is taken, and will not again be specifically cited. Some details of Janowski's time in New Carlisle were taken from 1945 newspaper accounts, esp. Lawrence Earl, 'No medals for Werner' (Montreal) *Standard*, 20 May 1945, and Earle J. Annett, 'Quebec spycatcher tells his own story,' *Toronto Daily Star*, 14 May 1945. Background on Abwehr agents in the United States came from David Kahn, *Hitler's Spies: German Military Intelligence in World War II* (New York: Macmillan 1978); Ladislas Farago, *The Game of the Foxes: The Untold Story of German Espionage in the United States and Great Britain during World War II* (New York: David McKay 1971); and William Breuer, *Nazi Spies in America: Hitler's Undercover War* (New York: St Martin's Press 1989). Information on the U.S. response to Janowski's landing is from the released sections of the Federal Bureau of Investigation file on Janowski, no. 98-14539, obtained under the U.S. Freedom of Information Act.

Chapter 3: A Fluent and Fertile Liar

Harvison's memoirs, *The Horsemen* (Toronto: McClelland and Stewart 1967), provided background on his RCMP career. Sections on pre-war Nazi activities in Canada, and on the RCMP's response, are from files obtained under the Access to Information Act from the Canadian Security Intelligence Service. Among these, an 86-page 1947 report by Corp. A. Alsvold, entitled 'The Nazi Party in Canada,' was particularly useful. I also drew on Robert H. Keyserlingk, '"Agents within the Gates": The Search for Nazi Subversives in Canada during World War II,' *Canadian Historical Review* 66, no. 2 (1985), 211–39. Background on Cpl. Joseph 'Pete' Bordeleau's career is from RCMP biographical files. The identification of Johnny is made in Juan Pujol with Nigel West, *Garbo* (London: Weidenfeld & Nicholson 1985). West kindly provided me with additional information on Treviranus's association with Capt. Sigismund Payne Best. The first public revelation of Dick Ellis's treachery came in Peter Wright's *Spy Catcher: The Candid Autobiography of a Senior Intelligence Officer* (New York: Viking 1987). Several requests to the RCMP and CSIS, both informal and through the Access to Information Act, have failed to produce any Canadian documentation on Treviranus. The author invites any readers with background on 'Johnny' to contact him through the publisher. Information about the veterans' Remembrance Day dinner is from the Justice Department file on the 'Inquiry into publication of a certain article in the Montreal Gazette of May 15, 1945,' obtained under the Access to Information Act. Comment from reporter Lawrence Conroy is from the same source. Details about the FBI's actions are from the FBI Watchdog file, cited above. Background on Walter Thomas Wren is from H. Montgomery Hyde, *Secret Intelligence Agent* (London: Constable 1982); Dusko Popov, *Spy/Counterspy* (New York: Grosset & Dunlop 1974); and F.H. Hinsley and C.A.G. Simkins, *British Intelligence in the Second World War, Vol 4: Security and Counter-Intelligence* (London: HMSO 1990), 145, though Wren is not specifically identified. There are many sources for the well-known Tricycle case; this account is based primarily on the last two sources cited above. Some background on Albrecht Gustav Engels is from Stanley E. Hilton, *Hitler's Secret War in South America, 1939–1945: German Military Espionage and Allied Counterespionage in Brazil* (Toronto: Random House 1982). Biographical and other material on Cyril Bertram Mills is from his published memoirs, *Bertram Mills Circus: Its Story* (London: Hutchinson & Co. 1967); Nigel West, ed., *The Faber Book of Espionage* (London: Faber and Faber 1993), 173–4; his obituary in *The*

Sources

Times (London), 22 July 1991, p. 16; letters from Cyril Mills to the author, dated 20 November 1990, 4 March 1991, 12 April 1991, and 4 May 1991 (Mills specifically declined to be interviewed, preferring letters); and from Pujol, *Garbo*, 87, 159–61. Lieut. Wilfred Samuel's initial interrogation report is from the Naval Intelligence file on Watchdog, cited above. Masterman's double-agent manual was later published as J.C. Masterman, *The Double-Cross System in the War of 1939 to 1945* (New Haven, Conn.: Yale University Press 1972). C. Herbert Little of Ottawa provided background on Samuel and on German and Naval Intelligence operations generally in an interview on 2 May 1995; Little's two articles, 'Early Days in Naval Intelligence, 1939–41,' *Salty Dips*, vol. 2 (Ottawa: Ottawa Branch, Naval Officers' Association of Canada 1985), 111–18, and 'Now It Can All Be Told,' *Salty Dips*, vol. 3, 213–37, also provided useful background.

Chapter 4: Bobbi Calls Home

Information about the FBI postal intercepts is from the agency's Watchdog file, cited above. On Abwehr agents' radios, see appendix 3 in Hinsley and Simkins, *British Intelligence in the Second World War, Vol. 4*, entitled 'Technical Problems Affecting Radio Communications by the Double-Cross Agents,' 309–13. The piece is reprinted, with author Ronald Reed's name restored, in West, ed., *The Faber Book of Espionage*, 206–10. Information on Capt. Edward Drake's Rockcliffe station is from Wesley K. Wark, 'Cryptographic Innocence: The Origins of Signals Intelligence in Canada in the Second World War,' *Journal of Contemporary History* 22 (1987), 643. Career background on Cpl. Ken Molyneaux is from RCMP biographical files. The well-known William Sebold case is discussed in Kahn, *Hitler's Spies*, 331–3, and Breuer, *Nazi Spies in America*, passim. Lieut. C.W. Skarstedt's report, in its draft form and final version, is from the Naval Intelligence file, cited above. Information about the U.S. intercepts of Watchdog transmissions is from the FBI file. Maj. Werner Trautmann's Hamburg station is described in Kahn's *Hitler's Spies*, 293–5. Career background on RCMP Commissioner Stuart Wood is from RCMP biographical files. The Cyril Mills quote about the flight to Canada is from *Bertram Mills Circus: Its Story*, 121–2, though Mills is scrupulously silent on his wartime intelligence role; remaining Mills quotations are from his correspondence with the author, cited above. A useful overview of RCMP intelligence functions in the early war years is the introduction in Gregory S. Kealey and Reg Whitaker, eds, *R.C.M.P. Security Bulletins: The War Series, 1939–41* (St John's, Nfld.:

Committee on Canadian Labour History 1989). The Camp 020 interrogation techniques are described in the Hinsley and Simkins volume cited above, appendix 10 (ii), 341–2; MI5's security liaisons in North America are discussed in the same source (144–8), as is the Garbo case (225–8). The fullest account of Garbo is in the Pujol book of the same name, cited above.

Chapter 5: C'est la guerre

Background on the Lehr Regiment is partly from Hinsley and Simkins, cited above, 298. The quote by Bert Keen, and other information about Janowski's first sojourn in Canada, is taken from James Y. Nichol, 'Gaspe spy bought his life by becoming Allied spy,' *Toronto Daily Star*, 9 Aug. 1945. Most of the biographical background on Olive Quance has been deleted from the RCMP's Watchdog file, but is found in full in the Naval Intelligence file on Watchdog.

Chapter 6: Collapse

Mills's comments on Janowski's SOS is from correspondence with the author; otherwise, all material is from the RCMP Watchdog file.

Chapter 7: Operation Grete

Material for this chapter is almost entirely from the Naval Intelligence file on Alfred Langbein/Haskins, obtained under the Access to Information Act from National Archives of Canada, RG 24 83–84/167 vol. 305 S-1487-H-1. Requests under the Access to Information Act for material on Langbein/Haskins were also made to the RCMP and to CSIS, but both agencies claimed not to have such a file. The section on the search for Langbein's buried radio is from Eric H. Wilson, 'A Wartime Incident,' *RCMP Quarterly*, 39, no. 4 (October 1974), 34–7. Hadley's *U-Boats against Canada* also provided some background on *U-213*'s voyage to Canada and subsequent destruction. Eric Yarrill, the naval lieutenant who accepted Langbein's surrender, provided some background information in an interview on 11 March 1995 from his Sherbrooke, Quebec, home.

Chapter 8: Autopsy

Information on the Annett purchase of the Gaspé shoreline comes from family interviews, cited above. Copies of all newspaper articles cited are in the RCMP's Watchdog file. Biographical information on Lawrence Conroy is largely from his obituary in the *Montreal Star*, 21 Aug. 1973. Much of the background on the Forsyth inquiry, as well as the transcript of proceedings and final report, is from the Justice Department file obtained under the Access to Information Act. The Cmdr. Eric Brand quotation is in the Naval Intelligence file on Janowski. The Springbok case is discussed in Hilton, *Hitler's Secret War in South America*; and in the Hinsley and Simkins volume, p. 228. The Canadian connection to the Garbo case is discussed in ibid., 225–8; and in Pujol's *Garbo*. The FBI's 24 Nov. 1942 report on Watchdog is in the FBI file, cited above. The suggestion that Canaris deliberately undermined his own operations is contained in Phillip Knightley, *The Second Oldest Profession: The Spy as Bureaucrat, Patriot, Fantasist and Whore* (London: Andre Deutsch 1986), chap. 7. Sawatsky's argument about the Janowski case is in *Men in the Shadows: The RCMP Security Service* (Toronto: Doubleday 1980), 69. Stevenson's argument is found in *Intrepid's Last Case* (New York: Ballantine 1984), 57–8. The Ronald Reed quote is from appendix 3 of the Hinsley and Simkins volume cited above. The Bremen post records on Bobbi's transmissions are in the FBI Watchdog file. See Hinsley and Simkins, p. 201, on U-boat Enigma and RSS intercepts. A concise account of the Maine spies is found in Kahn's *Hitler's Spies*, 3–26. The Mills quotations are from correspondence with the author. The Farago quotation is from *Game of the Foxes*, 761; the Kahn quotation from *Hitler's Spies*, 369. The internal RCMP history is Carl Betke and S.W. Horrall, *Canada's Security Service: An Historical Outline, 1864–1966* (Ottawa: RCMP Historical Section 1978), released under the Access to Information Act with many deletions; the quotation is from p. 479. Some information on Janowski's later life was obtained from the municipal registrar of Flensburg, Germany; otherwise, most of the material is contained in the RCMP Watchdog file, which was added to as late as the 1970s. Information on the 1952 Langbein revelations came from the Ottawa *Evening Citizen*, 14 March 1952, 5; and 15 March 1952, 1, 16. The account of Harvison's later life is based largely on his memoirs, *The Horsemen*. Copies of the 'True Comics' and *Real Heroes* comics are held by the Annett family; other information on Earle Annett Jr's later life is primarily from family interviews. The Murray article is Col. W.W. Murray, 'How We Tricked the Nazi Spies,' *Maclean's Magazine*, 15 Sept. 1949, 7, 64.

Index

Index

Index

Index

210

Index

Index

Index

Illustration Credits

John Annett, Halifax, NS: Rocky cliffs; Carlisle Hotel; Earle Annett Jr and Constable Duchesneau; New Carlisle courthouse and jail

Gordon Hardy, Ingonish, NS: Gordon Hardy; Wissmann and his four officers

Pierre Simard, Halifax, NS: Pierre Simard

National Archives of Canada: *Rose Castle* in convoy, PA-143173; Naval Intelligence map, C-142513; Belgian matchbox, C-104137; Barry German, PA-134322; mug shots of Janowski, C-107138; Janowski's effects, C-107133; Janowski's naval uniform, C-107136; letter and envelope, C-107143; Alfred Langbein, C-142502

Royal Canadian Mounted Police Archives: Stuart Taylor Wood, 1174; Cliff Harvison, 4825

Courtesy of the Mills family, London: Cyril Mills with brother Bernard